Dreamers
of the Valley
of Plenty

A PORTRAIT OF THE
NAPA VALLEY

CHERYLL AIMÉE BARRON

SCRIBNER

NEW YORK   LONDON   TORONTO   SYDNEY   TOKYO   SINGAPORE

SCRIBNER
1230 Avenue of the Americas
New York, NY 10020

DESIGNED BY ERICH HOBBING

Manufactured in the United States of America

1   3   5   7   9   10   8   6   4   2

Library of Congress Cataloging-in-Publication Data
Barron, Cheryll Aimée.
Dreamers of the valley of plenty : a history of the Napa Valley / by Cheryll Aimée Barron.
p.   cm.
Includes index.
1. Napa River Valley (Calif.)—History.
2. Wine and wine making—California—Napa River Valley—History.   I. Title.
F868.N2B37   1995
979.4'19—dc20
94-421122
CIP
ISBN 0-684-81295-9

To David
who was sure
I should write
this book and not
the other one

My fancy went out of my body in a way of speaking, I suppose, and I began thinking of myself as being at that moment in a city in Italy. . . . Americans are always up to such tricks because all of our old stories and dreams have come to us from over the sea and because we have no old stories and dreams of our own.

SHERWOOD ANDERSON

America of the Mirage was the best of all possible worlds—a new start for mankind and a revival of antique virtue, a model for revolution and a return to nature. . . .

The Old World's New World,
C. VANN WOODWARD

Contents

Acknowledgments

A BOOK'S BEST FRIEND goads its author to follow her hunches and persist past the many obstacles—real and imaginary—that hobble its progress. That friend was Jack Yelverton.

Other encouraging readers of whole or partial drafts of the manuscript were Dessa Brashear, Lewis Lapham, Sarwar Lateef, Merril Stevenson and Jeffrey Rose. Though not a test reader, Jack Leggett supplied sound literary advice.

My agent, the astute Frederick Hill, found me an exemplary editor in Lee Goerner, succeeded—in publishing's whimsical game of musical chairs—by Hamilton Cain, who saw the book through to the finish with great good cheer.

Scribblers toiling far from big cities are more indebted than most to expert reference librarians: Julia Fraser dazzles patrons of the Napa Valley Wine Library, including me, with her extraordinary instincts and speed. Fay Stahl is a professional cousin of hers at the Modoc County Library, where Betty Chism, Joanne Cain and Nancy De Ong arranged for many a vital interlibrary loan.

In Napa, my generous and long-suffering hosts were Marilyn and Jack Yelverton, and Renate Wright. I spent memorably delightful nights under roofs belonging to Maren and Mostapha Namdar, Dagmar de Pins Sullivan, Sally and Steve Gordon, Dawne and Howard Dickenson, and Bill and Lila Jaeger.

For innumerable acts of kindness hard to categorize, I am in debt to Robert and Roberta Henkel, Elvia and Federico Faggin, Chany and Lawrence Steinman—and by no means least, Jeanne Scott and Patrick and Mark Barron.

Dreamers
of the Valley
of Plenty

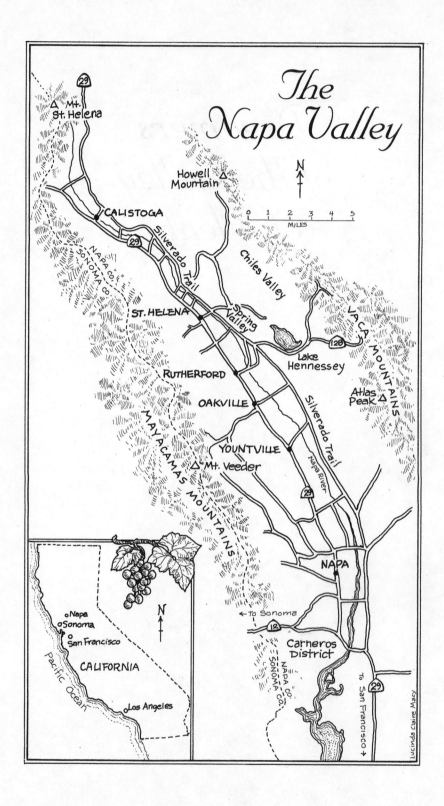

Compass

ONCE IN THE NAPA VALLEY you also find yourself in places in the world you have visited or left behind.

You go to Disneyland to wander in and out of other times and states of mind for a few hours, an entertainment like going to the movies or reading novels with exotic settings. But in the Napa Valley people live their fantasies day in, day out. To house his winery, each dreamer has built or acquired his own monument to his fantasy-made-real—in a style that is generally an import, because Napa is part of an America relatively starved of evocative connections to a past and culture all its own.

So, juxtaposed in a green slit between two mountain ranges are an all-white Greek monastery perched high on a hill (Sterling Vineyards), a massive construction modeled after a medieval fortress (once a winery, now the Culinary Institute of America) and a fussy Cape Dutch mansion (Chimney Rock), a gloomy scaled-down Rhenish castle (Beringer), assorted French châteaux—some chiefly clever veneers tacked onto plywood structures, others of genuine, imported cut stone—plus Spanish mission–style buildings, Italianate-Victorian and Victorian-Gothic mansions, copies of California barns, a postmodern pseudo-Minoan temple (Clos Pegase) and a tribute or two to the Bauhaus school.

To a stranger to Napa, the architectural eclecticism hints at the presence of foreigners. It is not misleading. I found, among full- or part-time residents of the place—all of them somehow involved in winemaking or grape growing—Mexicans, French, Germans, a Romanian, Iranians, an Israeli, Chileans, a Croatian, Swiss, an Argentinian, Japanese, a Chinese, Swedes, a Finn, Britons, an Austrian, South Africans, a New Zealander, Spaniards and Italians. The Napa Valley is unique in being a cosmopolitan segment of agriculture. Those of its dreamers who come from far away make it the one truly cosmopolitan bit of farm country anywhere in the world.

You may argue that that is because it is only an hour's drive north of San Francisco, but Napa does not feel like urban overspill or an extension of suburbs. It feels like countryside, even if it seems only distantly related to the rest of American farmland. Classic American farm country is a landscape of mechanically ordered sprawl, oceanic expanses of fields and far horizons punctuated by solitary farmhouses and barns. The Napa Valley, by contrast, might be the work of a Moghul miniaturist. Each row of vines looks crafted, suggestive of arrangements of hand-cut precious stones—even if here, too, machines help harvest vines, fight frost and tame the grasses and wild mustard that flourish between the rows.

After my first few visits, it struck me that the human face of Napa was a cultural curiosity like no other I had encountered. No book I read, no one I asked, could supply me with a satisfying answer to the question of what this polyglot collection of people was really doing there. The architectural extravaganzas rendered the obvious reply— why, making and hawking wine, of course—both superficial and unconvincing. Of the range of wishes that we of the late twentieth century entertain, which ones did these people in Napa embody?

Even as just wine country, the valley's context was odd. After all, America is not a wine-drinking nation, even if it does have wine snobs and oenophiles every bit as fanatical and encyclopedically informed as their European counterparts. The tremendous flow of foreign capital and winegrowing talent into Napa in the 1970s and 1980s was clearly not intended to serve the average American— someone not much more informed about wine than neighbors of mine at a concert in ranch country about three hundred miles from the Napa Valley.

He, newly divorced, overbearing and intent on making a new friend, asked if I preferred wine or beer and, given my answer, exulted, "Oh, me too! Now, do you believe in red wine for red meat, white wine for white meat—that sorta thing?"—as if the subject were UFOs or life beyond the grave. He was sure I had no choice but to agree with him and confident of being able to use my answer to prove that we were soul mates. I said that if I were eating garlicky roast chicken, I might want to drink a Beaujolais. "Oh, then you *really* know about wine," he said, crestfallen. "I haven't heard of that brand."

I was searching for a way to make him feel less yokelish without supplying romantic encouragement when the elfin, grandmotherly neighbor on my left cleared her throat. "I know about wine," she announced. "I've made it." Years ago, when she lived for a while in Los Angeles, she had made ninety gallons of "twenty-nine percent proof" wine in plastic garbage cans—"new and clean," she assured me. I asked what grapes she had used. "Concord," she said grandly. "You've got to have good grapes. I bought mine from someone I knew personally."

Dedicated oenophiles and professional winemakers would have done so reflexively, but I did not sneer at the mention of this variety alien to European wine country. I merely nodded. She explained that she froze her concoction in plastic milk jugs before she took it in to staff celebrations at the department store where she worked and let it thaw until party time. "It keeps fresher that way," she explained. The store was officially teetotal. "But I said it was sherbet and even the managers came back for seconds."

That cryogenic wine advocate hailed from the Central Valley, what Spanish colonists called the Valle Grande, the defining feature of California's inland geography. There's a massive mountain wall to the east, the Cascade and Sierra Nevada ranges, and a mountain wall to the west, the Coastal Range; they meet untidily at both ends. Sprawling between them is a farmer's paradise. Cotton and fruit, grains, nuts, rice, sugar beet and a mind-boggling array of vegetables grow on immense—and to a traveler, often tedious—flatlands watered by two great rivers.

To get to the Napa Valley from my home near California's border with Oregon, I drive down the northern half of the Central Valley and—near its middle—turn westward onto a highway that slices through the Vaca Mountains east of Napa. It takes less than half an hour to travel between the valleys. On a relief map, Napa looks like a miniature replica of the larger depression. They are both long and narrow and straddle a north-northwest south-southeast axis: the

Central Valley is about 450 miles long and, across, averages forty miles; the Napa Valley is roughly thirty-five miles long and between one and five miles wide.

Yet they engender strikingly different states of being. I endure the Central Valley by surrendering to its monotony—actually tune in to it by listening to country music stations, soothed by the flawless dovetailing of Garth Brooks intoning, "Ain't it funny how we come in kickin' giddyup/And go out hollerin' whoa," seemingly a dozen times, with the passing view: orchard, orchard, orchard . . . ; rice field, rice field, rice field . . . ; sunflowers, sunflowers, sunflowers.

Within minutes of emerging from the Vacas, though, the country music jars. I risk an accident, scrabbling around for a cassette tape with Schubert lieder or Indian ragas or something by Fauré. It's more than a matter of the Old World look of wine country. Here, too, are pickup trucks and four-wheel-drive vehicles in great numbers, but the pickups are glossier and new and—in a departure from the proud chauvinism of American agriculture—many of them are Japanese imports. There are Range Rovers among the all-wheel-drives and, flashing through the traffic like silverfish, the first Porsches, Lexuses and Alfa-Romeos I have seen for three hundred miles. Early on summer mornings, gaily striped hot air balloons are suspended above vineyards skirting Highway 29, the valley's principal north–south conduit: they carry champagne-sipping tourists out on a sort of larks' carnival.

To cross over into Napa (also the name of the county mostly made up of the valley, and of its largest town) is instantly to experience a forceful enlargement of perspective.

After a famous blind tasting of wines in Paris in 1976, the valley won world fame—became the one tiny slice of American farmland celebrated for its particularity. To the horror of their countrymen, French tasters judged Napa wines the best in both the red and white categories, against the products of the most illustrious French châteaux. Never mind that the French and fervent devotees of their wines later found innumerable tacks for discounting the results as all but worthless: Napa wines had at the very least demonstrated that some day, they could *conceivably* outrank France's by any criteria.

After that, well-heeled folk from all over the globe began to discover New World winemaking as a refined form of high adventure. A pilot who works for a small charter firm in Napa told me that in the late 1980s, he routinely flew back to San Francisco's airport disconsolate multimillionaires of far-flung provenance. They had arrived impatient to plant stakes in prime Napa Valley land or to snap up a winery, but had been outbid by fatter cats—or multinational corporations.

Napa's late-twentieth-century celebrity had a precedent roughly a hundred years before. The Californian wine country historian William Heintz has written that in 1889, at the Paris World's Fair, California wines, brandy and champagne were admitted for the first time to an international competition. Of the nearly three dozen awards that they garnered, the Napa Valley earned three-quarters.

Actually, the Napa Valley had been singled out as extraordinary even before it was widely planted to vines. A member of the U.S. and Mexican Boundary Commission, John Russell Bartlett, rode into Napa in 1852 and marveled at the valley and its nearby hills "covered with a luxurious growth of wild oats, and immense herds of cattle . . . roaming about feasting on them." He saw "ploughmen . . . at work turning up the soil, which was of the richest description."

Even by California's lavish standards, the valley has long been notable for exceptional fecundity—a sort of agricultural Eden—a gift of soils formed by relatively recent geological upheavals, and by alluvial deposits of the Napa River and its tributaries. The Wappo Indians to whom Napa belonged before the Spanish took it over were so spoiled by natural bounty that they never learned to farm. They are thought to have scarcely exerted themselves at all for their meals of fish, grasshoppers, worms and wild vegetation—so that "plenty" is understandably the most popular of competing translations of the obscure Wappo word *napa*.

The first Spanish explorers traveled through the valley in 1823. The Spanish colony of Mexico, at a loss for means of safeguarding this and other territory at the far limit of Alta California, granted massive *ranchos* of thousands of acres to loyal citizens—in another era of plenty.

Agriculture in the Napa Valley thus began with the *ranchos*, and two local historians, Denzil and Jennie Verardo, have recorded its

evolution since. In the mid-nineteenth century, the wild oats of the *ranchos* on the valley floor were grazed by vast herds of cattle reared for their hides and tallow. After 1848, the feeding of Gold Rush miners created a huge new market for flour: wheat became Napa's chief crop in California's early years as part of the United States (following the failed Bear Flag Revolt of 1846 and the end of the Mexican War in 1848). In the 1870s, slumping wheat prices had the nimblest farmers moving into orchards and vines; in 1879, a nasty root louse called phylloxera began to kill off vineyards in France, creating an opening for California grapes.

The Napa Valley saw in the twentieth century as an agricultural patchwork. Prunes were the dominant crop, but a few cattle ranches and tracts of wheat remained, and there were sizable acreages given over to other fruit and nut trees—and, increasingly, to grapevines.

From the beginning, the spread of grapevines through Napa progressed in fits and starts. Booms caused overproduction and busts. The inadvertent import of phylloxera caused a standstill in the early 1890s. One of the most bizarre features of the flight from common sense known as Prohibition is that in the fourteen years of its duration—1920–1933—wineries went bankrupt but grape growing expanded and grape growers thrived, thanks to an explosion in home winemaking. The last orchards were pulled up after the middle of the twentieth century, and today Napa's agricultural profile is pure, composed almost solely of vines that look as if they have always been there.

If it weren't for the fantastic architecture, a newcomer driving up Highway 29, passing one small town encircled by grapes after another, might assume that the valley's inhabitants make up that rarity for the West—a rooted, closely knit, homogeneous community. But even the seeming uniformity of the vines is an illusion. For viticulture, the valley divides into as many as four distinct zones or microclimates. The southernmost, the maritime region near San Pablo Bay, is cool, foggy in the summer and planted to early-ripening grape varieties like Chardonnay and Pinot Noir; at the upper end of the valley, near Calistoga, the diabolically hot summers are best tolerated by late-ripening Zinfandel. Mid-valley, around Rutherford, lies some of the finest Cabernet Sauvignon country in the world. Wines made from grapes harvested on the slopes of the Vacas, or the

Mayacamas Range to the west, have intense and sometimes wild flavors all their own.

The heterogeneous population includes classic "rednecks," Mexican farmworkers, second- and third-generation Italian immigrants—and foreigners who show no inclination to be absorbed into America the way earlier generations of immigrants were. They actually flaunt the ways in which their behavior differs from American norms. Winegrowing and wine connoisseurship, which have the charm of novelties for the valley's American wine people—for many of whom viticulture is a second career—are old hat to most of these outsiders.

Because of their greater ease with matters oenological, Napa's foreigners have tended to be models for the culture of the region. It amuses me to consider that precisely the opposite is true in an equally famous valley one hour south of San Francisco. Silicon Valley, too, was partly created by talented foreigners not driven there by economic necessity but magnetized by the creative possibilities it offered. But Silicon Valley's microchips and computers are quintessentially American industries of the future. Which means that its foreigners begin to sound like American tekkies before long. Too soon, their talk is sprinkled with such neologisms as "bootstrapping companies," having their plans "impacted" by unexpected developments and worrying about their creations being "obsoleted" by technological advance.

In Napa, by contrast, Frenchmen mutinously persist in calling their enterprises *caves* (meaning cellars) and their technical specialists *régisseurs*; some go further and publicly excoriate American inventions like "winery" and "winemaker" as feeble-minded and illogical. Few Mexican workers make the effort to learn English: it is gringo vineyard managers who improve their employment prospects by studying Spanish.

A foreigner myself, I doubt that I had thought of wine in connection with the land of Coca-Cola and the dry martini before I learned of Napa's existence—late in the 1970s, flipping through the pages of *National Geographic*. It was on a gray London day, one of such an immense succession of bleak days that I was resentfully depressed—and then envious, too, staring at aerial photographs of grassy, round-topped peaks and troughs inset with ripples of brilliant, emerald green vines. They seemed a long, long way away. As much as I longed to, I doubted I would ever be among them.

So much for pessimism. Two years later I was living in California, a two-hour drive south of Napa. On a wickedly hot August day I made a pilgrimage to the valley and decided I loathed it. It was not that the hills had turned from electric green to gold: I doubt that I really noticed them. Hordes of fellow-tourists, retailers of souvenir kitsch, slow-moving traffic and an impression of a local culture of cloying cuteness dominate my memory of the day.

I remember feeling as if I had found an overcrowded European beach nonsensically transposed to the hinterland: terrific heat, too many decibels, strutting bronzed bodies decked in lightweight clothing and a babel of accents. Restaurant menus had shrieked of voguishness in such listings as cornmeal pancakes with Tobiko caviar, quail with chilpotle marinade and gruesomely eclectic combinations like "pork loin with Thai style marinade and pesto, with hot sweet mustard."

I suppose I had expected to find an inland equivalent of the tranquilizing Pacific coast—where a token scattering of human beings is dwarfed and muted by the splendors of the littoral. My disappointment was extreme.

But for a love affair, I might never have returned. I was living near San Francisco, on the edge of the Bay, when time and again a profoundly reserved man would appear, open his heart to me and then—as if appalled by the exposure—simply vanish, like a White Rabbit of the emotions. Rushing to keep his figurative bobtail in my sights, one day I quite literally found myself not deeper in a subterranean Wonderland, but in a sunlit valley fully its equal in its appeal to the imagination. One branch of his family lived in Napa.

Our romance showed me other faces of Napa. I discovered back roads on which I could turn off the engine of my car and wrap myself in silence, solitude and vistas of vines in volcanic earth rolling away to the horizon in every direction. True, the tiny winery of my friend's family had a tasting room that even sold T-shirts, but I found that it was nature and not tourists to which working family members were enslaved.

In the spring they woke in the night to the clamor of frost alarms. Bundling themselves up against the cold, they rushed to check on automatic sprinklers or lit smudge pots to insulate the frail new leaves sprouting on brown canes against freezing temperatures. Some weeks, in March and April, they made do with fewer than five hours of sleep for several nights in a row. They spoke of fretting over too-late or too-early harvests, of agonies of indecision about the right day and hour to start picking grapes, about stretching too few Mexican hired hands over too many vines ripening all at once.

I knew that this family enmeshed itself with the roll-up-your-sleeves work of the vineyard and winery far more than most others in Napa did. Still, through it, I saw that there was grit behind the valley's glamour. Someone had told me that Robert Mondavi, Napa's most famous winery owner, had once hired helicopters to spray his vines with frost-defying droplets of water. And I suppose that story had led me to dismiss all the valley's winemakers as wealthy and effete dabblers in agriculture, insulated from its rigors by armories of expensive equipment.

When I first escaped Napa's main roads I felt a sudden sense of release. Time seemed abruptly to give up its manic hold on me. Perhaps because I was in love, the fragments of verse that floated into my head were ". . . and the roof of thy mouth, like the best wine for my beloved, that goeth down sweetly"—and, "let us get up early to the vineyards; let us see if the vine flourish. . . ." Vineyards, I saw, were entangled with my earliest recollections of arrangements of words, and were far older even than the Song of Solomon.

Later I was surprised to read Robert Louis Stevenson complain, in the late 1800s, that in Napa, he "did not feel the sacredness of ancient cultivation. It was still raw. . . ." For him, the savagery of the surrounding scenery obscured the link between the early vineyards and civilized man's oldest organized enterprise. In just the same way, the pseudosophistication, the creeping preciousness in much of what outsiders see of present-day Napa society, had thrown me off until unbidden, among the vines, those fragments from the Old Testament had drifted into conscious thought.

This was an important connection for me to make. Now I dimly understood at least one of the drives of Napa's wine people. Only a handful of them were born into the life; the others are migrants from other existences—from electronics, advertising, food-vending, drug-distributing businesses; from academia; from the professions of medicine, law, dentistry, ophthalmology, engineering. Something powerful pulled them out of the rodent race and into the unfamiliar rhythms of the agricultural year.

For several of them, that powerful something was an ageless set of symbols going back to the primal lure of land.

In the late 1960s and early 1970s, I knew, there had been a back-to-the-land movement in America. I also knew that for most of those dreamers of a return to a life pastoral, reality had resoundingly failed to cooperate.

To answer the question, Are there any back-to-the-land romantics left?, the nouveaux farmers of the Napa Valley are the only sizable group to which one might point. Because of the accident of a growing obsession with gastronomy and the good life among middle-class Americans after the Second World War, theirs has been the one instance of a successful living out of this fantasy of the industrial age.

Not that they have been spared their share of tribulations. In the mid-1990s, for example, the wine people were fighting two plagues. Phylloxera was creeping through their vineyards, wreaking devastation. The disease can only be eradicated by uprooting and replanting every last vine. This tremendous expense had to be borne at a time when winery owners' profits had been shriveled by keen price competition—the result of a glut of fine wine, and wine buyers turned tightfisted by a long economic recession. A winery or two went bankrupt.

Even so, these were afflictions of the affluent. Napa's dreamers have created the wealthiest agricultural community in America. Before the economic slump and outbreak of phylloxera, prime Napa land was selling for $50,000 an acre—then as now, the most valuable farmland in the country (roughly seventy-five times the national average).

Many of the valley's "lifestyle émigrés" had large or small fortunes to support their migration to agriculture. Indeed their message to the rest of us might be: yes, you can leave the city and do well—if you are persistent and hardworking, have a well-stuffed piggy bank, and choose a sector of farming in which a college education and urbanity give you an edge over traditional farmers.

Napa's large population of foreigners is proof that back-to-the-land romanticism was not a uniquely American phenomenon. Many of them came to the valley to create larger estates than they could ever afford in their overcrowded homelands—in a country with a stable government and currency and a less punitive rate of taxation.

Some foreigners, like the American lifestyle émigrés, are fascinated by the idea of getting a little dynasty going. Observing Napa's established winegrowing clans like the Martinis and Mondavis, they have seen people working all day long with blood relatives—something remarkable in the wake of a century-old trend of splintering families. Most of Napa's two-hundred-odd wineries are family-owned.

It's by no means a foregone conclusion that, in the future, these firms will remain in the same families: in Napa, as in other places, inheritance taxes make this difficult. As I show in a later chapter about the Martinis, later generations may not inherit enough of the founder's talents and enthusiasm to keep going. Other dynastic ambitions go unfulfilled simply because the founders cannot produce heirs: the chapter on Inglenook charts this fate of the most spectacular Napa winegrowing estate founded in the last century—by a rich Finnish seaman and trader, Captain Gustav Niebaum.

Yet for all the many causes for discouragement, dynastic dreams drive such second-career wine people as Jack and Jamie Davies of Schramsberg—just as much as they do Joe Heitz, who has spent almost his entire working life in wine.

Napa's foreigners have joined with American neighbors, from time to time, to fight political battles to keep the valley out of the clutches of housing developers and preserve it for agriculture. Since the Americans in Napa tend to be more sophisticated than most of their countrymen, they share with the foreigners an ambivalence about— or straightforward detestation of—the ordinary America of fast food and shopping malls.

But although some of the reasons that brought the Americans and foreigners in this book towards the Napa Valley are similar, others are as radically different as their private universes.

André Tchelistcheff, the man credited with starting the modern era of Napa winemaking at about the mid-century, came to California reluctantly—and chiefly because the job he was offered in Napa hap-

pened to be his least unattractive alternative. For all his progressive-
ness as a winemaker, the Tchelistcheff legend stems from his having
been far more a creature of the vanished world of czarist Russia than
of twentieth-century America.

André inadvertently taught Americans much about wine simply
by being himself. A later generation of foreigners, like Donald Hess,
Thomas and Anna Lundstrom, and Jan Shrem, were rather more
deliberate in seeking to demonstrate to New World folk the many
links between culture—in the rarefied sense of *kultur*, not mere cus-
toms or mores—and fine wine.

These transmissions affected the people they were beamed at in a
variety of ways.

Some Americans in wine, like the curmudgeonly Joe Heitz, were
little changed by them. His wines have won high praise from the
most exacting European critics. Yet he is a fragment of the old German Midwest transplanted to California, and denies being influenced in the smallest degree by the "damn furriners" around him.
Others, like the Davieses, are subtly Europeanized.

Each of the important subcultures that make up the Napa Valley sees
the place in its own peculiar way. To the Mexicans, who do virtually all
the hard work in the vineyards, it is a particularly baffling segment of
gringo-land—in which money and extraordinary care are lavished on
the manufacture of a substance not half as tasty as beer or tequila. They
stubbornly resist assimilation, and scarcely any of them are parlaying
their vine-tending skills into vineyard ownership or winemaking.

The Italian-Americans—who outnumbered immigrants from all
other European winegrowing countries at the end of the nineteenth
century—seem, on the outside, much like other American farm folk.
Their down-to-earth personas remind one that, in contrast to the
French in Napa, who have concentrated on wines of high quality, they
have sought to introduce ordinary Americans to the joys of wine
drinking. They spend far more time in family gatherings than in the
stylish fraternizing common among the second-career wine people.

Among the French, I found the severest critics of other members of
their group—also, the profoundest disdain for their surroundings
and for their neighbors' winemaking efforts. They gave the most
pragmatic explanations for their presence in Napa. Compared to Bor-

deaux, where an acre of prime vineyard land can cost at least three times
as much, Napa land is a bargain. They find both stimulating and deeply
depressing the exercise of trying to make fine wine in America, for a
population they see as composed chiefly of vulgarians.

From early on, these were some of the questions I had about the
Napa Valley, wine and their places in American life: Why did it take
a White Russian to teach Americans about making and appreciating
wine? Why were there still appreciable differences between French
and American wines after the years of progress in the New World?
Did winemakers' personalities and cultural affinities come through
in their wines? Napa's many imposing estates hinted at the existence
of a social elite: was there really such a thing? While it was clear to
me that scores of Napa folk were living out what were, for most people, impossible dreams, did they seem as successful and fulfilled to
themselves?

But investigating these mysteries came second to answering the
classic questions of curious travelers: what kind of place is this, who
lives here—and why?

A hybrid society—like any other sort of hybrid—is best described
by tackling its constituent parts individually. I felt I'd do best to
show facets of Napa in the course of setting down intricate impressions of a few carefully selected inhabitants of the place—some of
them famous, some not; some standing alone, others in groups. I
chose portraiture as my form because I saw no surer way of bringing
the valley to life. In years of globetrotting, trying to discover the
essential qualities of new places, I have found that any number of
days spent staring at the landscape, flitting around ruins and muse-
ums or hunched over histories of a region are time wasted—set
against a few rich encounters with its people.

My wish to make this a book of discovery explains one notable
omission from my collection of portraits. Robert Mondavi, who
started an ambitious Napa winery in 1966, imitated some of the
techniques of the finest French winemakers. Early on, he helped
prove the advantages of such little-tried innovations in winemaking
as controlling fermentation with refrigerated stainless steel tanks—
an improvement later adopted by venerable French châteaux. He

confirmed Napa's changed status in world winemaking by establishing a joint venture to produce a Cabernet Sauvignon in the valley with the Baron Philippe de Rothschild of Château Mouton-Rothschild, in 1981. A tireless publicist, he has done more than anyone else to spread the word about Napa's glories in places far away.

But in two long conversations with this short, ruggedly built and gnomishly handsome man in his seventies, I was disappointed to find that the private Robert Mondavi and the public one—about whom I had been reading for years—were apparently identical. And then, regardless of what I asked him, he directed the conversation in his charming, even endearing way, to what he wanted to tell me. Within days or weeks of our talks I saw almost everything he had said, seemingly spontaneously and entirely for my benefit, in newspaper and magazine articles about him. I did not find this objectionable; but a Warholesque exercise in portraiture through the deployment of too familiar images was not what I had in mind.

The sense of dislocation I expect readers will feel, moving from one portrait to the next, reflects my experience of the Napa Valley. There is so little of the melting pot about cosmopolitan Napa that as I moved from one group (or representative of it) to the next, trying on its point of view to deepen my understanding of it, I seemed to find myself in an entirely different valley.

Like their equivalents in paint, my portraits are true to the time of their "sittings" (how the Mona Lisa looked with wrinkles we shall never know).*

It helps, in studying portraits, to know something of the media through which they are executed, of the unwitting distortions that follow from the prejudices and experiences of the portraitist. So I tell something of myself here and there.

To sustain enthusiasm over the years of labor a book can demand, a writer must find the subject personally compelling. Although winemaking is an ancient art anciently symbolic of civilization and culture—and though it fascinates me—it was not the business of Napa that kept me going. It was what I had in common with some Napa folk.

---

*Hence André Tchelistcheff who, sadly, died in 1994, still lives in these pages.

I share with many of Napa's inhabitants a feeling of awe about the colossal spaces of the American West—and a wish to own some fraction of this landscape. In my childhood in India, a friend of my father's gave one of my brothers an impeccable scale model of a cattle ranch. We spent whole afternoons of a summer rearranging the split-rail fence and inventing adventures for the men and animals. When we grew bored with mounting the cowboys on their horses, I told my brothers stories about how the buckaroos had taken to training their cows to gallop and trot. We spread the cowboys' plastic legs wider for their unconventional mounts, and I didn't doubt that their real-life counterparts attempted similar experiments. Even at less than ten, it seemed to me that the West was synonymous with the freedom to be as innovative or daft as one wished.

Impecunious writers cannot even rent cottages in the Napa Valley. So though I have never lived there for long, an accumulation of hauntings—trivial yet unforgettable experiences of the place's beauty—has bound me to returning again and again.

I can remember driving away from Napa after a day of work in every spare moment of which I'd been brooding over a strange, wordless quarrel with a friend. Agitated as I was, I was startled suddenly to notice, looming massively to my left, the purple-red glow that the sinking sun had ignited in the valley's stark, craggy, eastern escarpment. Without the serene rows of vines to my right, I might have been exploring Venus.

My mood, myself, were forgotten in a growing awareness of an immense hush, like those moments of thunderstruck silence before wild applause in a concert hall after a virtuoso recital. At the valley's southern neck I turned west and saw that somewhere in the direction of San Francisco, ocean fog had encamped: above the ethereal blond pastureland in the foreground were piled layers of mauve and powder blue and silver mist in which a platinum half-moon swam like a lonely sea creature. Now I saw that the quarrel could mark the end of a precious friendship, or it might not, that I had done all I could to set things right. The outcome would, anyway, soon be part of the past.

Such is the power of great landscapes.

CHAPTER TWO

Civilizing Missionaries

In Xanadu did Kubla Khan
A stately pleasure-dome decree:
Where Alph, the sacred river, ran
Through caverns measureless to man
   Down to a sunless sea.
So twice five miles of fertile ground
With walls and towers were girdled round:
And there were gardens bright with sinuous rills
Where blossomed many an incense-bearing tree;
And here were forests ancient as the hills,
Enfolding sunny spots of greenery.

                        "Kubla Khan,"
                       SAMUEL TAYLOR COLERIDGE

AT MY SCHOOL IN BOMBAY, a Protestant missionary establishment, we sang from an English hymnal every morning. India had disentangled itself from British rule in 1947, but in the 1960s we children still piped in squeaky high voices William Blake's *Jerusalem*: "I will not cease from Mental Fight,/Nor shall my sword rest in my hand,/Till we have built Jer-u-sa-lem/In Eng-land's green and plea-sant land."

For myself and the scattering of other Eurasian, Protestant children in the school, this was eccentric enough: far more curiously, most of the pupils were from Bombay's plutocratic Hindu, Parsi, Muslim and Jain elite. They were not required to convert to Christianity to attend our school—and they did not—but gladly incorporated scraps of British public school ritual and tradition into the cultural mosaics of their lives. Political subjugation by the British had been unacceptable to Indians, but British institutions, from parliamentary democracy to snobbish clubs, had won the highest respect. British culture came as part of the package.

I remembered this eager eclecticism in Napa. America's cities are another matter, but it was startling to discover in a corner of American agriculture a recent attempt at something like cultural colonization—by not one but several would-be colonizers.

By one measure, foreigners completely dominated the valley by the late 1980s. Large foreign corporations in search of "strategic investments" had begun to buy vineyards and wineries in the 1960s. In the late 1970s, after the famous blind tasting in Paris in which Napa wines stole the highest honors from French rivals, the pace of acquisition stepped up, and by 1990, multinationals had the largest landholdings in Napa. The biggest outside investors by far are British. Yet, contrary to what such financial dominance might lead one to expect, British cultural markings are notably absent from the valley—unless you include the tradition of wine connoisseurship. From their headquarters in London, the conglomerates act as long-distance puppeteers manipulating local (American) managers in California.

No, the would-be avatars of culture I met in Napa were not faceless corporations but an entirely different species of foreigner. Their investments were personal, idiosyncratic affairs best illustrated with a few snapshots.

The astonishing building rises from one of the flatter stretches of vineyard land, just south of Calistoga, a mysterious terracotta excrescence that could be a palace or temple in a futurist fantasy. A stout, twenty-four-foot pillar dominates a rectangular portico crowned by a hollow cut in the shape of an arch. This is the entrance, which leads to a cool inner courtyard. I decide that the faint, neoclassicist echo is of Knossos, and am encouraged to imagine myself making a different sort of entrance, barefoot, bare-breasted and bejeweled, as a Minoan princess.

There is neither receptionist nor reception desk, so I wander beneath lofty ceilings into an office, to find a tiny, balding sparrowlike man bent over a desk, examining something with the help of a slender Freya with long blond hair, dressed in layers of diaphanous chiffon.

"I'm looking for Jan Shrem," I say. The man extends a welcoming hand and his smile reaches dark, intelligent eyes.

"I am Jan Shrem," he says softly, in a furry Lebanese accent.

Jan Shrem was born in Colombia. He grew up in Israel and America and made a fortune in publishing and real estate in Japan, where he turned to art collecting as a hobby. He went to Paris, started a second publishing company and became an oenophile, tutored in the finer points of connoisseurship by the likes of the Baron Philippe de Rothschild. In 1983, at fifty-one, he left Paris for Napa, where he bought fifty acres of land near Calistoga and started a winery called Clos Pegase. A publicity document written by Jan himself explains his choice of that name: "the sacred spring which issued forth from a grotto when Pegasus's hoofs broke the earth of Mt. Hellikon . . . not only gave birth to wine by irrigating the fields of Bacchus, but became the fountainhead of the arts."

"In ancient times, wine and art were inseparable," he almost whispers, with the air of one imparting an intensely personal confidence. "And in the same way, I have attempted to combine wine and art as one unit. Making wine *is* art."

The design for this outlandish Clos Pegase building—endowed with squat round turrets as well as soaring porticoes—won an architectural competition judged by the San Francisco Museum of Modern Art, on Jan Shrem's behalf. The winery's labels are decorated with a dark, moody painting of a white, winged Pegasus by the nineteenth-century French painter, Odilon Redon, a member of the Symbolist group of Impressionists.

"What made you migrate from book publishing into winemaking?" I ask. After twenty-five years, he replies, he was ready for something else. "I knew I could not produce art," he says humbly. "But I thought I could produce wine."

Before I leave, I am invited to a lecture he is giving to a gathering of wine and art appreciators on "Wine Through Art," to be illustrated with slides of works by Rembrandt, da Vinci and other old masters.

They chain-smoke as we admire the last of the sun's rays striking the white adobe tower at the far end of their swimming pool. Strips of suspended cloth flanking the structure could be stylized prayer-flags.

He is blond, blue-eyed—painfully diffident, hesitating over every other word—and lean, in well-tailored denim. She is blond and blue-eyed; tight-fitting white jeans and a minute matching waistcoat show off her tiny posterior, slender legs and an expanse of unclothed wasp-waist. A certain imperiousness keeps breaking through her mien of warm graciousness. It isn't clear whether it is her husband's tentativeness or mine that exasperates her more.

"Your father is the, er . . . Swedish consul in San Francisco. Yes, Anna?" I venture. It says something like that in the publicity file they have handed me, which I have been trying to skim-read.

"No. The ambassador. In Washington," she says in upper-class English staccato, delivered with faintly Swedish intonation. A few years ago, she was a journalist working for a leading Swedish newspaper in London, married to an Englishman; today she defines herself only as the daughter of Count Wilhelm and Countess Ulla Wachtmeister and mother of two children, married to Thomas Lundstrom, heir to the Swedish Wasabröd fortune. She claims to like Californian friendliness and yet seems out of place, plainly straining to be friendlier than she feels.

On the label of the bottle of their full-bodied Villa Zapu Chardonnay, resting on the outdoor table between us, is a brilliantly colored, pop-surrealist painting of the swimming pool and tower we are looking at: the artist has added a spaceship and a grinning cartoon-planet, and something that could be crimson primordial ooze, leaping up at the perimeter of the backyard. It is like no other wine label I have ever seen. The Lundstroms would have you say Zapu like Peru, but Thomas smiles broadly and does not contradict me when I say, "But surely zap-you was closer to your intentions, when you made up that name—?"

In its thickly forested, wild setting in the Mayacamas Range looming above the Napa Valley to the west, the Lundstrom house looks like the headquarters of a secret, countercultural cult. Various descriptions suggest themselves for the architectural style of the place. Haute punk. Pueblo punk. Postmodern punk. Certainly some kind of punk, that curious mix of ferocity and elegance that, improbably, hacked out a place for itself in the mainstream of British design in the 1980s.

The Lundstroms, who are in their mid-thirties, moved to Napa from London. A few years earlier Thomas, still a bachelor, had decided that a piece of Napa was the best real estate investment he could make in America. Then, having bought a 130-acre parcel of land, he decided he should "probably do something with it," and a winery seemed the obvious thing.

In the living room, unexpectedly furnished with an enormous Flemish tapestry and Louis XV furniture, I ask Thomas what he had done for a living in London.

"I had, er . . . other investments in London, but nothing terribly interesting. I mean, wine is far more interesting than . . . than doing a small bit here and there."

"So you were sort of . . . searching for the right thing in London— trying out different careers?"

"Yes."

"And now you think you've found *it?*"

"Oh, absolutely."

A winemaking consultant dissuaded him from leaping straight into the business, however. His advice, which Thomas took, was that he should feel his way into wine very gradually, starting by only buying grapes, hiring a winemaker to work on them in space rented in someone else's winery, and concentrating his energies on the biggest challenge facing a new entrant: establishing a market for an unknown label.

Pragmatic as it might have been, this strategy did not impress the newspaper of California's agricultural heartland, *The Sacramento Bee*:

> The denim is lightly faded, the chambray shirt is farmhand blue, the pointy-toed cowboy boots are polished to a rich, glossy brown. That's the rub: The boots bear no mud, no dust, no scars.
>
> Thomas Lundstrom is a member of the new breed of the state's vintners. He owns no vineyards. He has no winery. He's never taken a class in viticulture or enology.

Thomas had been a student at Sotheby's art school in London. "So I thought about doing art on the wine label even before I started building the house—in a way." He had commissioned an avant-garde English architect friend, David Connor, to design the house, even before he committed himself to getting into wine. The architect's original idea "was that one would come up the driveway and there would be freestanding walls that wouldn't be connected to each other, that would have holes in them you walk through, like in a maze. And coming up the road, he wanted to have stakes, with stuffed animals attached to them."

All that the final version of the Lundstrom house shares with that original conception is whimsicality: the facade is made up of one long rectangle interrupted by other overlapping and inset rectangles; symmetrical English Palladian details here and there are juxtaposed with playful asymmetry, like the mismatched sides of the frame for the front door. Thomas Lundstrom likes to say that the house looks like a sort of spaceship. And that the deliberate link between it and the art on the Villa Zapu labels is "um, a fantasy in a way, a fantasy into the next century that will stand on its own [merits] in the future—quite apart from the wine."

There are seven of us at dinner in an apartment full of expensive antique furniture and English hunting prints in the foothills east of the town of Napa. In the kitchen, everything is gleaming white except for the pale blond parquet floor on which Arari rugs in fiery colors float underfoot.

We are a reassembled fraction of a larger group from a small benefit dinner, two nights ago, at the Hess Collection Winery—a much larger neighbor of the Lundstrom estate in the Mayacamas. That dinner had shared the evening with an exquisite concert by the Camerata Bern, flown in from Switzerland at the expense of the Hess winery to help create a seed fund for its new offshoot, the nonprofit Napa Contemporary Arts Foundation.

NACA's launch followed by less than six months the glittering opening of the Hess winery, the creation of Donald Hess, a wealthy Swiss entrepreneur, and his wife, Joanna. A three-storied art gallery attached to the winery is crammed with Donald's personal collection of over a hundred abstract works—by Frank Stella, Robert Motherwell, Francis Bacon and Magdalena Abakanowicz, among other famous names—an assemblage that has recently earned a flattering sketch in the arts section of *The New York Times*.

Our hostess this evening is the mid-fiftyish daughter of one of Napa's most powerful grape growers, an octogenarian patriarch who put down roots in the valley half a century or so ago. She is hyper-vivacious, earthy, likable; is dressed in heavy satin and tartan. On the subject under discussion, she is as eager and excited as a child.

"I mean, that *camerata* the other night was just fabulous—*incredible*, don't you think?" she demands of us, and we nod in smiling agreement. "Well, we thought it was fan-*tas*-tic, even though, we've just started getting into opera recently and that's . . . uhhhhhhh! There's nothing like it."

A month before, I had met this blossoming *beau-mondaine* on a cotton farm in the Central Valley. There, she had been urging a relative from Nevada to visit the Hess gallery. "I mean, even if you hate modern art," she had said bafflingly, "it's worth going there to see that people actually pay millions of dollars for pieces of canvas."

A fellow guest tonight happens to be Leopoldo Maler, the slender, mustachioed and suave Argentinian director of NACA who commutes between Santo Domingo, his present home, and Napa. I can see him in a *New Yorker* cartoon with our host, a white-haired, old-fashioned accountant:

"I've always wanted to get one of you guys in a room—you modern art experts," he tells Leopoldo triumphantly. "Tell me, what have you got against beauty? What's *wrong* with *simple* beauty?"

I wonder whether Donald Hess did not envisage precisely this sort of ripple from his winery's debut.

Before we meet, I decide I will dislike Donald intensely. A San Francisco newspaper has run a picture of him leaning against a wall of his art gallery with a note about the winery's official opening. He looks blandly blond, faintly clownish, because of the way his hands in his pockets set the angles of his suit askew—and keen to please. Ah, I think cynically, another European rich boy who has discovered America as a safe playground and wants to be famous for it, too.

By our second encounter, I begin to worry that I might like him too much to see him clearly.

We meet shortly after eight on a chilly August morning on which the whole world seems caught in a wraithlike cobweb, an effect of the "fog"—frigid sea air confronting vapor from the inland inferno—that attenuates hot spells in coastal northern California. Nothing stirs, not the smallest leaf. The gray stillness is filled with the eerie echo of a barking dog as my truck crunches onto a gravel drive past a utilitarian metal gate. This is the entrance to Donald and Joanna's Napa house. It's a tiny redwood cottage surrounded by sloping vineyards and the forests of Mount Veeder, the tallest peak in the Mayacamas. I gape at the cottage disbelievingly, because nothing has led me to expect so humble a dwelling. I was sure of finding something all of a piece with the winery's crested, gold-embossed stationery and a black tie dinner I had attended at the sleek modern gallery adjoining Donald's offices.

Joanna is in Switzerland, so it is with boyish self-congratulation that Donald offers me coffee he has ground and brewed himself. He is by turns engaging and enthusiastic—and reserved and intense, with a high seriousness he tries to conceal behind ho-ho Swiss-German heartiness. He has, actually, gray hair; smooth, rosy, fine skin; and guarded, amber-colored eyes. He is tall and bulkily built, like a Swiss peasant, but with a scaled-down classical profile, and he has a youthful grace in motion—understandable when he says he has been a recreational boxer all his adult life.

Like an anxious relative—perhaps because of the coziness of our surroundings—he peppers me with questions about how I can possibly hope to survive on a freelance scribbler's earnings. He insists on knowing how, as a foreigner, I can live alone, deep in the American countryside, so far from European cultural stimuli. I feel a rush of identity with the stereotypical woman anthropologist struggling to explain to a wizened tribal chief why she has neither husband nor children.

Sipping my coffee, my eyes rove covetously from the warm red American Indian blanket in which a new Ralph Lauren sofa is upholstered to a Peruvian straw hat; quaint, orderly clusters of fresh zinnias set amidst dried flowers all cut to the same length; the stone fireplace; photographs of the Hesses' daughter, Alexandra, a lovely gazellelike girl; a pair of fine, subtle grape prints, about which Donald tells a tale of successful haggling with a snooty London antiquarian. Wan fog-light seeping through the skylights is defeated by the rich, ruddy glow the lamps conjure from the burnished redwood walls and ceiling whose warped, irregular beams and joints were set in place by the woodsman from whom Donald and Joanna bought the house. He says they enjoy the contrast between this place's easy intimacy and the formality of their great mansion, Roerswyl, near Bern, where servants flutter about them.

The questions Donald has been asking me about myself have kept interrupting the one I have put to him at least three times since I arrived: what keeps him coming back here, getting increasingly enmeshed in Napa and the winery, when he has an empire to run in Switzerland? The businesses of his conglomerate, based in Bern, range from the sale of mineral water and fresh trout to cattle ranches, holiday resorts and restaurants. Yet recently, he exchanged the job of chief executive for the figurehead role of chairman of Hess Holdings and, at our first meeting, told me he could end up spending more than half his time in California—compared to about a third, at present.

At last he sets down his coffee cup and leans forward, looking grave.

"We are all very interested in what is happening in Russia and China, but we are not interested anymore in what is happening in our villages," he says, frowning. "And it's in the villages I am living that I can influence something."

So, pick a "village" thousands of miles from your home as a sphere of influence? Why?

He does not answer my question. Instead, he swiftly reminds me that he can't give up Switzerland altogether. "The other businesses in Switzerland, obviously they are supporting this one," he says. "So I have to be very careful that they keep running."

Yes, but what are Napa's particular attractions for him?

The reasons he gives are impersonal, strictly businesslike—might lead a casual eavesdropper to assume I am his banker, a demanding Swiss-German banker no less, who must be answered precisely.

He says that whereas, for instance, the wines of Bordeaux—the world's greatest—are virtually at the limit of their potential for improvement, Napa's wines are only half as good as they will be someday.

Also, everywhere, the wine business is getting overcrowded. So marketing has become vital to give both winemaking regions and wineries an edge over their rivals. Of all the newer winemaking regions, he says, Napa—for twenty years—has been the most assiduously promoted.

Well, yes, he concedes, he could have invested closer to home—in a French château, say, "but for someone very innovative—it always bothered me, the way they say in Bordeaux, you know, we have made wine like this for at least two thousand years! It's one thing to stick to tradition and something else when you absolutely close your eyes to progress!"

He says he expects the return on his investment (around $26 million) to be slow. He finds himself constantly obliged to impress this on Swiss friends who would like to imitate him and start Napa wineries of their own—and he discourages them all, because they are so clearly in search of speedy gratification. In 1978, he bought 860 acres in the Mayacamas, of which 285 acres have since been planted to vines. More than ten years later, his winery is still losing money. He guesses that, realistically, it will take an operation the size of his—crushing the equivalent of fifteen thousand cases of wine a year, with plans to go up to fifty thousand cases gradually—roughly a quarter-century to recover the capital invested in it and make a name for outstanding quality. This slow payoff, he explains, is one reason why the big corporations trying to sink roots into Napa are all European or Japanese: they have patient money. Unlike the foreigners, American giants have shareholders stepping on their tails, demanding that they show a profit every three months.

Yes, yes, I say. But if a sound, farsighted investment was all he wanted from Napa, why attach an art gallery to his winery?

Sheer accident, he insists. "In Switzerland, there is never enough space. Whatever you do, the piece of land is too small, the road is too narrow, et cetera." There, he has many more paintings than walls for their display, so that most of his acquisitions were gathering dust in warehouses. In Napa, for the first time, he had more space than he needed. "And Joanna said, 'Why not house the art collection in the winery?' " He had always found the idea of linking art with business vaguely distasteful, he says edgily, but this did seem a brilliant solution to his problem.

"Did your interest in painting go back to your childhood?"

"No. I grew up in a house where there were absolutely *no* paintings. My father was a collector of Persian rugs and old furniture. My grandfather had collected beer mugs and my father told me never to spend any money on paintings. First of all, he said, a white wall is something absolutely beautiful. You can just sit and then, with your imagination, project whatever you want to on it. Still if you feel you want something, put a Persian rug on the wall. Then you have something you can always resell when the need arises. Whereas with a painting you have a used canvas and an old frame that you can't sell and paint you can't scrape off."

We set out on a walk. Before long, I am a little dizzy. Not only does the path beside the vines climb rapidly but, now that the fog has burned off, the glare and heat are prodigious. Seeing me lag behind, a beaming Donald informs me that he runs up these slopes every morning for an hour.

We walk in silence for a while and I consider what he has been saying. It seems I am expected to conclude that the winery in distant California is simply a clever ruse for converting Swiss francs into dollars for a sound, if sluggish, appreciation—and a salve for the frustration of not being powerful enough to influence matters in Russia or China. The art collection's relocation in Napa was merely a matter of convenience. And now he wants me to believe that his interest in modern art is just an act of filial rebellion, of self-assertion. Certainly these are plausible reasons, yet I cannot help thinking, the gentleman doth protest too much—there are surely deeper, interior motives for all of this.

Besides, nothing he has said so far casts any light on what Leopoldo Maler, his gallery director, had told me, burningly insistent: "You know, the Donald you see here is nothing like the Donald you would see in Switzerland. He's so *happy* here. And all his Swiss friends think he's become a cowboy!"

"How different would you be if we were having this conversation in Switzerland?" I ask him now, as he points to a jackrabbit flashing between vine stakes.

"Oh, completely different!" he says with mock severity. "I would address you always as Fräulein Barron. I would be seated behind a very large desk and certainly not walking with you like this, dressed in a jogging suit!" A hefty chuckle escapes him.

Minutes later, he is giving me a short lecture on how his mountain vineyards' irrigation system works when, out of the blue, he produces a metaphor that begs for yet more questions.

Explaining why, even in the midst of a hot, dry summer, it is important to irrigate a vineyard only sparingly, he says, "Good vines should always be under a little bit of stress, to have to struggle a little. It's like if a person has a life in cotton, he usually becomes a playboy, if he has enough money to become one. Whilst if somebody has a difficult childhood, has to struggle, has to fight—he usually has a bigger personality, a better personality . . ." I see, from a sidelong glance, the beginning of a smile on his face. ". . . sometimes a disagreeable one, but he will have a *personality*."

Donald's presence in Napa begins to be less mystifying once he starts telling me about his family's peripatetic history—of which his own life appears to be a seamless extension.

We meet again, weeks later. He has just flown in from Switzerland and, though he looks exhausted, declines, with a small grimace, to drink "bad American coffee" for an artificial boost of adrenaline. His eyes are red-rimmed and they stare as he strains to seem his usual ebullient self. There's a striking disjunction between the mood created by his office's pulsating delphinium blue furnishings and his immense fatigue. He recounts the facts of his life in a hollow voice.

He was born in 1936 to an American mother, Louise McNeir; his father, Hector, was the grandson of a member of the sixth generation of a Bavarian brewery-owning family, who emigrated to Switzerland. "There was just no room for him," Donald says of this ancestor.

I ask what his mother was like. "Ah . . . my mother," he says with a faraway look. "She was really a very unhappy woman who was enormously gifted in many ways but she never wanted, or worked hard enough, to achieve something. She spoke four or five languages—for an American, quite extraordinary. She was a very good artist. She was a very old person when she was young—never had the passion of children or young people."

"She painted, then?"

"Yes."

"But you'd seemed to say, the other day, that you'd had no connection with painting, in your childhood."

"Well, my mother was not very close to me, because she left when I was seven. And I hardly ever saw her, really."

"She was from the East Coast?"

"New York. Apparently three hundred years in America. A very old family."

"So you feel that, because she left, it would be mistaken to attribute to her influence these things that have become important to you as an adult?"

"Mm hmm. I had a hard time relating to her and she left when I was too small. I saw her maybe until I was eleven. Kind of for short vacations, when she lived in Switzerland. Then she married again and went to California and from eleven until I was twenty I never saw her. I don't think she really influenced me. In fact I always said that the only nationality of woman I would never marry was American." He pauses. "But that's exactly what I did!"

He bursts out laughing. I look astonished.

"I sure did. My wife is American. She's from Boston."

Donald's father was a romantic, an adventurer. In his youth he was a purchasing agent for an English firm of rug merchants, traveling into the mountains of Persia to exchange gold for rugs with about a hundred camels and an armed escort of forty-odd men for protection against raiding tribes. This phase of his life lasted about eight years, ending abruptly in 1917, when his own father threatened to sell the family brewery if he did not return to relieve him of the burden of running it. He obeyed the summons but never was comfortable in Switzerland.

"It was all too small for him," Donald remembers. "He had an awfully hard time with Swiss functionaries after he'd had an experience of Persia—kind of like the Wild West—where he and his assistants did whatever they wanted to and *they were* law and order."

His father was a martinet and, as Donald was disobedient, lively, and a reluctant and poor student, their relationship was mutually trying. Donald was not permitted to invite his friends to play, and was expected instead to perform a strict rota of character-building chores. There were no other relatives to plead moderation with his father. The only other participants in his upbringing were servants: he remembers the family cook with particular affection.

He was just twenty when his father died. It was a loss that came as a relief: it had its redemptive aspect, too, since Hector Hess and his son were reconciled in the last six months before his death. Donald felt he finally won his father's respect by holding his ground against him in their differences, at the end. Even so, "I felt at that moment, when I was alone, that life was very, very easy. I thought, finally I can do what I want to."

A task of heroic proportions had to be tackled immediately afterwards. The collection of small companies his father had assembled was losing money. Donald had not had a college education and his business experience was limited to six months working as a clerk in the Crédit Suisse Bank in Bern and a brief stint as a brewmaster's apprentice in Bavaria. But with sink-or-swim bravado, he flung himself at the challenge of disposing of some of the enterprises and trying to turn a profit in others.

By the time he was thirty-two, he had accomplished his goals: he had even started thriving new ventures, including a business built around a mineral water spring he discovered—ferreting through nineteenth-century library books on natural water sources—and made his Valser St. Petersquelle into Switzerland's second-ranking brand. He attributes his success to the counsel of experienced older managers he hired to assist him, to whom he humbly confessed his ignorance.

Still, even early on, he had enough confidence to institute highly eccentric managerial practices. For several years, he invited applicants to managerial posts to go a few rounds with him in a boxing ring, offering to pay for them to take ten boxing lessons as preparation, if they felt they needed any.

In a seven-week gap between meetings with Donald, I can't stop marveling—incredulously—at an art collector turning to pugilism to pick his managers. So, of course, I raise the subject again at lunch in the luxurious library of the Hess winery with Donald and Joanna.

"Boxing gives you self-confidence, which I didn't have as a boy," he says. "And it helped me a lot to quickly analyze a situation under big pressure."

But after some years of hiring henchmen in the boxing ring, he was forced to stop. People began to warn prospective employees against submitting to this trial. "They said, 'Watch out! What he really wants to do is hit you on the head.' So it got a little more difficult. I now box with people more mentally. It's enough for me to imagine him in a ring." After a moment's reflection, he adds, "I think this is my fortieth year boxing."

"I think we should celebrate that with a little ring in the ballroom," Joanna murmurs, a decisive note in her voice.

She is a most surprising wife for Donald. He told me he was often tempted to make California his home, but that his wife wanted him to be in Europe. So I had imagined a sternly classical beauty, a blond twin of Donald's, a Grunhilde or Brünnhilde Hess—or certainly a Johanna, not this diminutive, rail-thin, half-Italian Joanna, née Marcaitelli, with shoulder-length chestnut hair, hazel-gold eyes emitting mischievous flashes, a perfect aquiline profile and intriguing, irregular teeth. She is dressed as I had expected her to be, having heard that she was living in London, working at *Vogue* and painting at home when she met Donald, roughly twenty years ago.

She wears a small-waisted vermilion dress with a wide belt and dramatic swirling skirt, and matching shoes; a bumblebee brooch in gold and diamonds decorates the low-cut neck. Her earrings are dainty gold stars suspended from fine filaments.

She sits straight-backed and queenly; she is fey; she is canny. I discover that she has been making a cool assessment of me behind her *douce*, empathetic ways when one day she says, pointedly, "You've had *quite* some time with Donald, now."

The ecstatic summer passage in Vivaldi's *Four Seasons* is being piped in over the sound system; we nibble at wild mushrooms on toast, sipping a lean and perky three-year-old Hess Chardonnay, when suddenly Donald is summoned to take a telephone call. "When I met Donald I had been painting nudes for many years," Joanna says. "So, to meet a man who collected only what are called hard-edged paintings—I thought, look, here's the other side of me, probably. The question was, why was he attracted to paintings of squares? And he said, if he'd had a hard day at the office, he'd come home and stare at one of these paintings—that he actually *used* them to create a calm within himself. I'd never thought of *using* art in that way."

Donald, reseating himself at our little round table, soon catches her drift. "It was my psychiatry," he says about his attraction to the colored squares. "Instead of paying psychiatrists to relieve my pressures, I would look at those paintings."

His career as a collector of art began by chance. When he was thirty-two, a woman who owned an art gallery took a fancy to him and told him he really ought to own some paintings. She said that if he gave her only three afternoons, she would teach him all she knew about art, and that he would owe her nothing. Before that watershed encounter, he had only ever bought one picture: he saw a painting of a face he liked, and later was embarrassed when he had to say to a friend who knew all about it, "What Picasso? Suite Vollard?" He had no idea that the picture was one of the painter's famous studies of the Parisian art dealer Ambroise Vollard.

He only collects works by living artists; he prizes his friendships with a few of them. He says that his evenings in their company have opened up to him windows on the world he did not know existed.

"I have a different conception of the future since I got to know them—theirs is predominantly a negative view and mine is a positive one, but still I have built their little raised fingers into my conception of things. So the art has really become important for me in my business decisions." Asked for an example, he pauses. "Well, I think one direct thought was that you shouldn't have all your eggs in one basket—that the whole continent of Europe was involved in both world wars . . ." His voice fades and he tries again. "I think I got more sensitive to problems a businessman doesn't usually think of. Like overpopulation and pollution."

That explanation sounds flimsy, as if it could account for no more than half the intensity with which he talks about his artist friends. I think about the paintings themselves. Donald likes to stress that he looks at each work "very emotionally. I like to let it work on *me*—so it's very personal." The introduction to the Hess gallery's catalogue emphasizes that most of the paintings and sculpture in it are "difficult and disturbing."

The gallery embraces the polar extremes in moods—from mania to depression. It has in it vibrant and joyful paintings by Robert Motherwell and Alfred Jensen and serene and playful works by Markus Raetz. Works by other artists, like Francis Bacon and the Dutchman Armando and the Austrian Arnulf Rainer, are testimony to modernism's obsession with the dark side of the psyche—anomie, neurosis, psychosis, depravity and existential pessimism.

After lunch, Joanna and I stroll out onto the balcony beyond the library: Donald, having given us each a peck on one cheek, has left.

"Here's something I find interesting about him," she says. "What is it in his psyche that attracts him to these paintings? It's interesting because it's not a part of him that's visible on the exterior. Many of the paintings are really disturbing, but they touch something in him and he can't resist them. And it isn't a matter of their being known or famous. It is that he *is* attracted to them."

One of the artists in the Hess collection, the Swiss Louis Soutter, did most of his work in a lunatic asylum, she says. Another spent some time in a concentration camp.

I consider the possibilities of second-hand catharsis, vicarious catharsis.

Looking over the edge of the balcony, we spy Donald standing near a door leading to the winery's office, profoundly absorbed by a conversation with a winery employee.

"It must be a subject of earthshaking importance!" I say lightly.

"Oh, but he's always like that—he always gives all of himself," Joanna says, adding, worriedly, "I just don't know how long he can keep this up."

Success in Napa requires a genteel hawking of a winery owner's own persona. In Switzerland, Donald does not have to subject himself to endless interviews with wine and food writers and play host at one tasting after another, or give and attend dinner parties, to sell his Valser St. Petersquelle—or anything else. But as a latecomer who hopes to win for his wines the celebrity—among cognoscenti—of names like Robert Mondavi or Clos du Val or Schramsberg—he must submit to a partial cannibalizing of himself.

Because he thrives on contact with people, he does not see this as quite the sacrifice Joanna does. "We live in a very low-key way in

Switzerland and we have the most beautiful house there," she says, a little wistfully. "The gardens are at their peak right now. There's a rhythm one misses when one travels so much." It is only September, but she has already flown to California and back five times this year: the next round-trip, in October, will be her seventh. "It's basically a physical problem—I'm just tired," she says.

"Then you wish Donald would just stay in Switzerland?"

"Well I've never lived in one place. Your home is within yourself," she replies.

Later, she is blunter. "Switzerland gets on my nerves. You know, it's all so *perfect*—I'd like to go, unhuuunh!—mess it up a little bit," she says, twinkling, with a sweeping motion of one hand.

"Then you must like having a Californian dimension to your life," I say.

"What pulls us here is this land. It's just giving back to you so much. Just being in the vineyards or going for a walk gives you this feeling of expansion which is so difficult to get in Europe. Everything is so built up in Switzerland, even on the outskirts of Bern.

"But," she adds after a considering pause, "it's very important to keep the window open here so we can fly out again. I would find it difficult to live here full-time. I would miss Europe very much."

I have recently read somewhere that people free themselves of the yoke of necessity only to be saddled with the burden of choice. Listening to Joanna, I am suddenly grateful that hers is not my load to tote. On the other hand, I know just what she means about the feeling of expansion on this continent.

"The emptiness of the West was . . . a geography of possibility," the writer Gretel Ehrlich reflects in an essay. She goes on to lament that once barbed-wire fencing bounded and fragmented the landscape, "the 'anything is possible' fever . . . was constricted." But for people from the cramped and rule-bound Old World, the magic still works—still amplifies a sense of personal latitude, still opens minds to the unexpected and nonconformist.

Donald Hess likes to think of himself as sui generis. Most of us do, I suppose, but Donald's dislike of being consigned to a group is fierce. He countered every parallel I drew between his and Jan Shrem's and

Thomas Lundstrom's style of engagement with the Napa Valley with a listing of the differences between them.

So much is unarguable: They are all foreigners. They could all have afforded to be career lotus-eaters, had they chosen to—and each of them had run other kinds of businesses, with varying degrees of success—when they lit on winemaking as a focus for their energies, a creative conduit. Winemaking is a way of getting someone else to make art for them, a sort of secondary self-expression: each has hired a talented winemaker whose work communicates his employer's most precise and subtle ideas about what wine should taste like.

They are all art collectors. Collecting art, for them, is an avocation of passion, and contact with works of art seems to help appease a craving for purpose. In Napa it gained another dimension for them. The valley became irresistible to them when they found, in the notion of sharing their art treasures and sense of style with the natives, a higher purpose—something like a latter-day variant of the White Man's Burden, or the *mission civilisatrice* of French colonists.

Donald's design of his own larger mission is guided by Joanna—his *femme inspiratrice*. She had little to do with his work until he bought his stake in Napa. The winery interests her more than any of his other businesses, she tells me, "because it has such potential to grow in many, many different artistic directions—not just as a winery. Look at the possibilities," she says breathlessly, "—the film festivals, concerts and the art courses. We could even have environmental discussions here and seminars. About what we're doing to the planet, to the land. What can we do to get away from using pesticides and herbicides. It has such incredible scope.

"It's a chance to make a different awareness happen—within the, let's say, *mundane* success story of a vineyard."

We are whizzing round Mount Veeder's many blind curves, Joanna at the wheel of a spiffy all-black Jeep, driving with élan. We are on our way to an immensely old oak tree she wants me to see—a "menstruation tree" for the coastal Miwok Indians to whom this land, now owned by her and Donald, once belonged.

"Donald thinks a lot. He's growing a lot. He's becoming more and more aware—in a global direction," she says. "And that makes me very happy."

We stop beside a padlocked gate beyond which a mud track has been scraped out of the fold between hilltops colonized by widely spaced oaks casting long, graceful afternoon shadows. Joanna pauses on her way to tackle the lock. "We both feel that we have to make some kind of mark in ecological matters. This is probably a very good time in our lives to go in the direction of giving rather than making money.

"Donald is looking for a new challenge—and it's an inner challenge," she says, proud and somber.

I think back on her account of a conversation she recently had with a dinner partner, a man who, having made a fortune through the sale of the winery he established, was wondering whether he should start a second. "But there's been so much success in this valley," she told him. "Why don't you take it a step further and become a center for conscious effort for [fighting] what is destroying the earth? The valley needs a conscience."

So Donald is not the only person she incites to dream bigger dreams. Yet she has led her husband on treks into the transcendental blue yonder of a sort no other successful businessman I have met has ever told. "We are all a little bit believers in reincarnation in our family," Donald has announced. He has his own commonsensical, Swiss-German take on the matter. "I never quite understood why, when everything else is so well used in this world, that the most complicated part of us, our soul, would just be buried and not reused."

We arrive at the menstruation tree and I begin to see why Donald goes along on her capers. In years of admiring oak trees, I have never seen anything resembling this one. Its trunk is too thick for any tree-hugger to get his arms around, and its perfectly symmetrical branches descend, their tips not far above the ground: like a banyan tree's, the limbs and leaves create something like a numinous arboreal cave.

So here I am with an elegant, tweed-clad Joanna cutting a distinctly surreal figure as she dives in and out of the oak.

"You see, it has its own sphere," she says. "When you're under those branches, you're in it. I can imagine the women just squatting here, with the children running around and playing and laughing, and probably feeling that they were feeding the earth, recycling their energies.

"But it's very *dense* under the tree, a very dense energy. Not bad, just *very* heavy. Really *earth*," she says in a throaty whisper. "It pulls me down."

Later, Donald and I are standing on the brow of a hillock, encircled by other hillocks rising to hills that graduate mistily to mountains at the distant perimeter of the circle. Land under vines makes for a patch here and a patch there, interrupting a panorama of undulant meadows and scattered stands of live oak, Douglas fir and redwood, and thickets of manzanita. This spread Donald bought on Mount Veeder, though formally included in the Napa Valley in the appellation rules, is actually a twenty-minute drive from the valley's floor. He points to the boundaries of his land and, because some of them coincide with the circle's edge, I think fiefdom, principality, kingdom even: the mountains make up exactly the sort of barrier you would want to keep the barbarians at bay. Scarcely any buildings interrupt the greenery—just his winery and the red-tiled structures and bell tower of the chapel owned by the Christian Brothers, the order of monks that ran a winery under its name for nearly a century.

For both a vineyardist and a progressive Napa winemaker, these mountainside vines present challenges that call for steely spines. Untamed, the mountain wines are harsh, because Napa's high-altitude vines typically grow in poorer, faster-draining soils than those on the valley floor, and produce, as the fruit of this struggle, smaller berries in which aromas, flavors and especially tannins are intensely concentrated. Donald and his winemaker, Randle Johnson, have transformed these liabilities into veins of character and distinction in Cabernet and Chardonnay wines that are otherwise velvet-smooth, in the best French tradition. Even before the winery's official debut—when the Hess wines were being made in rented facilities—the most feared of American wine pundits, Robert Parker, had predicted that its Cabernets could "turn out to be among the very finest made in California."

Neither Donald Hess nor Jan Shrem nor Thomas Lundstrom is from any of the world's great wine countries. Yet part of their civilizing mission in Napa is to insinuate European—principally French—styles of winemaking into Californian barrels. Although in the last century German, French and Italian émigrés brought over both the craft of winemaking and cuttings of traditional varieties of grapevines—like Riesling, Cabernet Sauvignon, Merlot, Sauvignon Blanc—Californian wines made from the fruit of those vines have their own distinctive flavors. Differences in soil, climate and winemaking techniques inevitably alter the final product of a crush. There is also a grape variety virtually unique to America (its European antecedents are obscure) that produces a wine of remarkable range called Zinfandel, which can be subtle and even delicate but, traditionally, has been rough and hearty.

Quintessential Zinfandel epitomizes the extreme of the Californian style—big, overstated, crashingly orchestral. This is, anyway, how wines made the traditional Californian way strike someone whose palate has been conditioned by good French wine. The newcomers all speak of trying to bring a more refined sensibility to Napa winemaking—ideally, a careful balancing of daring innovation with harmony and restraint.

They did not pioneer delicacy in Californian winemaking. Bernard Portet, the French manager-winemaker at Clos du Val, and Robert Mondavi are two names associated with leading the shift in style for well over a decade before the foreign millionaire-aesthetes came on the scene. But it was clear, from their very debuts, that their winemaking ambitions were consistent with their broader civilizing crusades.

Donald has made his winegrowing as difficult as can be. It is obvious even to eyes as inexperienced as mine that the obstacles to working his land verge on the quixotic. Not only is the terrain steep-sloped but it can fall away at two or three different angles in a single section of vineyard. Mechanical harvesting—a labor-saving route that even some of the elite wineries on the valley floor have been obliged to take, which is even practiced in Bordeaux—is out of the question here. The grape pickers are paid by the ton, and it makes me lightheaded to imagine them staggering uphill and downhill between grapevine and gondola, racing to boost their day's wages.

The grape picking at Hess is more expensive because it is so heavily dependent on human effort. The work of planting and establishing terraced vineyards is far more arduous and more than twice as costly as putting down roots on the valley floor (where the yields are more bountiful, too—an average of five tons an acre, compared to three or four in the hills).

"Our biggest problem on our steep hills is erosion in the winter rains," Donald tells me, showing me a long gash in the ground at the bottom of a section of vineyard. "What you see here is part of the drainage lines we have to dig to prevent it. We go down anywhere from ten feet to eighteen feet—we dig big trenches, which we fill with stones and, where the ground is too rocky, we put in pipes instead, and in this way we take the water down to our reservoir."

All of these extra costs have been carefully fitted into his profit-and-loss plan for the winery.

His goals for what his wines should taste like are defined just as meticulously. In wine's chemistry, it is mostly through the action of tannins that aging wine acquires its depth and many facets of flavor. The tannin in the Hess mountain Cabernet could make a "heavy" wine that would be superb after ten years of aging. But few Americans have cellars and a tradition of buying wine years ahead of its consumption: virtually all the wine bought in America is drunk in less than two days. On the other hand, no winery could hope to be profitable, storing an expanding stock of wine for ten years before its first release. This calls for "lighter" and more "forward" wines that are ready to drink in, at most, five years. "But still we want them to have elegance and complexity—like a diamond with a lot of little sparkles—like Bordeaux wines, but without slavishly copying the Bordeaux people," Donald says.

His hopes for his winery's success are tied up with an ambition that has haunted him for years—"doing right what I did wrong at twenty." One of the businesses in the collection he inherited was a winemaking château near Geneva with fifty acres under the vine. The château's roof was leaking and in need of urgent repair, so one of his first decisions as the new head of Hess Holdings was to sell that stake in Swiss viticulture. For years after that he failed to find a replacement where he hoped to, in France or Italy.

His first trip to the Napa Valley, in 1978, was actually an abortive quest for a spring of mineral water. The day he gave up the search, he found himself sitting with Joanna in a restaurant where he asked the proprietor to bring him the very best local Chardonnay and

Cabernet wines he had. He remembers that a 1976 Château Monte-lena and the 1970 Private Reserve Cabernet from Beaulieu were set before him. "And I was astounded because until then I'd thought, you know, that California wines were probably like Moroccan or Algerian wines—too fruity and too heavy, with not enough acidity."

He returned to California a short while later and spent seven weeks visiting Napa as well as rival winegrowing regions near Mendocino and Monterey and in Sonoma County. He chose Napa coolly and logically—because, as the most famous stretch of American wine country, its wines would be easiest to find customers for. Of the most desirable land on the valley floor, parcels that were for sale he thought overpriced.

Then, he says, he wandered up into the hills and instantly fell in love. "I abs-o-lute-ly had the *coup de foudre* when I saw those steep hills." Business-minded rationalizations, such as the interesting impressions that the mountain wines make on palates, came later.

Art frames and tidies life in the raw at the Hess Collection Winery. Ornamental beds planted with too precisely spaced flowering plants and shrubs greet the visitor at the front of the complex. In the central inner courtyard, strips of concrete enclose a rectangular "meadow" of wildflowers and grasses.

The winery and art gallery are housed in a sandstone structure of clean, simple lines, built in 1903: it was expanded and remodeled by the Swiss architect Beat Jordi. The extension, for the gallery and tasting room, has neoclassical flourishes like a wrought-iron-and-glass awning above the main, round-arched glass doorway.

In the starkly stylish tasting and sales room, there is none of the clutter of tourist knickknacks you find elsewhere in Napa. Your attention is riveted by the abstract "mural" high up one wall: a window that looks onto stacked oak barrels from Nuits-Saint-Georges in Burgundy.

Inside the white-walled art gallery—softly incandescent during the day, because of sunshine filtering through skylights and an abundance of windows—large glass panels expose sections of the winery's innards. Viewed from this perspective, the immaculate steel fermentation tanks seem Beaubourg-ish. On the top floor of the gallery, wine bottles glide silently along a semicircular conveyor belt—the automatic bottler—that looks like a kinetic sculpture. Parts of the hilly vineyards are visible from some of the gallery's windows. Beside one window hang two Frank Stella lithographs, geometric arrangements of parallel lines of solid color on bone-white backgrounds that seem like distorted modernist mirrorings of the vine rows.

After the drive here along narrow roads snaking through forest and thick brush, the gallery is as improbable as, say, coming upon a Hermès boutique in the Amazon jungle. The works here are about as cerebral as modern art gets, and yet it is as if they and the grapevines outside are each straining to capture something of the essence of the other. Through their splodges and splashes and whorls and teasing asymmetries, the modernist *objets* expose what is most wild and untamed in their creators—stand for a shaking off of classical conventions for the sake of viscerality. Whereas the vine rows express ancient agricultural conventions and must fight untamed nature, tooth for tooth, claw for claw, to exist at all. So, nature and civilization are here married in a peculiar harmony.

Everything dispatched from the Hess Collection Winery to the outside world reflects Donald's wish for his wines to acquire a reputation for quality that will far outlive him. Joanna sketched the blueprint for the wine label, which is decorated with raised gilt letters in a plain Roman typeface. Above the label on each bottle is a detail intended to attract browsing shoppers: a gold coat of arms featuring a pair of lions with outstretched claws.

It's the same crest that embellishes the Hess notepaper—borrowed from Roerswyl, the country mansion outside Bern that Donald's father bought in 1929, built in 1308 for a religious order of women called Frau Brunner. (Donald's own crest, designed for the original family business, did not seem right for Napa: it consists of three hops.)

Such connections to the past plainly gratify him. He has told me he misses the keener European appreciation of historical context when he is in California. So one day I ask whether it might not have been more satisfying to have located the Hess winery—art and all—in Switzerland.

He shakes his head. "I feel I have a much better audience here than in Europe. If somebody is successful here, people look up to him, whereas in Europe, they look down on him. They say, what a parasite, he must be a drug trafficker. Our European socialist system tries to drag everyone down to a lower level.

"I said to my managers in Switzerland—you know, one day I want to make my art collection public, and I would want to do it somewhere close to our headquarters. Do you think that's a good idea? They spontaneously said, that's great, but within two or three months, five of my six managers came up to me and said that as much as they liked the idea, they thought it would harm our business more than it would do it any good. You see, they said, people might think that this is proof that Hess sells his products far too expensively, that he is making far too much money.

"The American, when it comes to culture, has almost an inferiority complex that he shouldn't really have, but that makes him want and need to *learn*."

But sadly, in the course of conversations with Donald spread out over two years, I discover that the green-eyed monster has caught up with him in Napa. Because there are few private art collections like his anywhere and certainly none that are open to the public in rural California, art critics have written about him adoringly, as have glossy women's magazines. Other wineries make wine as good as his but few winery owners are as lively, expansive and photogenic— which means he is a darling of the wine press; has even been given the cover of *The Wine Spectator*, an honor yet to be accorded many longer-established Napa notables. The head of another winery, another urbane foreigner and a friend of Donald's, complained to me that Donald used his art collection unfairly, to grab more than his proper share of attention.

So, ever alert to the changing mood of his public, Donald began to cut back sharply on attention-getting cultural events—such as flying over the fourteen members of the Camerata Bern to perform. He told me he sympathized with the valley's large population of regular Joes—people who were neither oenophiles nor art lovers and were "a bit sick of hearing about the wine, of the traffic density from all the visitors attracted to the area, and of the culture the wineries want to push down their throats for PR reasons."

Roughly two years after his winery's grand opening, Donald had limited its cultural propagandizing to an occasional class in art appreciation and the sponsorship of a series of lectures at nearby state universities—on such esoteric but presumably useful subjects as "Terminal Reality and the Disembodied Presence" and "The Sensuality of Packaging."

But he had no wish to relinquish his Napa fiefdom and retreat to Bern.

"You know, I feel sad for Europe," he said once, a rare, brooding expression clouding his face. "We lost the child in us. You can't make a fellow laugh in Switzerland anymore, except with a dirty joke or alcohol.

"But here, you see even old people dance. And how they enjoy themselves!"

CHAPTER THREE

A Very Old Pioneer

"In my youth I wanted to become a literary man—and didn't; I wanted to speak well—and I spoke horribly badly. . . . I wanted to get married—and I didn't; I always wanted to live in town and here I am ending my life in the country—and so on."

> Sorin in *The Sea Gull*,
> ANTON CHEKHOV

"A Russian is peculiarly given to exalted ideas, but why is it he always falls so short in life? Why?"

> Vershinin in *The Three Sisters*,
> ANTON CHEKHOV

IT IS ALL SO VERY SAD.

After a year and a half of waiting to see him—of being told that he was ill yet again, or convalescing, or frantically catching up with his work—I am seated beside the grand old man of Napa Valley winemaking, André Tchelistcheff, on his polka-dotted living room sofa. It is late spring in Napa. Beyond the sliding glass door of the room, arresting patches of deep pink and red azaleas remind me that André's wife, Dorothy, told me on the telephone that "his garden is where he works off his frustrations."

Take what he says literally and he is a disappointed man, passionately aggrieved, bitter even, and his frail, slight frame—he could scarcely be more than five feet tall—seems in danger of being shaken asunder by the force of his emotions. Exclamation marks seem the most natural form of punctuation for his sentences. "I am *not* a part of Napa Valley. I am NOT a part of Napa Valley!" he insists, bending towards me from the waist and striking the expanse of sofa between us with the back of one hand. His milky jade green eyes have an angry glaze, and the dark, thick, winglike eyebrows above them seem poised to shoot off his face. "I am *very* foreign—*ve-rrry* Russian! Aristocratic. That's my tragedy."

Yes, he understands that I wish to talk to him about the disproportionate role he is said to have played in transforming Napa's status in world winemaking. About his philosophy as a winemaker. Even so, "One thing I hope you will understand. I have a very little opinion of myself in importance as a personality of Napa Valley. And wine as such, as a profession, has had very little influence on me as a person. Okay, I've been doing my job for sixty years of my life, but it's never absorbed me to such a point where I'm really part of this damn, overpriced Napa Valley!"

The years that he has, in spite of himself, devoted to winemaking, have been wasted. "My *maître*—my professor—in France said, 'André, you could have been an excellent research man. But do not go into industry because if you do, you'll become a servant of industry.' And I am a servant of industry—instead of being myself in the excitement of academic research—when you don't sleep, or you only sleep for half one night, because you are working! I would have loved microbiology as a profession!"

There is certainly no visible evidence of spectacular material rewards for this woefully misdirected life, chez Tchelistcheff. "Recently someone said to me, very probably, in the past, you used to have vineyards, a winery, et cetera. I said, no. See what I have— this house? Little tiny thing? Little garden. And space in a cemetery in St. Helena—for tomorrow—which has everything on it: André Tchelistcheff {he pronounces it ch*ell*-cheff}, with my date of birth, and my wife or my son will add the final words. That's it—my real estate investment! Because I understand that everyone is finishing up exactly the same way!"

Absorbing all of this, it strikes me that I should at least be mildly depressed, in sympathy with what is being said. Instead I feel the elation of being completely engaged—enthralled—by a conversation. For even at just seven months shy of eighty-eight, André is magnetizing his audience of one with his exotic intensity, and with the sort of charm that flows from a burning curiosity about other people. "Tell me," he had demanded only minutes after I sat down, "maybe this is not polite or even ethical, but I'm going to ask you a question. What have you been doing in your life that you have reached this point in it—of taking on this challenge?" Because the answers were not what he expected, he had chuckled delightedly.

I am struck by his having no trouble whatever hearing or understanding me, even though I am talking fast and idiomatically, with an English accent, and he in his own idiosyncratic English, with what he describes as his "heavy Franco-Russian accent."

Only last night, he and Dorothy entertained a visiting Georgian, fresh off the plane from Moscow, until one o'clock in the morning. The visit began at six. "An exciting evening!" André says, twinkling and smiling broadly. "We consumed a great amount of wines and cognacs and armagnacs! And continuous conversation, and singing together! We quoted Pushkin—Eugene Onegin! And an endless toasting. Toasting of the past. Toasting of the future. Toasting of the fact of life and inheritance!"

So it occurs to me that much of his breast-beating about roads not taken stems not from literal disappointment or a sense of actual failure but from Russian temperament. It is an aspect of the peculiarly Russian indulgence of the untranslatable *toska*, an undefined longing, the feeling that what you most deeply want and need is somewhere else.

And yet André Tchelistcheff radiates the restfulness of a man profoundly comfortable in his home, which is startlingly modest for one whose name invariably appears prefaced by the adjective "legendary" in historical accounts of Californian winemaking. The plain gray shingle-roofed Tchelistcheff dwelling sits on perhaps a quarter of an acre in a row of well-tended cottages snuggled up to one another along a gentle rise in a funky suburb of the city of Napa.

Most of the Napa Valley's distinguished denizens live surrounded by vineyards on their estates, many of them further "up valley," closer to the rustically genteel and plutocratic town of St. Helena, or off in the hills. André and his wife, Dorothy, live within the limits of predominantly working-class and lower-middle-class Napa, at the valley's southern neck.

Visitors enter the Tchelistcheff home through a yard smothered in gleaming ivy, then proceed through the screen door of a Lilliputian kitchen. The living room, perhaps fourteen feet long and twelve feet wide, is tidy and homely (in the English sense of the word: pertaining to home; unpretentious). There are lacquer boxes on end tables, a bold blue and white Chinese rug to one side, and scattered, garish, decoy ducks. Framed portrait photographs of André hang on one wall; watercolors of bunches of grapes by a local artist on another. Above the fireplace is a large, imposing crest, cast in bronze turned black.

Dorothy explains that it is the Romanoff crest—the double-headed imperial Russian eagle. One of André's consulting clients, Brooks Firestone—the tire company heir who left the family business to start a winery—recently presented it to him at a dinner given in his honor. It was acquired from the uncle of an American merchant seaman who found it in Leningrad in the last world war: "The story was that the little Czarovich was a hemophiliac. So at the summer palace, the father had a railroad built on the grounds for the youngster. And on the smokestack of the railroad were two emblems—and that's one of them."

A saucy cuckoo clock sings out the hour at the Tchelistcheffs'. Twittering birds in the garden sound like an exuberant Latin extended family on an outing. Expressions of Slavic gloom and anomie—however sincere—are unconvincing here.

I knew that André Tchelistcheff was in his late eighties and I did not go to see him with much hope. The very old can make rambling conversationalists: because I have a voice that old men do not hear well, it is difficult for me to interrupt them and steer them back on course. I had made my appointment dutifully—had been urged to do so by others in the reverential tones in which people discuss living historical figures. I went along like a first-time visitor to Paris dragging herself to the Eiffel Tower without the smallest hope of enjoying the experience.

Halfway through the first afternoon we spent together I confessed my low expectations for our meeting. He shook with silent laughter. "You said to yourself, 'It is going to be *murder* interviewing André Tchelistcheff,' didn't you? *Hell!*" he added, with keen relish.

The short history of California as a winemaking region—in which André, diminutive as he is, looms so large—has five eras.

In the first, the mission era, wine was made by Franciscan missionaries for their altars and dinner tables, most of them in southern California. This era began around 1769 and continued through the 1830s.

In the second, the pioneer era, cowboys outdid the clerics. American ranchers cultivated vines as one of several agricultural pursuits and sold modest quantities of wine from cellars that were mostly tiny. The California historian Kevin Starr has noted that in this phase, which ended in the early 1860s, few of the wine producers had Mediterranean ancestry: they were principally of Yankee or Irish stock. This era, too, was predominantly a southern Californian phenomenon. In the Napa Valley, the first grapevines were planted by George Yount, a trapper from North Carolina, in 1838. The state of California took the lead in American wine production in 1870.

In the third era, roughly the last quarter of the nineteenth century, the growing popularity of Californian wines led to two phases of breakneck expansion in the business, followed by spectacular busts. Kevin Starr tells of vineyards being leased to pig farmers who grazed their animals on ripe grapes during those collapses. This was the period in which recent émigrés from the traditional European wine-producing countries began to plant vineyards and contribute their superior instincts for viticulture and winemaking to California's developing wine country. In the mini-booms in production, so many corners were cut that quality plummeted and Californian wines were stuck with a reputation for inferiority. Still, in 1889, in this same historical phase, Californian wines won their first gold medals at the Paris exposition.

Between 1880 and 1900, approximately, owners of Californian vineyards fought the spread of phylloxera—by which European wine country was even more severely damaged.

The fourth era followed Prohibition, which lasted from 1920 until 1933—a fourteen-year stretch in which a defiant surge in home winemaking led to greatly expanded wine grape acreages. But less than a quarter of commercial Californian wineries survived by Prohibition's end. So the fourth, post-Repeal, phase in the industry's life was a sort of convalescence in which it struggled to reestablish itself. The Second World War proved helpful. Imports were severely restricted and several European vineyards were destroyed, which meant that some Americans tried Californian wines for the first time and were surprised to find they liked them.

These converted taste buds made for a base on which the modern era was gradually established. The 1950s and 1960s were marked by a sort of shuffling progress in the maturing of Californian winemaking, with intervals of backsliding—until 1966. That was when Robert Mondavi built his winery at Oakville, and his optimistic splurging on stainless steel fermentation tanks, French oak barrels and up-to-the-minute laboratory equipment was a prescient statement of faith in a brilliant future.

It was in 1937, about halfway through the post-Repeal era—stretching from 1933 to 1946—that André came to California from France to work for Beaulieu Vineyard. Through the 1940s, 1950s and early 1960s, he gradually acquired the status of the best-known Californian winemaker, the brightest star in an admittedly small and rather obscure galaxy—since the talents of winemakers, like those of chefs, were not then recognized outside their places of work. In the provincial and parochial Napa Valley of the day, "we all wanted to be André," a former apprentice of his told me. "But none of us had the personality to match his."

Roy Andries de Groot, in *The Wines of California, the Pacific Northwest and New York*, has described André as "a supremely imaginative and innovative winemaker and teacher of most of the important technicians of our time."

Beaulieu's "winemaking style of elegance and finesse, shaped by the legendary André Tchelistcheff, influenced an entire school of winemakers, from the 1950's to the present day," wrote James Laube in *California's Great Cabernets*. The Private Reserve wines, he noted, "rarely departed from the rich concentration of ripe fruit, delicate balance and fine tannins that made the wine eminently drinkable on release yet remarkably ageworthy, gaining elegance, complexity and finesse with age."

Perhaps inevitably, there are cognoscenti who do not rate André's talents as a winemaker quite so highly—critics and rivals who insist that he was merely a good rather than supremely gifted winemaker who had the luck of perfect timing for his arrival in California. But far beyond question is this: that he brought with him and taught to Californians who entered his orbit—taught them by example rather than by fiat—the culture of wine appreciation, the wine-loving sensibility, that were part of his upbringing.

When Joe Heitz, a former protégé, worked for André in the 1950s and early 1960s, he had yet to make a single pilgrimage to the great winemaking regions of the Old World. Listening to his superior analyze wines, André remembers, Joe's honest-to-goodness American reaction was "to treat everything I said satirically. He used to tell people, everything he is saying in tasting the wines is artificial! He is trying to make a fuss out of it—to make it a very complex business! He was very sarcastic about my teaching him about the *feeling* of wine!"

A seeming digression.

Soon after I left London to live in California in 1981, it struck me that one of the strangenesses of the New World was the extraordinary earnestness with which Americans I dined with discussed wine.

A native-born Californian friend asked me how the English treated the subject in similar circumstances. I sketched an impression of the difference. At a London meal, an exceptional wine was briefly applauded with something like, "Mmmmm. Very nice!" or "Lovely!" and "Jolly well ought to be, at the price!"

Occasionally two oenophiles might indeed conduct an exchange something like one of these, in *Brideshead Revisited*:

"... It is a little, shy wine like a gazelle."
"Like a leprechaun."
"Dappled, in a tapestry meadow."
"Like a flute by still water."
"... And this is a wise old wine."
"A prophet in a cave."
"... And this is a necklace of pearls."
"Like a swan."
"Like the last unicorn."

Other guests would treat those remarks as hobbyists' esoterica not intended for their ears.

In California, a chance remark about the wine seemed frequently to convert the dinner table into a miniature lecture hall for a good half hour.

"Yes, I thought it was a Chardonnay! Let's see now, it says Frog's Leap on the label. But I'm so ashamed—I really know practically nothing about wine. Hey, Paul, you're the expert—tell me whether this winery's any good."

There nearly always was a Paul present—someone able to tell what he knew of the winery's reputation, who would obligingly dissect the wine into its component oak and vanilla and fruit flavors and (most astonishingly, to the Old World ear) say a few words about anything he knew of the winery's "marketing strategy." The other guests listened with rapt attention—I no less than anyone else, because these wine sippers in America tended to be engagingly didactic members of the intelligentsia.

Yet I was baffled by why expert opinions on the quality of a wine seemed to matter to Americans far more than the impression it made on their taste buds. The obsession with correctness was difficult to reconcile with what—viewed from an English perspective—were the cheerful, everyday barbarisms of Americans at the table: eating toast spread with jam between mouthfuls of bacon and eggs, for heaven's sake, instead of treating jam on toast as a separate course. Or downing glutinous milkshakes with their hamburgers, instead of saving them for later, as a sweet course.

Wine did appear to occupy entirely different places in life across the Atlantic.

In London it had helped to make of meals isolated pools of light and warmth in an unending bleakness. Wine made chinks in English reticence and made it possible for people to open their hearts to one another. Such interludes were a dire necessity—to get you through winter and even more so, the desolation of yet another summer-that-wasn't. You stretched out memories of these respites for as long as you could. Wrapping them around you like a luxurious extra layer of insulation, you used them to shut out the depressed, shut-in faces of your fellow human beings and the rest of your surroundings, commuting on the grim and squalid Underground—or trudging through a drizzle, grocery-stuffed plastic bags slicing into your hands, an umbrella handle wedged in the crook of one arm.

In California, wine was not needed as a salve for the psyche, succor for the soul: landscape and the climate met these needs, it seemed to me. The Californians with whom I drank treated it as a substance primarily designed to be run through their intellectual and aesthetic faculties, for which their palates dutifully gathered data.

As for myself, I felt as if I could taste the beneficence of California in the exuberant, ripe flavors of the local wines. European connoisseurs might sneer at the too generous oak barrel infusions in the Chardonnays, but I was swallowing platinum hillsides shimmering in summer heat and studded with grand gnarled old oak trees. In the early days of my expatriation I can remember a glass of wine helping, for an hour or two, to take the edge off my guilt about living in an earthly outpost of paradise without having done a thing to deserve it.

Time and again, I have been struck by how, to Americans, the connection between wine and pleasure does not seem to be self-evident. Indeed there seems to be a tradition of Europeans assuring anxious Americans to just relax and enjoy wines that their taste buds find congenial.

For instance. In 1983, Christian Mouiex, the Bordeaux *négociant* associated, most famously, with Château Pétrus—the most expensive wine in the world in the 1980s—answered questions put to him by two interviewers from L'Académie du Vin in New York. He said: "What is a great wine? For me it is a wine that pleases you. Pleasure is a part of life and we should not forget that, you know."

Admittedly, Americans continually amaze people from the Old World by the kinds of advice they seek from experts. "Can you believe it, a whole wall of books just about how to *live*!" I remember a Greek woman exclaiming disgustedly after an expedition to the self-help section of a bookshop on her first visit to the United States.

In Europe, people suffer silently for their ignorance of matters that society deems instinctive—as if knowledge of them can only be passed on in their mothers' milk. Particular sorts of knowledge are the preserve of particular social classes. In a short story called "Copenhagen Season," Isak Dinesen tidily assigns an intimate familiarity with wine to its proper place in Europe's past—which still casts a long shadow over the present:

> In the great country houses . . . the sons of territorial magnates . . . were open-air people; their predominant interests were hunting, with the care of stock or game on their estates, horses, good wine, forestry and farming, and fair women.

Mulling over all of this, I gradually set aside my puzzlement over why, at the mid-century, it should have taken a White Russian to teach Americans how to savor the fruit of the vine. André Tchelistcheff was exactly right for the job. He was born into Russia's rural gentry, which had much in common with the aristocracy.

Besides, of all the European wine-drinking peoples, the Russians, with their sepia-tinted souls, would seem most easily and profoundly able to grasp the many facets of the myth of Dionysus. Death and rebirth are associated with the Greek god of the grape: the idea of arriving at an affirmation of life through the experience of being torn apart.

Wine's mythical resonances make it almost a foregone conclusion that the life of the man that led Napa into the modern era of wine-making should contain strange lands and separations, princes and princesses, disastrous acts of nature and a political revolution. The idea of a life making wine was far removed from the ambitions of his childhood: the road that led him to it was tortuous.

André Tchelistcheff was born in Moscow on November 24, 1901. Up to the age of eleven, he was brought up on the family estate about one hundred miles southwest of Moscow in the province of Kaluga. The difficulty of maintaining family members in the country in the manner to which they were accustomed had begun a move off the land and into the professions in the generation before André's. In an interview with the archivist Ruth Teiser of the Regional Oral History Office of Berkeley's Bancroft Library, he said:

"I remember, for instance, early-maturing cherries near the house, and I remember the years that the cost of harvesting was already prohibitive to the point that the cherries were left to the birds. The same thing happened to dairy products, and life became very difficult on the property. All these families of the—I hate to say, aristocratic origin, because it's not true—but all the families of old origins have all kinds of privileges. They raise horses, they raise hounds, and the horses and the hunting dogs consume a tremendous amount of money."

Certainly wine was one of the good things in this way of life. There was always Madeira and port in crystal decanters in the drawing room, and French or Crimean wines were drunk with meals. Some of the Crimean wines came from the estates of the imperial family and from land owned by the family of Prince Golitzin (who later married André's sister Alexandra Victorovna). André remembers getting drunk for the first time, as a child—illicitly draining the dregs of champagne glasses returned to the kitchen with his sister Anne one New Year's Eve. A present from a godfather made him the juvenile absentee landlord of a vineyard in the Crimea.

He was confined to bed with tuberculosis and peritonitis for four years of his childhood, which meant that his parents paid him even more attention than was considered his due as the eldest son. He read the newspaper to his father at breakfast, after which a tutor appeared to teach him his day's lessons.

André's father, Viktor Tchelistcheff, a jurist who eventually became chief justice of the court of appeal in Moscow, was a liberal who openly favored a revolution. André believes that, like other highly cultivated intellectuals of the same persuasion, his father had only a tenuous grasp on reality and so failed tragically to foresee the consequences of overthrowing the old order—for his country or his family. He was offered a high position in the short-lived Kerensky government. When it collapsed and the Reds took over, the family had to flee to the Ukraine, where the civil war began. Viktor Tchelistcheff became a secretary of justice in the White government.

Meanwhile André himself enrolled in the officer's course at the White Army's military academy in Ekaterinodar (now Krasnodar). Two and a half years after he joined the army, when the Reds had the White Army on the run, he was evacuated by way of the Black Sea with thousands of other soldiers. They subsisted aboard ship on near-starvation rations for many days while they waited for the Allies to decide what to do with them.

That evacuation foreshadowed years of enforced wandering, when fate dictated André's life to such a degree as to make the idea of free will laughable.

For over a year, André's regiment languished in the Dardanelles, awaiting orders. It was dispatched to Bulgaria to work, first, in the coal mines and later, to help put Czar Boris back on the Bulgarian throne. André put in a stint as a frontier guard for Yugoslavia's King Alexander. Then the Nansen Committee of the League of Nations set about helping young refugees to complete their education. André found himself in Czechoslovakia studying for the college entrance examination and, when he passed it, literally drew in a lottery a place at the Institute of Agricultural Technology in Brunn (now Brno): overwhelmed by the crush of young refugees, the authorities could not match their vocational preferences to places at universities.

From his boyhood, André had dreamed of being a doctor. Now he decided to make the best of a career as an agronomist with a particular interest in animal husbandry. In 1929, he started work at an experimental agronomy station in Yugoslavia, where he had moved with his father and siblings. Before this migration, there had been an important six-month interlude in the Tokay region of Hungary, where he got some training in viticulture and winemaking. He emphasizes that, then, winemaking only appealed to him as a sideline. His chief hope was to have a farm of his own on which he would rear animals.

That wish was realized in 1933—in France. Another displaced White Russian family with which the Tchelistcheffs had stayed in touch was that of Prince Sergey Troubetskoy, a graduate of a French agricultural institute. He and André went into partnership with a group of other agronomists, farming an estate in the Ile-de-France.

André's work on the farm led him into a deepening fascination with poultry, about which he wrote and had two books published in French. Then, in the partnership's second year, a catastrophic shower of hailstones the size of "about a pigeon's egg destroyed all our fields, everything," André told the Bancroft Library interviewer. The partners were forced out of business.

André decided he would have to return to his winemaking studies. He supported himself working part-time for large wineries while he immersed himself in experimental viticulture and in the science of fermentation. In 1938, Georges de Latour, the founder of Beaulieu Vineyard—one of the two resplendent Napa wineries of the day—called on one of André's professors at the Pasteur Institute in Paris.

Beaulieu's owner was looking for a specialist—someone who could help him put an end to frequent, tiresome chemical breakdowns of his wine. The professor immediately suggested his cosmopolitan White Russian student for the job.

André hardly leapt at the chance. Before Georges de Latour appeared on the scene, he had decided he should make a career in research in France. He had the requisite curiosity and intense, obsessive interest in the work—and he had ruled out commercial winemaking in France as an option because, "in those particular days, foreigners were looked upon with a very dirty eye by the French people. So I knew I had to emigrate or stay with the research institution."

What tipped the balance in favor of California was that the parents of André's first wife, Alexandria Jassinsky—whom he had met and married in France—had moved to America and wanted their daughter closer to them. True, he had been intrigued by some of the first Californian wines he had ever tasted—at an international exposition held in Paris the year before Georges de Latour arrived on his quest. One or two of the wines had struck Frenchmen as well as André as astonishingly beautiful and original.

Yet it was with only faint enthusiasm that he set sail for America with his wife and son, Dimitri. His reluctance stemmed mostly from the Old World view of the United States as the world's largest cultural desert interrupted, perplexingly, by oases of artistic accomplishment and aesthetic refinement.

There was also the matter of relative status to consider, in accepting the Beaulieu job. It was not a winemaking star that Georges de Latour sought, but a talented technician. A career in research at the Pasteur Institute in Paris had far more prestige than even the post of manager-winemaker at Beaulieu, to which André was promoted a few months after his arrival in California in the autumn of 1938.

Years later, when André was ready to retire, Dimitri—recognized as an outstanding winemaker in his own right—refused to succeed his father at Beaulieu, to André's considerable disappointment. When I asked why, Dimitri said:

"It's ten o'clock at night and Madame de Pins [Georges de Latour's daughter, who ran the winery after his death] goes out for a stroll in her garden. She sees a faucet leaking and runs to the telephone and calls my father to fix it. And he goes. No, I'm not joking. That's what the general manager had to do, working for the family."

André Tchelistcheff's first taste of Napa dealt his pessimism about the move something like a sharp jab in the solar plexus.

On his first evening at Beaulieu, his host, Georges de Latour, sported a dinner jacket and bow tie. Resting on the head of Fernande de Latour—every inch the grande dame—was one of her elegant dinner hats, altogether distinctive from the hats she wore for lunch every day.

The first course consisted of crayfish caught by servants earlier in the day in a stream that ran through the family estate. With it came a wine that Georges de Latour had misidentified—and labeled—as a Chablis, that André recognized as being, actually, a cross between a Graves and a Sauternes.

Another locally made wine, a Sauternes, was poured for the second course of trout that André had been invited to fish for with his host, just before dinner.

Pheasant from the de Latour estate followed, accompanied by a well-made Cabernet. This main course of the meal might just as easily have been partridge or beef reared at Beaulieu, and also prepared skillfully enough to do the tradition of French cuisine proud. Georges was a great gourmet. Fernande was a brilliant cook and instructed the kitchen staff minutely.

For an immigrant watching his pennies—one who had tried to put out of mind the comforts of the Russian *haute bourgoisie* with which he had grown up—the de Latour estate was "the most unbelievable paradise."

André spoke no English, but that hardly mattered here in little-France-in-California. Georges de Latour's secretary spoke French as did Jean Ponti, the superintendent of the vineyards. So did the Italian gardener. French was indeed the only language spoken at the de Latours' table.

Beyond Beaulieu and a winemaking neighbor or two lay farmland—the sort of territory that, everywhere in his travels, André had found most congenial. Visually, there were professional reminders of Europe in the Napa Valley of the late 1930s: many of the vineyards were planted in the Italian manner. But the valley was not then the exclusive preserve of vineyards that it is today. Vines broke up stretches of cattle ranch country and great expanses of fruit orchards—and, as in Europe, the vineyards were worked chiefly with horses and oxen. There was only one early-model Ford tractor at Beaulieu, for instance. The town of Napa, a "little tiny settlement" to André, still looked sufficiently homespun to make it easy to imagine the field of beans on the west bank of the wide, winding Napa River that had been the original site less than a hundred years earlier.

Had the Latours merely been wealthy and living in high style, the Old World snob in André would have made him miserable at Beaulieu after his initial surprise had worn off. But he had already learned in Paris that Georges was a gentleman and had a keen mind honed by the Jesuit school he attended as a child. Also, on the head-hunting trip on which he found André, Georges had been accompanied by his son-in-law, the Marquis Henri Galcerand de Pins, an aristocrat and former cavalry officer that André liked immediately.

André's admiration for his first Californian employer bordered on worshipful. On the Bancroft Library tapes he says, "He was a man of unbelievable culture. His library and his knowledge of music, his knowledge of international literature, his knowledge of philosophy, his knowledge of theology, was unbelievable. His classical training in Latin and Greek was, I say, as good as of my father. . . . He could quote you by memory the *Odyssey*, *Julius Caesar*, by chapters."

Fate had severed Georges, too, from countryside roots in his native land and led him to seek a living abroad. He was from the Périgord. As a young man, he had had to invent an alternative to the career he had always assumed he would pursue after phylloxera destroyed the inheritance of a parcel of vineyards that his widowed mother had been saving for him.

Soon after Georges had graduated from the Ecole Centrale—one of a handful of prestigious colleges known as the *grandes écoles* at which French bureaucrats were trained—he left for California. The gold rush had petered out in the 1860s, about twenty years earlier, but he somehow got sucked into a gold-prospecting expedition to Nevada into which he sank and lost the entire nest egg of gold napoléons that his mother had hoarded for him.

Far from spelling disaster, this loss was merely the equivalent of one of many discarded canvases for a painter on his way to bringing off a masterpiece. Only a few years after the Nevada debacle, he had begun to amass a fortune of his own, running a business that converted argol—crude deposits of tartar that encrust the insides of wine tanks—into baking powder.

One of Georges's argol-gathering trips took him to Rutherford, where he fell under the spell of a 120-acre spread of farmland that he later bought, that Fernande named Beaulieu (the beautiful place). At first, wine was made on the new estate from lees—the settlings or dregs in the winemaking process—purchased from other wineries. Later, land was cleared and planted with cuttings of vines that Georges and Fernande brought back from trips to France.

For the first few years, Georges himself gave the orders in the preparation of the wines: his training in chemistry at the Ecole Centrale came in handy. When the winery began to grow, he hired as winemaker Léon Bonnet from Narbonne in the south of France, who was teaching viticulture at the University of California at Davis when Georges offered him a job. When Léon became ill and retired, he was replaced by Jean Ponti, who had—improbably enough— trained as a stonemason and gradually migrated from the building trade in Switzerland to toiling in the vineyards of California. At Beaulieu, he rose to be winemaker as well as superintendent.

Tell this to someone who only knows about Napa that some of its wines are thought by experts to be the equal of Europe's finest: a Frenchman from a part of France where wine and the best foie gras are produced was making wine in Napa near the start of the valley's modern era. Your listener will assume that the Frenchman was probably responsible for Napa wines scaling the heights of expert esteem. But that conclusion would only be very partially true.

Within Georges de Latour an idealistic aesthete and a pragmatist apparently battled to dictate the decisions he made. Those rival selves gaze out of a formal portrait of him in old age.

The white-haired, wide-browed man in the photograph wears a dark suit: a pale carnation sprouts from the edge of the wide left lapel. He has a broad, square-looking face that contains suggestions of a generous spirit, practicality and conservatism. The nose is bony, with a pronounced bump for a bridge. There is humor in the dark eyes—an assessing quality, too, and a touch of proud reserve. The mouth is thin, suggestive of a stern discrimination, but it is also wide, seemingly telling of at least an appetite for sensual indulgence.

It was certainly Georges the pragmatist that decided it would be cheaper to make Jean Ponti winemaker than to travel all the way to France to find a top-notch replacement for Léon Bonnet. After all, as André tells it, his ambition for Beaulieu was no grander than to produce merely sound wines acceptable to a French palate, and that Americans would be willing to buy.

The equipment in the winery revealed his goal as modest. Georges the aesthete had imported grapevine cuttings from France, but the pragmatist did not permit the expense of replicating French techniques, equipment and facilities. In the second half of the century, several people would begin to do this in Napa—importing French oak or finished French cooperage at considerable cost.

When André Tchelistcheff arrived, he found the winemaking facilities and procedures at Beaulieu to be decidedly makeshift: why the wines spoiled so frequently was obvious. It was, of course, Georges the aesthete that had eventually grown disgusted with the deteriorating quality of the vintages of the Ponti era, and had set off on the search for expertise that yielded André.

But it was the pragmatic Georges that provided André with the platform from which he was able gradually to influence winemaking techniques and wine appreciation in America. Without Georges's business acumen, Beaulieu might not have existed at all—or might only have been an inconsequential fraction of its size in the late 1930s. Beaulieu's story would have been rather different if he had not made a killing in the same Prohibition years that were a waking nightmare for most American winery owners.

His Jesuit schooling, charm and intelligence endeared him to clerics of the highest rank in the Catholic church in America. In the Prohibition years, when other wineries were forced to shut down,

Beaulieu prospered and grew: San Francisco's Archbishop Patrick Riordan, a friend of Georges's, issued a special bull appointing his winery as a supplier of altar wines (which were exempt from the ban on alcoholic consumption). When Prohibition ended and the skeletons of other Napa wineries were tottering to their feet, Beaulieu was able to satisfy pent-up demand with large stocks of aged wine.

There is never any suggestion, in accounts of this coup, that Georges manipulated the bull out of the archbishop unfairly. Nor was Beaulieu the only Californian winery to be awarded one: Beringer and Christian Brothers won them, too. But neither does anyone ever suggest that M. de Latour was a notably devout or charitable man. No, he just happened to have the ideal balance of qualities that success in Napa demands to this day. It is unlikely that his specially imported Russian expert, for instance, could have done as well on his own.

Slightly more than half a century after André arrived in America, he is bouncing up and down on his sofa in acute agitation. The objects of his ire are American values—materialism ("defined as rapid creation sans foundation," he explains crisply, unasked) and incessant striving. He says he has found these utterly alienating. As always, understanding him calls for a rapid decoding of his ingenious, improvised English sentences.

"I do not understand this routine of accomplishment—individuals constantly pushing up and up! I do not agree with this thing!"

The "thing," as he sees it, is inimical to the state of being wine induces, the misting over of sights trained firmly on the tangible, everyday world; the dive into interior thoughts and feelings—especially feelings; the unhurried, fine-grade filtering of the qualities of the hour through the senses.

With a relishing glint in his eye and a strangled chuckle, he tells me a story of Russian unworldliness, which, he feels, is far more compatible with a true love of wine.

"My brother-in-law, a Serbian cossack, came here in the 1920s and decided to offer the business—a dairy product business—in the streets of San Francisco, close to the population of Polish and Russian and Jewish people. At this time, every decent American eats at least

two fried eggs for breakfast! But in the Depression, business was
very poor. So he was buying the eggs in Petaluma and cracking
them—artificially breaking—because the business was in broken
eggs. Cheaper. So he was doing this with the idea to have a successful—yes, to have a sale! That's a Russian businessman! He went
bankrupt two months later!"

While André's craft and expertise were valued in his early years at
Beaulieu—"Georges de Latour told me, I give you carte blanche!"—
his pleasure in them was diminished by the absence of the social and
cultural context he was used to. He missed an environment capable
of producing a man like his and Dorothy's Georgian visitor of the
night before—"a man with a *tremendous* love of life! Every day, every
second, every expression, trace of shadow or sunshine—this causes
sentiment in him!"

Exasperatingly, fifty-three years after he first set foot in California,
not enough had changed: "We have *never* reached the point of giving
wine the status of a family beverage. Americans, my dear, are very,
very puritanical. In this country, we *love* the extremes of sanitation
and cleanness—spiritual cleanness. How are you expected to promote here such a beverage as wine?"

There is no question that when André arrived at Beaulieu he was a
rarity, locally—in simply being able to recognize that some of the
wines served at Georges de Latour's table were mislabeled. But even
so, there were enough scattered instances of Californian winemaking
yielding remarkable results to excite the craftsman in him. From the
start, he had competition.

Only next door to Beaulieu, a German called George Deuer
labored to satisfy the perfectionist owner of Inglenook, John
Daniel—who was both a model and something of a hero for André.
John Daniel's idealism, by all accounts, bordered on the saintly.
Unlike Georges de Latour, he was no businessman—indeed his
approach to running Inglenook (see Chapter 7) eventually spelled
financial ruin for his winery.

Of the twenty-eight wines made at Beaulieu, André had, from the
start, selected the Cabernet Sauvignon as the finest. He first came
across it in New York, on his way to his new job in California, in the

distribution cellar the winery maintained there. He tasted his way through the generic (rather than varietally labeled) wines—the Burgundies and clarets—then came to the Cabernet and selected it as "the best Beaulieu red wine in the cellar, which actually was the master key to all my future career in California. . . . That became, really, my success."

Most of the Beaulieu red wines of the day were strong, sweet and uncomplicated, reflecting popular American taste. But with his Cabernet Sauvignon, Georges de Latour intended to make wines of character that could stand comparison with Bordeaux's greatest.

In 1936, Georges and the stonemaker-turned-winemaker Jean Ponti had pampered one particular line of Cabernet wines by aging it in small oak barrels: later, Georges's and André's taste buds concurred in estimating this to be potentially an extraordinary wine. When Georges died in 1940—surely after reflecting with immense satisfaction on Beaulieu, the creation that crowned his career and was visited by the likes of Winston Churchill, Herbert Hoover and Lord Salisbury—the wine was released as the Georges de Latour Private Reserve.

André directed the making of the Private Reserve for virtually all of the thirty-six years of his tenure at Beaulieu. He improved on the mold that Georges de Latour and Jean Ponti had established, greatly refining the sculpture of successive vintages. Winemakers who worked under André after his promotion to general manager also did their bit towards making the Reserve the California Cabernet with the longest and most distinguished record. But to professional winemakers, there is no question that André is responsible for the wine's distinctive elegance.

This is, for instance, the view of Bernard Portet, the canny French-born and French-trained chief of the Clos du Val winery in Napa, who always speaks of André with a smile of such radiant affection that he might be discussing his best beloved old relative. He told me that "the Private Reserve plainly shows that Mr. Tchelistcheff has a softer palate, which is why his has always been the best of the Californian hundred percent Cabernet Sauvignons."

Also consistent with André's "soft" palate is his vote in the ages-old debate about whether it is the best red wines from Bordeaux or Burgundy that are truly *ne plus ultra*, the ultimate glory. They are like aristocrats with diametrically opposed styles. Bordeaux—which the English came to call "claret" in the middle of the sixteenth century—resembles a member of the nobility who is uncompromisingly arrogant and difficult to get to know: except when greatly aged, its aggressive tannins and acidity mean that it only gradually reveals the nuances of its austere charm to the novice wine drinker.

Great Burgundy, by contrast, is all velvety, perfumed grace and welcoming graciousness: it wears its complexity lightly, and is more straightforwardly sensuous than Bordeaux.

It is pointless for someone new to wine to ask connoisseurs which style they consider superior: they unfailingly tell you it is a matter of individual taste. And yet, in the hair-fine cracks in this sweet reasonableness, an exquisitely restrained sniping goes on interminably, as in this example from the definitive book on claret, Edmund Penning-Rowsell's *The Wines of Bordeaux*:

> The late Maurice Healy who wrote as engagingly and enthusiastically about claret as any man, and who sharpened my early knowledge and appreciation of Bordeaux, yet proved an apostate at the last jump. In his *Stay Me With Flagons* (1940) he wrote: "For let there be no doubt about it: Burgundy at its best overtops claret at *its* best." . . .
>
> . . . It comes down to the kind of taste and flavour one ultimately prefers. There is no need to denigrate Burgundy—to me the second of red wines—to express a preference for red Bordeaux. There is more flavour, more variety and distinction about claret; it is a more interesting wine than Burgundy; a violin compared with a trumpet, a baritone as against a bass. But then some prefer basses.

André Tchelistcheff prefers Burgundy and says he has done so "starting from education of boyhood." Most English connoisseurs—presumed impartial, and therefore most reliable—have always preferred claret. So, too, did Georges de Latour. But Dick Peterson, who worked as Beaulieu's winemaker under André's supervision in the early 1960s, told me that the grapes from the particular vineyard that is the source for the Private Reserve make a Cabernet Sauvignon that is intrinsically less aggressive and less Bordeaux-like.

So, to some degree, the Private Reserve's charms have more to do with nature than nurture. But André's renown among oenophiles and winemaking professionals rests on a good deal more than a single wine.

From the 1960s onward, Americans streaked ahead of Europeans in applying modern technology to the craft of winemaking. Earlier, though, in the late 1930s, science came to American winemaking with Georges de Latour's White Russian. On the morning after his arrival at Rutherford, a white-coat-clad André did indeed conduct laboratory tests on Beaulieu's wines for the first time in the winery's history. Yet it was not so much science, in the sense of formal observation and experiment, as knowledge, the older meaning of the word, that he taught.

An example: the Napa Valley's lush growing conditions meant that Europeans who missed the wines of their native lands rooted cuttings of vines associated with those wines in the fertile soil and were virtually guaranteed a harvest of fruit. With greater or less skill, they attempted facsimiles. Mostly the results were poor imitations of the originals because a wine is shaped not only by particular grapes and the winemaker's art but by the "taste" of the environment with which it is typically associated—the chemical and geological characteristics of the soil, the disposition of the climate and the whims of weather.

In Napa, vines associated with delicate, lean, fragrant wines were planted cheek-by-jowl with vines linked with hearty, full-bodied wines. They flourished in the same ordinary-extraordinary way that palm trees and primroses co-exist in even modest Californian gardens. But to a classically trained viticulturist, this indiscriminate horticultural hospitality was a dubious blessing.

"I revolted, when I came here, against this liberalism of interpretation of the law of ecology," André told the Bancroft Library interviewer in one session. In another, he returned to the theme: "I was a revolutionary-minded man in the field of viticulture in Napa Valley. As I came in, I said, 'There must be something wrong with you people, because in my European mind, you can't build a reputation of Burgundy in the Bordeaux, and you can't build the reputation of the Rhine in the Burgundy, and you are trying to build a reputation of

Burgundy and Bordeaux and Sauternes within the same geographical area within the same soil.' "

At Beaulieu, André gradually moved all the Burgundian varieties to new vineyards bought and planted, at his behest, in the cooler, fog-prone Carneros district about twenty-five miles southwest of Rutherford. He expanded the acreages given over to Cabernet Sauvignon. His matching of varieties to soils and what later came to be known as microclimates—the meteorological idiosyncracies that vary with the lay and elevation of sections of land—was noted and imitated.

There were all sorts of other newfangled vinicultural practices associated with André. Some he lifted from research in which he had assisted in his training—that, even in France, had scarcely found their way out of the laboratory.

Take, for instance, malolactic fermentation—the gruesome technical term for rounding out and softening the acidity of red wine by deliberately introducing bacteria that convert astringent malic acids to velvety lactic acids. In France, André had investigated the phenomenon in looking for ways to prevent bacterial spoilage: then, malolactic fermentation only ever happened spontaneously and went too far. In this investigation, he came across a paper by a Swiss chemist who, after a transatlantic journey, stated firmly that the problem did not exist in California. At Beaulieu, André established that she was dead wrong and went on to demonstrate to Californians how the bacteria could deliberately be exploited in a second fermentation—after the conventional one, triggered by adding yeast—to yield wines of greater character and subtlety.

He pioneered in seeking ways to protect tender young vines from sharp-toothed spring frosts—tinkering with techniques that ranged from burning rubber tires and oil-soaked sawdust bricks to wind machines whose propellers infiltrated the freezing air at ground level with blasts of warm air from above.

André was one of the first in California to apply German research showing how the quality of white wines was improved by fermenting them at cooler temperatures through refrigeration.

Beaulieu's bankers wrung their hands over the expenses he ran up in introducing his innovations, expenses that other Napa wineries did not have. They warned Fernande de Latour, Georges's widow, that the young man from France would be the ruin of her. Almost every experiment embroiled him in a long battle for funds with Madame— and not only because of the bankers breathing down her neck.

From the beginning, parsimony, just as much as luxury, had been a hallmark of the life at Beaulieu. Georges had scolded family members for tempting the servants by leaving quarters lying around, and he urged André not to use two matchsticks to light a cigar when one lit carefully enough would do.

Part of André warmly approved of this. Frugality is a quality he respects and associates with the restraint and simplicity of true nobility. It is as a living embodiment of these virtues, among others, that he admires Dagmar de Pins Sullivan, the granddaughter of Georges de Latour, whom he insisted I pay a visit. "She is typical French aristocrat girl—she has simplicity of French peasant girl," he said.

First, an aerial tracking shot of the larger scene. I am the speck making its way westward down an immensely long drive that shoots off from Highway 29, slices through wide flat vineyards, and vanishes in rooftops and a clump of trees clustered at the base of the blue-green tangle of the Mayacamas. Certainly the scale of this approach inspires respect, down on the ground, but no great awe, because the road is unpaved and deeply rutted and the sycamore trees lining it mere saplings.

Let us move in closer now. Here is a converted bunkhouse dressed in an immaculate coat of white paint and black-green trim; it peers out of the dense shade of massive towering elms. The wire-screened windows admit little of what light there is, so that the interior of the house—in which the furniture is stoutly elegant and comfortable—is womblike, chthonic. The year could be 1950 just as easily as 1990: there are none of the flags of contemporary style, nor is there any distancing aesthetic scheme contrived around antiques. Though its owners are only here part of the time, this is a house that feels thoroughly lived in.

We are in the cluttered kitchen, sitting at a table covered in shiny recipe books and a vase casually arranged—but by an expert eye— with pale pink, mauve and white garden flowers. To top up our glasses, something she does alarmingly often, Dagmar de Pins Sullivan leans back in her chair and reaches into the refrigerator behind her for the bottle of Mumm's. She looks closer to fifty than to her sixty-five years, with satiny pale olive skin, inquisitive brown eyes and thick black hair with a single streak of pearl gray. The ample curves of her body fit her earth-motherly ease and straightforwardness.

I tell Dagmar that it strikes me as interesting that while other Napa wineries make much ado about their European origins or connections in their marketing, Beaulieu scarcely exploits its links to France at all. I say that when I met Legh Knowles, the aggressively plebeian manager her mother found to run the winery in the 1960s, he said he had insisted on doing the commercials for the wine himself because he "didn't want anyone with an accent" frightening Americans intimidated enough by the foreignness of wine. Before him, Georges de Latour apparently was not tempted to erect any building that recalled France in its design. And here is Dagmar, now, with the ripest of French accents—and, though I have been drinking so-called BV wines for years, I have no more associated Beaulieu with France than, well, "English muffins" with England.

I tell her about a French couple, owners of a newish Napa winery, that markets its wine with a sketch of the family château in France on the label.

"Well you see, things have changed so! There was no such thing as marketing in Grandfather's day," she says emphatically. "A lot of these people—it really makes me angry at times—who have come from the world of oil, of this, that and the other thing, who have made piles of money and who invade this valley—they are building boutique wineries that are, er, statues, er . . . yes, shrines to themselves! Each one is out to outdo the other one.

"They try to copy French châteaux, which don't belong here—Grandpa didn't feel he wanted to or needed to. I mean, these are the simplest wooden houses we have here."

Perhaps Dagmar sees the transformation all the more clearly for having severed almost all connections to her grandfather's winery. The winegrowing estate Georges de Latour built was sold for $8 million to Heublein, a giant American purveyor of alcoholic spirits, in 1969—not long after Heublein snapped up Beaulieu's equally illustrious neighbor, Inglenook. This was the first sign of an interest that would later become a devouring appetite for Napa wineries among conglomerates, both American and foreign. It was whetted by the impression that more Americans were losing their inhibitions about experimenting with wine and were even beginning to like the stuff.

Dagmar, her American husband, Walter Sullivan, and their four children, have retained the main house at Beaulieu, half a dozen or so related buildings and about a hundred acres of land—including the vineyards that have, from the start, been the source for the Private Reserve wine. The harvest is sold to the winery every year under a long-term contract.

I ask Dagmar why her family sold Beaulieu. She sighs almost imperceptibly and looks away. Her face takes on a look of stoical resignation. Walter was already well established in a career in real estate when they met, she says, and had no interest in changing careers to run Beaulieu after they married. Nor did their son or daughters have any desire to succeed Dagmar's mother, Madame de Pins, as the winery's head.

Beaulieu could have been run on the family's behalf by a professional manager—but to attract a good one, large sums of money would have had to be borrowed to modernize the run-down equipment, and on giving the winery's sales and promotional efforts real teeth. Over the post-Prohibition years, Beaulieu had gradually been acquiring younger and more ambitious competitors—most notably, the Robert Mondavi Winery—that were raising standards in every sphere of operations. Keeping up with them called for capital, of which the business had been starved for years.

"My grandparents and my parents *never* wanted to borrow money," Dagmar tells me, with a satisfied air. "Besides, we have a rather large property in France to look after." She inherited from the Marquis de Pins seven hundred acres in Gascony that are given over to the cultivation of wheat, corn and sunflowers.

To help keep up what is left of the de Latour estate, Dagmar and a friend give cooking classes to an elite clientele in the main house, to the left of the converted bunkhouse that is her home. She and Walter travel between Napa, a house in San Francisco, another in London and her father's estate in Gascony. She doubts that any of their children will ever want to use the ninety-seven-odd acres of vineyards that her family owns to found a new winery.

"Now, you know, you have to fight the big international companies like Taittinger, Nestlé and Seagram's that have put people that have been here a long time—like Martini, et cetera, et cetera—on the defensive. Don't get me on that!"

The champagne has made me hungry. I excuse myself, go out to my truck and return with a crusty baguette—explain to Dagmar that I do not want her to have an inebriated guest on her hands. I can think of grand and starchy houses built with new money in Napa where I would not want to ask for a teaspoon. Dagmar's face only registers calm amusement about my making myself at home. She twists from her waist to retrieve from the refrigerator a tiny bowl of extravagantly garlicky eggplant "caviar," as she calls it, left over from the morning's cooking class. We spread it on the bread and she raises an eyebrow to convey a true Frenchwoman's surprise that an American-made imitation of the staple food of France can be as good as this.

We turn to the reason for my visit.

"I *love* André," she says, her voice growing warm and dropping a register. They met when he first came to California—when he was thirty-seven and she a child of twelve who, having had polio, had only recently begun to "walk on my own two feet. He and my father got along very well and I adored my father. I used to tell André about all my little love affairs and he used to teach me a little bit of this and that—about raising the grapes and making the wine."

I remark that André was not then the luminary he is now—that winemakers have risen in status since.

"Well, there's no question about that!" she bursts out, as if she had been longing for the chance to say as much. "And he was *very* humble and he was married, as I suppose you know, to a Siberian woman from Lake Baikal."

I ask whether Dagmar has kept in touch with the first Mrs. Tchelistcheff.

"I don't even know if she's still alive. Because we never see her anymore—not even in the grocery store. And now it's really—maybe a little bit before they were divorced—that he is the winemaker's winemaker and everyone kowtows to him." Dagmar, immensely dignified, and therefore less like a gossip than like a wise woman telling a mildly cautionary tale to a younger member of her tribe, settles into the story. "And his present wife used to be the secretary down there [at Beaulieu] and she was married to a nice guy in the army and then—"

"She fell in love with André?"

"Evidently. And he with her. And now she is *very* Madame André Tchelistcheff and wants everybody to know it. He's much more modest than she, I think."

I sift through my impressions of Dorothy Tchelistcheff and reflect on the possibilities of love. Even in her low-heeled brown brogues, she looms above her husband by at least a foot. She wears no makeup. Her face, composed of neat, small features, pleases because it is kindly and frank. The day we met, her ample bosom was clothed in a simple tailored blouse, her hips draped in a denim skirt. She had at least twice André's bulk, but was Amazonian rather than fat, to my eye. Trying to imagine the start of their romance, I can't help but ask Dagmar—irrelevantly—whether Dorothy was sylphlike then.

"Oh, no no no! And I'm no one to say, because I'm fat, too. But she has lost a lot of weight."

I remember a lugubrious Dorothy telling me it is a good thing she has "a broad back that can take many kicks," in her life with her moody husband. I remember André grinning like a demented elf as this scrap of information is imparted to me.

It is hard for me to imagine Dorothy as a relentlessly ambitious spouse prodding André to seek fame and glory. I can imagine her being generous in her admiration of him, helping him through episodes of Chekhovian despair by encouraging him to think more highly of himself—perhaps going as far as delivering the conversational equivalent of a rap on the knuckles to people that do not accord him enough respect. Still, it does seem plausible that she is more ambitious for him than he can allow himself to be. After all, it is peculiarly Russian to look on ambition as virtually a vice.

But then I grasp the reason for Dagmar's irritation with Dorothy. "I think at times André has been so . . . *monter en l'épingle de cravate*— you know, when in the old days, you put a pearl in your tie [translation: made much of]. At times . . ." She comes to a complete halt before she can continue. "I adore him, you know. But I resent that my grandfather has been put a little aside, sometimes."

She is careful to repeat that she does not hold André himself responsible.

After the champagne, I accept an invitation to dine with Dagmar in an Anglofied Mexican restaurant in St. Helena, about ten minutes north of her home. She learns that I intend to drive at least half the three-hundred-odd miles to my own home after dinner and puts her foot down: it would be far, far, more sensible for me to sleep at Beaulieu and leave early in the morning, she insists.

I am assigned to a small bedroom arranged with French provincial furniture that has flowers and birds hand-painted in gilt on a turquoise background. The curtains and bedspread, made in a matching Provençale print, are elegantly cheery. I drop off to sleep smiling at Dagmar's insistence that I ask for a doggie bag for the food I could not finish at the restaurant and then, before we retired to our bedrooms, reminding me not to forget it in the morning.

No wonder André always speaks of the de Latours with the devotion of a vassal—is my last clear thought before dreams take over.

At Beaulieu, after the acquisition, André was invariably trotted out by the managers in charge of sales and promotion to impress East Coast wine snobs—visiting wine writers, wine distributors, proprietors of snooty restaurants. "André is really an artist—and one with a lot of flair," a former protégé of his told me. "You know, so many artists are good artists but they can't sell their work—put it across. André does—almost by trying not to sell it. It's just that his personality and natural approach in talking about wine actually sells it."

Another old colleague, a marketing specialist, chortled about how André "talks about wines as females and males. For instance, he might say about a Gamay Beaujolais, 'This lady's not dressed in black and white'!" He continued, "What do I mean by saying he's a salesman? Well, when you met him, did he kiss your hand? Right. Now how many guys kiss your hand. See what I mean?"

Yet André's years working under Beaulieu's corporate owner were acutely unhappy: he found the species "organization man" and its ways profoundly alienating. Legh Knowles, who continued to run Beaulieu after the takeover, frequently found himself straining to account for behavior by André that was virtually indefensible under the new regime. Once, Heublein executives summoned Legh Knowles to explain "some memos between André and me. And they said, we see you sent him a memo, and in his reply, in the first paragraph, he changed direction *ten* times!"

Even though André had excelled at tasks in research and applied winemaking that called for precision, a flagrant inconsistency is part of the essential Tchelistcheff personality. Another former associate always illustrates this with an imaginary dialogue in which, when he asks André how tall a beer can is, he slices the air horizontally with one hand—roughly ten inches above the surface of a table. Asked the same question the next day, he marks the air about two inches above the table top. "Now if you take the average of those two, it's the right answer, sure enough," the former colleague told me, ruefully affectionate. "And that's how you learned to work with him."

The Heublein men did not feel they should have to make any such accommodations. But they were at least as infuriating to him. The cast of mind that prevented these good corporate citizens from seeing him as more than an exotic promotional device also apparently precluded any glimmer of understanding of the wine business. One financial expert sent out from company headquarters in Connecticut returned from a trip to Napa and wrote a report recommending that since, of all Beaulieu's best-selling wines, the Gamay Beaujolais was the most economical to produce, the winery should drop every other wine on its list to concentrate on making that one varietal alone. Never mind that the Private Reserve Cabernet Sauvignon had covered itself in glory from the start.

People who worked closely with him at the time remember that André was bitterly disgusted by being manipulated—for the sake of Beaulieu's image—into taking credit for making its wine for a short period before his retirement when he no longer oversaw the vineyards or the winery. This turned to cast iron his conviction that promotion is inherently dishonest.

From the late 1960s onward, Robert Mondavi gradually began to steal from André the mantle of ambassador-at-large to the world beyond Napa. His is a markedly different personal style, what might be called seduction by active pursuit—as opposed to André's stately magnetization. The huggy-bear, Italian peasant-patriarch persona of the younger man makes his tireless proselytizing almost indecently successful. André, for one, does not see it in the kindest light.

At the gleaming dining table in the Tchelistcheffs' doll's house, we are chatting over the remains of a thoroughly European conclusion to a meal, one still little imitated even in Napa: we sip a four-year-old Napa Merlot between nibbles at cheese and water biscuits. I can't remember lingering over cheese and biscuits since I was last in London. But André has already explained that he and Dorothy live different lives from the ones around them. "We shut ourselves in this fortress. *Yanh*, this is fortress!" he had said. "I go off into my own world!"

It has been two years since my first visit and we are lucky to have him here at all. A few days ago he left the fortress, alone, at the wheel of a yellow Datsun 280Z that flipped over and crash-landed him in a ditch, shaken but unhurt. Dorothy says he has been feeling humiliated about having his driving privileges snatched from him at only eighty-nine.

André is comparing himself with others now famous in Napa. "They are coming in Napa Valley with a purpose; I came to Napa Valley without a purpose—just to do a job. Now, Mondavi. Very typical. Purpose of glorification. In all ways. Not only materialistically. Philosophically. Spiritually. Et cetera. Every day, the process of lifting up, pushing further. And, as a matter of fact, one of the very first secretaries of his told me personally—*daily* he comes to work and he asks what are the news in the papers, magazines, et cetera, about him. And the days there is not such a thing, he is *mis*erable and lonely!"

As for himself, André regrets that his work in wine has loomed quite as large as it has in his life. No true aristocrat can be a consummate professional anything—let alone a winemaker—because this usually means taking something far too seriously. André seems in earnest—not merely conventionally gloomy, in the Russian fashion—in regretting that his career in wine left him too little time to cultivate the range of interests that made his father, for instance, André's model of the supremely cultivated man. Having been brought up "in a very intellectual family," he told the Bancroft Library interviewer, "I was exposed to politics, history, art, music—

far more than I was able to expose myself to as an industrial man, working in one single industry."

He went on: "The basic fact of success—you got to learn to live with the grapes and with the wines—very interesting thing—giving everything of my time to them, to understand their desires, their feelings, their pains, and their demands. Conversation with the individual vine in the field and conversation with the individual barrel, the common knowledge of acquiring a mutual language of understanding between the products and the producer. . . . I used to go in the evenings alone in the vineyards and just relax by talking to them, to my world."

Much as he might decry it, and as late in life as he came to it, a passionate sense of vocation resonates in the tortured poetry of that declamation.

Children do sometimes carry out the unfulfilled wishes of their parents. At a rendezvous with André's only child, Dimitri—a short, pale-eyed, etiolated, endomorphic man of fifty-eight—I wonder whether he might not have led parts of André's unlived life of foreshortened achievement and noble drift.

Dimitri was a teenager when he started helping his father with his work. As an adult, he acquired a reputation for being an even finer winemaker than André. Rather than shine in Napa, however, he chose exile in Mexico at the age of thirty—after six years toiling at America's largest maker of bulk wine, E&J Gallo, in California's Central Valley. He spent fifteen years managing production at the Bodegas de Santo Tomás Winery in Baja California, which he left for Hawaii, where he designed a process for producing, of all things, pineapple wine and champagne, and established the Tedeschi Winery in Maui for their manufacture.

After nine years in Hawaii, an aversion to paying taxes led Dimitri to move, with his Japanese second wife, to the state of Nevada, which levies no taxes on income. From his base in sagebrush country on the border with California, he took up the life of an itinerant consultant to wineries all over the world. His résumé baldly states: "I prefer to work in a low profile posture and let the winemaker and owner get all the praise and publicity." Between consulting trips, he hunts and struggles to farm his inhospitable patch of desert at five thousand feet above the sea.

He tells me he thinks the line of Tchelistcheff winemakers will end with him. Of the two sons "that I recognize as mine," he says, keeping a close eye on my reaction, one fishes for salmon in the Pacific; the other, a recovering alcoholic, is living off his grandmother's Social Security checks.

His plaintive, high-pitched voice has an innocence that makes a startling contrast with his faintly dissipated, cynical air. He tells me he is a womanizer: "What's wrong with it? At least you know you're alive!"

I have been forewarned of this—by André, as well as by two old friends of Dimitri's. "Be careful of my son. He likes women!" André had twinkled. I said I thought he was married. "That makes no difference to him." Well, why was he a womanizer, I couldn't help but ask.

Earlier in the conversation, André had lamented Dimitri's American upbringing—"It is very bad to grow up in the philosophy of a foreign culture—a *mis*ery! There is nothing common between us, between America and Russia!" But now his smile of unadulterated glee turned his face into a map of about a million wrinkles.

"You know how they say," he gurgled archly. "An apple does not fall very far from the tree!"

CHAPTER FOUR

An All–American Winemaker

IN HIGH SUMMER the Napa Valley is a viridian gash in a strawscape of sun-bleached hills. This morning I find myself in Spring Valley, a small and intimate adjunct to it, about two thirds of the way up its eastern flank. I sped here along the meandering Silverado Trail, once known simply as the Old Back Road, the vine-covered Napa Valley floor to my left—still and mostly flat, suggestive of a calming green lake. Streaking around a blind curve, I almost missed the tree-shrouded turnoff to Spring Valley, also carpeted with vines and bordered by oakwoods, with the feel of a secluded backwater.

I was last here in the witching season for which this subsidiary valley was named: then, the light was all translucence, the air moist and stirred by zephyrs and the colors a medley of scintillating fresh greens and ecstatic wild mustard-yellow—telling of sap rising everywhere and of dewy young shoots sprouting, improbably, from gnarled, stumpy brown canes in the vine rows. Now, nine weeks or so past midsummer, the light is flat and dull, the grapevines dusty and yellowing in patches. It is the same lovely landscape of course, and I can only explain my sense of let-down by drawing a parallel to a man who, having met a beauty all got up in evening finery and full makeup, glowing with convivial excitement, must adjust to seeing her as her drabber, everyday self.

As compensation, there is the sharp, sweet, faintly rank scent of the crush, drifting on currents of torpifying air. It is a sensuous smell. So even in what is, for me, the least enchanting time of year in Napa, it is hard not to attend to goings-on in the natural world. To function in parts of the world, like Bombay's streets or most of Manhattan, is automatically to shut out of awareness most of the environment, because it is so unpleasant. Here in Spring Valley, even in the wrong season, I am fighting my surroundings in a battle for concentration.

For I am not alone. I am reminded of a tortoise by the arrangement of creases and bulges in the face into which I am gazing, a little defiantly. Especially in this dour mood, Joe Heitz looks as much like a disaffected tortoise as any human being could. There is an expression both baleful and sad in the drooping brown eyes framed by heavy lids and baggy pouches. The mouth scowls. I scan this face for some hint that its owner is secretly teasing me—entertaining himself by only acting the curmudgeon—but find none.

The trouble began a few minutes ago, when we strolled up to the gray stone building beside which we are standing—which, with its rectangular base and inverted V for a roof, is as simple a structure as a conventional child's illustration of the word "house." He explained that in it, Heitz Wine Cellars today vinifies some white grapes and does a portion of its cellaring, and that it was built in 1898 to replace a wooden winery in which ten thousand gallons of wine were made in 1880.

I ask if he had any idea of what the inspiration for this building was. I don't know the European wine countries well enough, I say, so I am curious—"Would the original have been in Bordeaux? Or Italy?"

He laughs scornfully. "I don't know what the hell their inspiration was!"

"It does have a somewhat European look about it though, doesn't it?"

"Well. The California wine industry was founded by Europeans. The Indians didn't start the wine business," he says in the tone of one addressing an unreconstructed twit.

"I'm just trying to get my European references right," I say mildly.

"Well, I'm about as far removed from it as you. I'm fourth-generation American."

"But you've traveled to the European wine countries a lot, haven't you?"

"A bit."

"How many trips, roughly?"

Our conversation veers off its rails and plunges into a ravine lined with spiny cacti.

"Well, I sure as hell didn't go there to pick up and study wine-making. I was there as a tourist or a wine merchant, not studying wine architecture. I didn't pattern myself after Europeans," he says, his manner both insinuating and choleric—as if he has caught me red-handed, setting a devious trap for him.

"Well yes, but you will hear people say that the inspiration for this building or that one came from this or that European country. And there are people like André Tchelistcheff who came here and apparently contributed a lot."

I am hinting that I know perfectly well that Joe worked under Tchelistcheff for eight years, near the start of his career in wine.

His voice rises in exasperation. "He's been coasting on his . . . "

"His European heritage?" I suggest.

"On his European speech—for years! When I worked with him at Beaulieu [in the 1950s] he could speak very good English, but now he's using his French accent more and more, for that approach."

I adopt a humoring tone. "Well then, let's take your approach to an extreme and just say that there was this group of cattle ranchers that came out from Montana and started here and—"

Rockets go off. "We're really getting off to a bad start today! You ask me about one thing and then you turn it around and talk about everything else! What was the term you used about the building?"

"Inspiration?"

"How would I know?" he demands, exasperatedly incredulous. "It was built in 1898! I wasn't born until 1919."

"Maybe there's a document lying around—or a local historian might know . . . ?"

"No! They built it like that because everybody else was building like that."

"That's good enough," I say, guessing I will get no further.

"Go up and down the valley. A lot of them exist. They were built into a hillside to save labor and be as cool as possible. I don't think that's *inspirational*! It's very *practical*. Anton Rossi built it. That's why his name's on the front. He was a farmer and winemaker."

"From where in Italy?"

"I don't know. A lot of Italians claim to be Swiss, you know."

That night, falling asleep in a yellow faux-Victorian guest cottage on the edge of a vineyard, I am woken bolt upright by the thought that I do not know where my tape recorder or tapes are. Fighting panic, I search the dimmest corners of the house, to no avail. I humiliate myself by rousing my hostess to ask if the family has a dog for whom recording equipment might be choice provender. A call to the Heitz winery early the next morning confirms what I had begun to suspect near dawn—that Joe's crankiness had so rattled me that I had forgotten my most precious possessions in his lair.

Why had no one warned me he might behave the way he had? I would have to wait two years for an elderly widow, the owner of another Napa winery, to tell me he had made her cry more than once. "I'm a lot older than he is," she said. "But he still thinks of me as a young girl he can discipline. And he bosses his own children around something fierce!"

Joe hardly seems to fit in the Napa Valley—or does he?

In Napa, nature's splendors and the lurking spirit of Dionysus combine to exaggerate Californian friendliness so much that it cloys, at times. Where wine is made and drunk in the Mediterranean, Greek pessimism or Italian cynicism—for instance—exist on the flip side of the bonhomie to restore a sense of balance. Whereas Napa has been settled by people determined somehow to coax reality into the Californian dream of unending felicity.

From this perspective Joe Heitz is out of place, unless he is seen as a rare counterweight to Napa's superabundance of sweetness and light—a goblin-gargoyle lunging from a Gothic gable lavishly ornamented with ivy leaves, flowers and birds.

Foreigners' opinions may make no odds with Joe, but he has earned high praise from Britain's king-making wine connoisseurs (a natural role for natives of islands too cool and dank to yield much good wine—who are therefore bound to be objective, judging other nations' efforts). One eminent British authority, Hugh Johnson, notes in his *Pocket Encyclopedia of Wine* that Joe is "in many eyes the first name in California. An inspired individual winemaker who has set standards for the whole industry." The same entry characterizes the red wines for which he is renowned as "dark, deep and emphatic."

I arranged to see Joe after complaining to Bernard Portet—

unquestionably the most able of Napa's expatriate French winemakers—that I was tired of meeting jet-setting pseudosophisticates in the valley, and that I should love to find a highly regarded, honest-to-goodness American maker of wine. Joe was my man exactly, Bernard assured me.

I asked Bernard what he thought of the Heitz wines and he said they violated certain basic principles of the French winemaking tradition. For instance, they are usually based entirely on grapes of a single varietal—whereas in France, it is customary to dilute the characteristics of a particular grape by blending wine made from it with other wines. At Clos du Val, where Bernard is winemaker, "we feel we've got to tone down the character of our Cabernet Sauvignon with some Merlot," he said. "Some other people, on the other hand, want the Cabernet characteristics to jump out of the glass."

But one aspect of Joe's technique of which Bernard is in awe is that "he really brings out the character of the soil in his wines. That is something very special that not everybody can do." Why not, I ask. "I don't know. Maybe he is searching with more intensity than other people."

The wine for which Joe is most renowned is his Martha's Vineyard Cabernet Sauvignon. Early in 1990, he had sold all of the quota he had set for that year's sale of the 1985 vintage (about 2,250 cases) roughly two weeks before the wine's official release date. Wine lovers had queued outside the Heitz tasting room for as long as two hours to be sure of getting their share, and paid $50 a bottle for it. At about the same time, American wine's journal of record, *The Wine Spectator*, hailed the Martha's Vineyard Cabernet as "America's most collectible wine" and, in a later article, suggested that the 1985 vintage would have sold out just as fast at twice the price.

A nonexpert can only intuit the meaning of some of the adjectives that pepper the wine taster's patter: since the *Spectator* aims to be understood by people barely literate in the language, here is the magazine's detailed description of the 1985 Martha's wine:

> A truly magnificent Cabernet, this deeply colored wine shows rich, powerful aromas of currant, mint, spice and plum, wonderfully rich, elegant, supple and concentrated fruit flavors and smooth, polished

tannins and impeccable balance. The '85 . . . is destined to join the ranks of the great '68, '70, '74 and '84 Martha's bottlings as uncommonly spectacular wines.

Such words as "big," "rich," "complex," "intense" and "concentrated" recur almost tiresomely in the experts' descriptions of the Heitz Cabernets. These are classics of the old school of California winemaking, wines that often seem less like accompaniments for food than like heftily ambrosial meals in themselves.

It is not too farfetched to see in them distillations of the character and personality of their maker. Until I met Joe, I did not think I would ever, in real life, find a human being as much like a variety of wine to warrant anything like the ingenious vinous metaphor chosen for an enigmatic character, who sometimes goes by the name Rosalba, in the Isak Dinesen story "The Dreamers." One of three ardent admirers of Rosalba thrown together in Switzerland describes her like this to the other two:

> . . . to obtain perfection in the special white wines of this district, they leave the grapes on the vines longer than for other wines. In this way, they dry up a little, become over-ripe and very sweet. Furthermore, they develop a peculiar condition which is called in France *pourriture noble* . . . which gives the flavour to the wine. In the atmosphere of Rosalba . . . there is a flavour which there is about no other woman. It may be the true odor of sanctity, or it may be the noble putrefaction, the royal corrodent rust of a strong and rare wine. . . . Or it may be both, in a soul two-parted white and black.

Cabernets can be harsh and even curmudgeonly, hard and tight and closed—those are reasonable descriptions of ones with a high content of acid and tannin, the astringent, puckery substance in some wines. But if they are great Cabernets, these are only qualities of their youth. As they age, their tannins grow round and smooth and lend the wine body and luxuriance. Joe Heitz, I gathered from conversations with people who know him well, has such potential: some spoke of detecting signs of mellowing in him, and I imagine a gentling of Joe might be generally noticeable if he were laid down in a cool cellar for, say, another seventy years.

I was snapped and barked at when I asked him which aspects of himself might be reflected in his winemaking—and I put the question to him more than once, in different guises. He made it clear that he thought it a contemptible line of inquiry. Once, he contorted his face into an exaggeratedly foolish grin, bent his arms and flapped his hands, creating an impression something like a senile baby. "I'm not one of those artsy-craftsy, tiddly-diddly people who have come into the business. No, I'm a scientist," he said, glowering.

What makes a great American winemaker? Joe Heitz's, to most of his countrymen, is just another tale in the honorable Horatio Alger tradition. To Europeans, his huge ability as a winemaker—in someone not bred to an appreciation of wine, who deliberately cultivates an image of uncouthness and philistinism—is something as wondrously inexplicable as the talent of an idiot savant.

Sickly sweet homemade wines wrought from Concord and Delaware grapes (which are not *Vitis vinifera*, the only kind that merit consideration by serious wine drinkers) were all Joe had ever sipped before his first taste of a commercially manufactured wine in a job he stumbled into in his early twenties.

He grew up where he was born in Princeton, Illinois, on his family's farm, where his parents lived with his grandparents—and where corn, oats and alfalfa were cultivated and cows, pigs, chickens and sheep reared. In spite of being the adored youngest child of the family, the only son born after four daughters, he had his share of the chores. One was to wash the tools of the family winemaking, including the barrels and the press. As both of his parents were of German stock, he was taught to bring Teutonic thoroughness to the task. He does not believe that this limited childhood involvement with vinification in any way prefigured his later career, since he could not stand the taste of the family tipple, "and if I tasted it today I wouldn't care for it either." But he does believe that scrupulous cleanliness and meticulousness are essential underpinnings of his success as a winemaker, and that "maybe some of my affinity for cleanliness came from that gofer work I did as a kid."

There is a great dreariness in Joe's voice as he speaks of his years as a young adult—partly because he is bored with repeating the facts about them and because it was not a happy time. America had slid into the Depression the year of his tenth birthday and though he had hoped to be a veterinarian, could not afford to attend any of the out-of-state universities that had a school of veterinary medicine. He had a scholarship to the University of Illinois and so was enrolled there, studying "just general agriculture, heavy on animal science, hoping that something would happen and sure enough, we got World War II." After two years of college, lacking the funds to continue his studies, he enlisted in the air force, only to discover that he would not make a pilot. He was discharged and hitchhiked to southern California.

That trip was momentous: "Once you see California you kind of lose interest in Illinois, if you have any sense at all." He worked in the aircraft industry as a quality control inspector on the P-61, the Northrop Black Widow night fighter—an experience that further honed his attention to detail "because in aircraft, you look ve-ry darn close for minor defects." In this new role, he was drafted into the army air corps and sent to Fresno—a hot, flat and colorless spot in the Central Valley—where he worked as ground crew chief on the P-61.

It was in Fresno that he accidentally discovered his métier or, as he says, "I got vaccinated with the wine needle." Short of cash, he walked this small town's streets at night, looking for an evening job, any job. One of the doors on which he knocked belonged to the La Paloma plant of the Italian Swiss Colony Winery, and it was here that he at last found work—running an evaporator, making concentrated grape juice.

It is at this juncture in his story that I belatedly glimpse the equivalent of bedrock in his ability as a winemaker. His voice inexplicably gains energy and good humor as he recounts, "I would come in from the [air force] base around six or six-thirty. And of course, when I would get tired and have to go home, I'd have to shut down the equipment—shut down the boiler, the source of steam. And as they built up confidence in me, why, they'd leave a filter running, or a heat exchanger or something. And you know, when you go home, you pull switch A, close valve B, just to shut it down. You didn't have to know anything—just to read simple recipe instructions. And sometimes the manager would come out and see what I was doing and he would take me into the laboratory and show me a little bit of the technology of winemaking, and gradually I got to run a few simple tests there."

I ask, "So then, at what point in all of this were you, as you said, vaccinated with the needle? Were you bored doing these things you've described?"

He looks at me in stark amazement. "Well, it [the job] changed my life. That's what I've been trying to tell you."

I feel I must have missed some vital detail about his duties at this bulk wine plant: "Was it when you went to the laboratory, then, that it began to be fun?"

"No," he growls, glaring at me as if I am being willfully obtuse. "Not the laboratory. The laboratory is only ten percent of winemaking. I liked *all* of the operations. The sounds of the winery at night— a huge winery. Concrete tanks as large as this whole office complex and two or three times as high, and row upon row of fermenting and bubbling and smelling delicious. It's a total experience. Not just a flash in the pan, but something that lasts."

Now I get it. It was certainly not the challenge of replicating the flavors in any of the world's great wines that had ignited his interest in winemaking. Nor was it, apparently, a fascination with the mysteries of the chemical changes involved. It was a sheer love of *process*—the here and now of the business. And I had been so very slow to grasp this because the joys of process—especially in relation to the material world—leave me quite cold.

It is just such differences in innate orientation that so often make other people's dreams incomprehensible—both their hopeful schemes for their lives and the stories they tell themselves in their sleep.

Now I see that Joe was not being especially evasive a half hour or so ago when he had insisted, truculently, "There's no secrets to winemaking. I think everybody knows how to make wine—or they should. I think my wine is better than other people's because I pay attention to those little, shitty details—little details that you don't like to do, sometimes. You know you should but, oh well, nobody will know the difference."

The war ended. Joe was discharged from the army air corps and knew he did not want to return to Los Angeles and aircraft manufacturing. The manager at the Fresno winery urged him to get a degree at the University of California at Davis, where the most advanced research in oenology and viticulture in America was being done. In 1945, Joe met and married Alice Maloney, also posted to Fresno—from South Dakota—to do her part in the war effort. After Joe spent a summer working at the aircraft plant in southern California, he began to attend Davis and Alice worked as a secretary to support them. He graduated from Davis in 1948 and, for two years, worked as a chemist for bulk wineries in the Central Valley. Then he got a job at Beaulieu Vineyard as assistant winemaker to André Tchelistcheff—among cognoscenti, the century's most famous name in American wine before Robert Mondavi came along.

Joe worked under the small, dark, elflike Tchelistcheff for over eight years—years that unquestionably helped to shape him as a winemaker because they constituted his first experience of top-notch winemaking. But this is not something easily gleaned from talking to Joe. Ruth Teiser, from the Regional Oral History Office of Berkeley's Bancroft Library, tackled him on the subject in 1985:

RT: Do you feel it was something of value, to be learning at Beaulieu?

JH: Oh yes, sure. It's helping me now.

RT: André Tchelistcheff is, I guess, a very good teacher, of viticulture, also, is he not?

JH: Yes.

And that was all he had to say about the great master in three lengthy tape-recorded sessions with his interviewer.

At one stage of my own conversations with him I tell him I would like to return to discuss in detail certain subjects, such as his years with Tchelistcheff, and he answers irritably: "Well, Tchelistcheff I can summarize now. He's been a great winemaker and a great addition to the Napa Valley. And I worked with him for seven or eight years and learned a great deal from him and love and respect him. Now what else do you want to know?"

I ask if he can tell me where his technique of winemaking departed from Tchelistcheff's, how he evolved his own distinctive style.

"I put a Heitz label on our bottles. When I worked for Tchelis-

tcheff, we put a Beaulieu label on our bottles. That's the only difference I can think of."

"You mean, in all other respects, your techniques were identical?"

"Of course not! This has been a slow evolution. I didn't say, well,
Tchelistcheff, you're full of prunes on this subject and I'm going to do
this differently. No. Come on. And I didn't only learn from Tche-
listcheff. I went to the university. I worked for many other wineries.
I taught winemaking. I've done consulting with André and without
André."

A photograph of the Heitz family in *The Wine Spectator* in 1990 could
easily be an updated retake of that arch portrayal of a Midwestern
farming couple, *American Gothic*—with the addition of a few more
family members. The smiles of Joe and Alice, standing in the foreground, are wintry, unconvincing. Behind them, the faces of the three
Heitz children, unsmiling or set in faint scowls, are truer reflections of
the family's sentiments about publicity. The distancing frown on the
face of thirty-five-year-old Kathleen—pretty in a strong-jawed,
tanned, sturdy sort of way with straight, short, sand-colored hair
streaked blond, dressed in a tailored white blouse that matches the
strand of pearls around her neck—is close to an exact replication of the
knit brow of the farmer's daughter in the Grant Wood study.

She is flanked by her expressionless, round-faced, balding, bespectacled, roly-poly brothers, David, thirty-nine, and Rollie, thirty-one.
Like their father, they wear simple, open-necked, short-sleeved cotton shirts. Alice, the shortest, roundest member of the family, looks
like a matriarch both gentle and stern. Her broad, pale pink face is
framed by white hair, cut just below her cheekbones, and a long-
sleeved blouse—a miniature floral print on pale pink cotton.

In this photographic portrait, too, the props and set help explain
the subjects, in the way the pitchfork, buttoned-up work clothes and
the carpenter Gothic building in the Grant Wood work somehow
convey moral rectitude, thrift and lives of dignified toil. The simplicity of the gray stone winery building behind the Heitz family fits
well with its members' disdain for show—with their frugality and
stubborn integrity; this is a family as firmly set in its ways as the
stone blocks in their plaster molding.

Actually, all of these are most quintessentially qualities of Joe's. Alice, when I ask her what makes Joe a great winemaker, says dryly, "We always tell him it's his family behind him. And he says, 'Oh, sure.'" Yet the other family members do come across as shadowy adjuncts of Joe—as satellites, buttresses, sounding boards.

Joe and Alice, for all their years in quasi-urbane Napa, still speak of each other in the preshrunk, laconic utterances of deeply rural folk.

On an August afternoon in Napa, the heat is crushing: shielded from the harsh light outside, the interior of the tasting room is crepuscular, intimate. But the atmosphere does not encourage the Heitzes to share confidences. Alice says she was born and raised in South Dakota and no, people there weren't interested in wine in her childhood. Like Joe, she first tasted "real" wine in her early twenties. She was his only helper, finishing and then making wine, from scratch, beside him, in the first few years of Heitz Wine Cellars' existence. Later, her responsibilities narrowed to handling public relations for the winery, and endless entertaining—dropping whatever she was doing to whip up meals for visitors from all over the world at the drop of a hat.

The experts on such matters usually warn against husbands and wives trying to work together, I tell them. How did they manage to stay out of each other's hair in the early days?

"Sharing a bottle helps a lot," Joe says. "Her background is Irish, so she's got a well-oiled elbow. That's important." He does not look at her as he says this, but his tone is crustily affectionate.

Earlier in the day, impressing on me the importance of attention to detail in wine, he said: "Of course when I married Alice, she used to get so angry with me. Because she'd serve me dinner and I'd see a little, tiny spot of dried egg from breakfast—or something like that, you know."

"Of course both your parents having been of German descent probably explains the perfectionism, yes?"

"No. Alice says, that's why I am an old grouch. Whereas she, of course, being Irish, is a bit more easygoing."

I ask how they happened to meet in Fresno, and am effectively told to mind my own business. Alice says it was so long ago, they don't remember anymore. Joe says they didn't take notes about the event.

After a few other routinely personal questions get stonewalling responses, I decide the problem is that Joe's presence is inhibiting Alice. But she is just as guarded when I return to talk to her, alone, on a long, golden day in September. Again, I try to discover what she believes to be the secret of his success in wine.

"He's very particular, and everything has to be just right. Then we have some very good grapes, too," she answers.

Persist, persist, I tell myself, and later, try yet again.

"He was just a good student at Davis. He has a good palate, and that kind of helped."

I say I was a little startled, on my last visit, to have made him so angry—merely asking about Napa winemaking's European links. She was a witness to my excoriation.

"Yes," she says gently. "I wanted to run away."

Would it have helped, if I had asked my questions differently?

"No. I think it was just the wrong day, that's all. You must have a terrible impression of him."

And that is all she will say on the subject. She is obviously devoted to this husband of forty-six years. A grouch he may be, but he is her grouch.

We discuss the children—the question, much debated in Napa, of whether the second generation of Heitzes will succeed in keeping the winery's standard flying as high, after their parents' day. I know that her answer will have to be prudent. I have been told, by a close acquaintance of the family, that for well over a decade, financial advisors have been pressing Joe to loosen his hold on the reins, to let the children demonstrate their ability to run the business—that this was essential if the winery was not to be starved for capital because of investors' anxieties about its future.

Alice, on this subject, comes as close as she can to smiling expansiveness. "Well, David has always loved the winemaking. He has a wonderful palate and is very conscientious. In 1974, his first year in college, Joe was in the hospital and he did all the winemaking, and it was one of the better wines [an understatement: *The Wine Spectator* rates it as one of Heitz's greatest]. He'd worked with his father year after year, in the crush, so he knew how." It was long ago decided that David would succeed his father as winemaker.

I say, I find it a little surprising that his critical and demanding father did not drive David into a line of work far removed from wine. "No. He was never deterred. Brave soul, huh," Alice says proudly. Joe, in the Bancroft Library transcript, is excruciatingly frank about David's pursuit of a degree in oenology: "He's really a home boy, so he went to junior college, then he went to Davis for two quarters, and he got Cs and Bs, but he was just working his tail off to do that. So he took the third quarter off to help us when we were building the new winery. And then . . . he went to Fresno State where the academic standards are a little lower. As far as the oenology program, it's more practical and less scientific. . . . There, instead of Cs and Bs, he got As and Bs . . . "

It was far from preordained that all three children would throw in their lot with the family business. Kathleen earned a degree in biology, taught the subject in high school, and flirted with the idea of a career in biological research before she went to Davis to take a curious combination of courses in oenology, viticulture and Japanese art history. At the end of this, aged twenty-four, she chose to join the winery, where she is responsible for maintaining diplomatic relations with Heitz's distributors, overseeing the Heitz retail salesroom, and writing sales and publicity documents—a collection of charges that adds up to marketing at Heitz. When I try to make an appointment to see her, an obstacle proves to be a steady stream of overnight guests: one of her jobs, she tells me, is to clean the cottage after the visitors leave. I find this extraordinary: most of the guests are connected with the business, which has a net value estimated at around $10 million, and I cannot help but think, surely a maid can be hired for the job.

Rollie, born in 1958, took a degree in business studies at Santa Clara University, and is responsible for managing finance, the vineyards and property. At harvest time, when the winery staff are working flat out, he pitches in to help with production. He was, briefly, an entrepreneur in the spice business before he went to work for the family: that fledgling venture expired, Joe bluntly informed the Bancroft Library's Ruth Teiser, because "you have to have a lot of individual initiative to start a business and it didn't pan out."

The children share their parents' marked preference for the familiar over the exotic: I ask David what food he would serve guests on a desert island where he had only one bottle of Martha's Cabernet and one of Bella Oaks (any vintage) and an offer to parachute to him the ingredients for just one dish. I have him on tape, saying in a faintly amused monotone: "I think the two wines would be pretty inter-changeable, so far as what you would serve with them—both of them are Cabernets. I'm kind of partial to heavy stews myself."

I try to get Kathleen to expound on what prompted her, in the end, to choose the family business over research or teaching. "Well, I've always enjoyed it," she says. "It's a beautiful area and lifestyle." Like David, she is unembarrassed about stating the obvious without any enlivening fillip of humor or finesse: this is distinctly Midwestern.

Rollie is more his own man, with a youngest child's greater sense of latitude. What is it like, working with his father, I ask. "Well, some days are definitely better than others," he says. "It was very hard, initially, because you'd be doing things you were doing every day and he would tell you to do them different, when he hadn't the recent experience of them. That still happens to a degree, but he's able to step back a little more now, and have more confidence in us."

We discuss the likelihood of family-owned wineries—and the Napa Valley's rurality—lasting for many more generations. He laughs when I tell him someone suggested that the only sure way to preserve these things would be for the children of the valley's winery and land-owning families to intermarry. His father, he said, had once thought "it might be good if David married Carolyn Martini, to get the tie there, and Kathleen would marry one of the Mondavis and I could marry Paula Kornell—we'd have the whole valley wrapped up. But it didn't work out that way."

Did he expect that his brother, the winemaker, would one day want to change the winery's style of making wines—to express his own taste and ideas? There would be gradual stylistic changes, he imagined. "But you know, a lot of the stylistic questions—a lot of them are decided almost by committee now—by the three of us and by Joe and Alice."

One after another, friends of the Heitzes spoke of the excruciating reluctance with which Joe has been stepping out of the way to let the children run the winery. About the past, so much is clear: Joe Heitz does not want his accomplishments diminished by the slightest exaggeration of his debt to anyone else.

The subject of André Tchelistcheff is especially sensitive—despite Joe's affection for his former boss—because of his extreme touchiness about any inference that Napa owes its success to European knowhow, suitably adapted for Californian conditions and raw materials. And Tchelistcheff, after all, was educated in his craft in the Old World.

I am persuaded that Joe's defensiveness on this score is not unwarranted by a conversation with another highly regarded Napa winemaker. John Thacher, at thirty-five, half Joe's age, has already made a name for himself at Cuvaison, a small winery owned by members of the Schmid-Heiny family, one of Switzerland's richest and most powerful clans. Unlike Joe, he is introspective and entirely at ease with the role of winemaker-as-artist-craftsman. But then John's are rather different roots: sculpture and geology were emphasized in his studies as an undergraduate at Berkeley, and he grew up in Sonoma, the county west of Napa, where as a teenager he helped tend a small vineyard owned by his parents. He is thin, dark-haired, pale-skinned and intense, and talks in staccato bursts of enthusiasm in the relaxed Californian vernacular.

In the days when Joe worked at Beaulieu, he says, "wine would routinely go bad, and they didn't know what was causing it. I mean, I can see where he's coming from—he probably sits there and goes, 'Wait a minute, I can remember very clearly when none of us could figure out why all this wine was spoiling'—and he and Tchelistcheff and other guys of his generation figured all this stuff out. You can imagine him saying, 'What debt do we owe Europe when we solved all these problems on our own?' I mean, they solved *huge* technical problems. The industry couldn't even put a wine in bottles without things happening to it.

"Imagine not having a single clue about that. Nowadays, we may never quite know exactly how the wines are going to develop, but we at least know the probabilities of stability and stuff. But can you imagine making wine and not knowing if it's going to develop molds or weird things going on with iron deposits or all this chemical stuff.

It's pretty impressive what they came up with—and the accomplishment really was here."

There is no gainsaying the disproportionate contribution California made to framing and driving the modern era of winemaking. Before the advent of the new era, wine was fermented in open wooden barrels or sometimes in cement tanks, without any temperature control. This was all very well in the cooler climates of French wine country. In California, fermentations were frequently too hot, which encouraged the spread of bacteria that were anyway ubiquitous, because sanitation was poor. Wines too often developed "off-flavors" and a silky cloudiness. Research showed how these gremlins could be eliminated and wines rendered more stable: the most striking of many advances was the introduction of "cold" fermentation in spotless stainless steel tanks equipped with special jackets that maintained temperatures within ranges that had been discovered to produce the right results.

Most of the research in the 1940s and 1950s was done at Davis and at private, progressive laboratories like André Tchelistcheff's at Beaulieu or at E&J Gallo, now the world's largest producer of (industrial) wine—based not in Napa but in the Central Valley. The new practices were later copied by the oldest and most haughtily traditional European producers.

One of the paradoxes about the behavior of Joe Heitz is this: defensive as he is about the merest hint that the Californians learned their trade at the feet of the European masters, he forgoes innumerable chances to educate ignoramuses like myself about California's contributions to the technology of winemaking. In my mind's eye, I can see him leading me through the various stages of winemaking and bottling at Heitz: showing me the jacketed tanks in which fermentation takes place, he could explain that Californian wineries led the way in cold fermentation, but he fails to do so. Possibly because he finds this far more entertaining, he chooses instead to make me pay for foolishly inquiring after his stone winery's European lineage.

"Certainly in America, winemaking is built on science," he tells me in the course of a short stroll we take through a vineyard. "We don't like to forget the little romance involved, but you try and build on the romance and the history of wine alone and you won't be in business very damn long!"

He is of course implying that the Europeans are misguidedly romantic about the business. Yet it was émigrés from the Old World who first brought science to American winemaking. André Tchelistcheff, arriving at Beaulieu in 1938, was appalled by the backwardness of what was then one of the most prestigious California wineries. In a 1979 interview with Ruth Teiser, for the oral history project, he said: "I was amazed to see . . . such an obsolete system of winemaking, without any sign of scientific-industrial interpretation. . . . The first thing I said was, 'Now, I've got to have a complete inventory of wines, and I have to have complete samples, and before that I will run the chemical and microbiological analysis and see what is there."

It is hard to see how Joe could fail to have been strongly influenced by André Tchelistcheff when you consider the striking similarities between their predilections and biases. Both men have made other wines successfully and there was a time, in the 1970s, when Joe's most admired wine was his Chardonnay. But it is his Cabernets, finally, that have earned him his grandmaster status, and the same is true of André. They are both renowned for Cabernets in the big and lush-bordering-on-overripe California style. But there is a more subtle and important similarity, too.

One younger Napa winemaker with whom I have discussed Joe's approach to making wine believes that most practitioners of this craft fall into two categories—pursuers of truth or of beauty. The latter group consists of romantic idealists who strive to bend and twist their raw materials to approximate as closely as they can a notion of a perfect wine that they carry within themselves. Members of this group, in which the young winemaker includes himself, tend to lie to themselves a lot. As a result, he says, their wines usually do not age very well: fundamental precepts for the treatment and blending of particular varietals are broken in the straining after the beautiful ideal. By contrast, members of the other group are ruthlessly honest with themselves: in making their wines, they limit their ambitions to the possibilities inherent in their ingredients, and much of their effort goes towards obtaining the right grapes to begin with. Their wines are structurally sound and so withstand well the passage of time. Joe Heitz, according to this theorist, is the supreme exemplar in Napa of the second approach—and, for the same reason as John Keats ("Beauty is truth, truth beauty"), would certainly consider the dichotomy to be false.

One species of demarcation between generations is the degree of restraint with which ambition is expressed. "At Cuvaison our goal is to be the Lafite-Rothschild of the Napa Valley," John Thacher says, without a flicker of embarrassment. Also, openly aspiring to emulate one of the most hallowed names in Bordeaux does not seem, to him, to put his own talent—or his countrymen's—in question.

But of course it had fallen to earlier generations of Napa wine-makers, like Joe Heitz's, to fight the old prejudices and earn for California wines their place above the salt. Their prickliness on the question of what Napa owes Europe is a leftover from that time. And, because two cataclysms of their growing-up years shattered many of their original aspirations, caution and a certain fearfulness are far more characteristic of Joe's generation than naked ambition. In an elegant encapsulation of its experience, John Updike has written of having been "reared in the static, defensive world of the Depression, to which the World War added a coloring of embattlement and patriotic pride."

With that as the backdrop, it is possible to see why Joe Heitz speaks of every stage of his advancement in the wine business as something he backed into inadvertently. This fits oddly with his reputation for individualism and arrogance. But it is not inexplicable. It is a little like acts of heroism born of desperation or hopelessness: a person who feels he has nothing to lose, who has had his first high hopes utterly dashed, is often someone who ricochets, willy-nilly, between the extremes of inhibition and a devil-may-care defiance.

Around 1958, near the end of his thirties and his time at Beaulieu, Joe was profoundly bored. "It was a nice job but the wine industry was asleep and I was just poopin' along at half speed." A college friend from his Davis days had set up a viticulture department at Fresno State College; when plans for an oenology department were being drafted, he recommended that Joe be put in charge of it.

Joe was delighted with the offer. He had enjoyed his education and liked the idea of teaching. A year after the move, though, he knew it to be a mistake. He heartily disliked Fresno's intemperate climate and, far from compensating for it, the job brought many more frustrations than satisfactions: dealings with the state educational bureaucracy were demoralizing. There was a minor outcry from members of the public who believed that the establishment of an oenology department at the college was tantamount to encouraging young people to guzzle alcohol. He began a discreet search for a job in Napa.

While he waited, he distracted himself from the drudgery in Fresno by earning a master's degree in food science from Davis. Three and a half years after his return to Fresno as a lecturer, when one weekend after another of job hunting in Napa failed to turn up anything, he decided he would have to start his own operation. As he tells it, this decision to be an entrepreneur was made very much *faute de mieux*: with a wife and three children to support, the idea was less than compelling.

Besides, in 1961, the California wine business was dowdily insignificant. Banks had no interest in lending to it and scarcely any new wineries were being started. An increasingly outraged Joe Heitz was turned down for a loan by one bank after another. Eventually, with $5,000 borrowed from friends, he made a down payment on a small wooden building on the main Napa highway. With Alice working by his side—the only other pair of hands involved at this stage—he began by "finishing" surplus wine acquired from other wineries. It was a time of glut, which meant that the Heitzes were able to buy a few barrels of partially processed wine for very little money. They then took it through the final stages of refinement, bottled it and sold it under their own label.

From this humble start, the new winery thrived, owing chiefly to Joe's exceptionally discriminating palate—which some rate as his greatest asset (and, others say, was greatly assisted in its judgments by the taste buds of Alice). It meant that he was good at selecting his wines from the choices available, estimating how he could improve them and—perhaps most usefully of all—at guessing what shockingly high price he could get away with charging for them.

Even though, in this phase of his life as an entrepreneur, he was "crawling on his belly"—a phrase several people who know him use to describe his struggle—the grand scale of his aspirations is perfectly clear in retrospect. Indeed, in *Vintage: The Story of Wine*, Hugh Johnson describes the young Joe as "one of the most far-sighted and ambitious young men in the Napa Valley." Making nonsense of his claim to owe little, if anything, to the European winemaking tradition, this English connoisseur explains how it was Joe who demonstrated to Americans the "French flavors" that could be imparted to wines by aging them in barrels imported from France. He casts him for the ages as "the apostle of French oak."

Joe steadily raised his prices until they were markedly higher than those of long-established large wineries and discovered that his wines sold better with each hike. This took a most curious sort of confidence. It was rather as if the owner-chef of an eatery accommodated in a shack were to charge more for the same three-course meal than the luxuriously appointed three-star restaurant next door. And it made Joe's reputation as the pioneer in seeking for California wines prices commensurate with their quality: up to then, these were probably sold for less than their true worth, reflecting American oenophiles' typically condescending view of domestic wines, and the inferiority complexes of their makers.

The wines that command the highest prices are French and most of them are so-called first growths of Bordeaux. This group can be seen as somewhat like wine's equivalent of the ancients' Seven Wonders of the World: in 1855, in connection with an international exposition held in Paris, Bordeaux brokers were asked to come up with a short list of the best of the hundreds of wines produced in their region. Having investigated the question of which wines had earned the top prices over the preceding half-century, they compiled a list of sixty-one producers of claret and classified the châteaux into five "crus" or "growths." A few of the châteaux among those classified no longer exist, and some of today's finest (and costliest) Bordeaux wines are not on the list at all. At any rate, since Joe's pioneering push for an upgrading of the market value of Napa's wines, the gap has continued to narrow, and other California wineries have commanded even higher prices.

In 1994, when Joe's 1989 Martha's Vineyard Cabernet was changing hands at $65, the Cabernets of Stag's Leap Wine Cellars and Caymus Vineyards were going for $80 to $90 a bottle; the same year, most of Bordeaux's first growths were fetching $90 to $100 in American stores. Hugh Johnson notes that, roughly thirty years earlier, when Joe started out on his own, "he had the audacity to charge $6 when the going price was $2.50 or $3."

Joe's outlandish cockiness was also evident, from the start, in making his own wine. "He came up with a style—he didn't waver and he didn't second-guess himself," John Thacher explains. "Once he locked on to that, he just maintained it, where a lot of us would say, okay, we're impressed with the style, but we'll push the edges all the time. The rest of us are kind of in the same boat—we're chasing the style of what's popular. Whereas in his case, it paid to be incredibly dogmatic and opinionated about one style. For every Joe Heitz, there are probably a lot of people for which that hasn't worked, because they didn't want to change with the times."

Part of Joe's style involves demanding of his grape growers that the fruit he uses in his Cabernets be exceptionally ripe. The other vital ingredient of it is that, even before the first release, he ages it far longer than most other wineries—including many of Bordeaux's famous names. From the beginning, Joe has aged his Cabernets for five years before their debuts—storing them first in large vats of American oak and then in small oak barrels from Limousin in France—so that they are considerably softened before they reach the world outside. "I've heard him lecture people on how they release their wines too young," John Thacher says, grinning at the memory. "He feels that if he could take the risk when he had no money, to age all this wine, why can't everybody else?" And this is part of the explanation for his being able to charge high prices for his wines from the outset: by the time he was ready to ship his first vintage, he was able to let merchants and wine-lovers sample, from five years in a row, consistently superior wines.

There is a high degree of concurrence in dissections of Joe's technique as a winemaker. Which demands this question: why does he not have more imitators? One reason John Thacher gives suggests that winemakers approach their task in the spirit of true artists: "Once something's been done, you've got to keep moving on, right?" Besides, he concedes reluctantly, "there is only one Martha's Vineyard, and [its wine] is very distinctive. It's got this more minty flavor—why is a source of endless conjecture—whether or not it's because it's near a eucalyptus orchard, for instance. It's not at all a simple wine."

A favorite anecdote that travels along the Napa grapevine is Joe's terse assessment of the eucalyptus grove theory: "Eucalyptus groves smell like tomcat piss."

Heitz Wine Cellars' connection with Martha's Vineyard began in 1965, the year the company was formally incorporated—also the year in which Joe and Alice acquired and moved to the Spring Valley estate, complete with stone winery—and the first in which the Heitzes crushed grapes for a wine made from scratch. Some of those grapes came from a small (twelve-acre) vineyard named for Martha May, who had recently bought it with her husband, Tom, a teacher. The Mays were not winemakers and were looking for customers for their grapes. Joe believes that adding the words "Martha's Vineyard," set in a small oval, to the label on the Cabernet, mysteriously enhanced its appeal—even though it had nothing to do with its namesake, the genteel East Coast summer resort. As for Martha herself, she does not suggest an aristocratic wine so much as a joyful *paysanne*: she is sturdily built, open-faced, someone easy to imagine making swaying progress through her vine rows, a basket of grapes on her head.

Far from minding that the source of grapes for his most famous Cabernet is someone else's vineyard, Joe has always insisted that he finds this a relief. Possibly because he had had all he could take of farming as a boy in Illinois, he prefers to leave viticulture to others—in principle, anyway. The transcript of his interview with Ruth Teiser contains this exchange:

JH: I repeat. I think I've said this half a dozen times: I like to consider myself a winemaker and not a vineyardist.

RT: But in spite of yourself you're a vineyardist.

JH: No, not really. We hire that work done.

RT: Yes, but you have to direct it. Don't you make the decisions?

JH: Just what to plant. I'm not out there on a daily basis.

RT: But you do decide what to plant.

JH: Oh, sure, and when to pick.

He believes, implicitly, that the winery is relatively more important than the vineyard in the creation of great wines—not a point of view that is popular in Napa. "I mean, you talk to any of us and people will tell you, yeah, wine's made in the vineyard," John Thacher says. "He's the lone rock trying to hold off from what the rest of us are saying these days."

Yet Joe is famously fussy about grapes he will and won't accept from growers: they must meet his exacting requirements for extreme ripeness, and consignments of fruit containing leaves and other materials are summarily sent back. Indeed, terminated relationships with some growers of Joe's Chardonnay grapes explain why his white wines of that strain are no longer the claim to fame for him that they were in the 1960s and most of the 1970s.

Despite Joe's lack of enthusiasm for viticulture, success has enabled Heitz Wine Cellars steadily to expand its Napa holdings to 150 acres of vineyards. A lot of the Heitz harvest of grapes is sold to other wineries.

In 1989, Heitz Cellars bought 560 acres of land in the scorching and virginal Pope Valley, northeast of the Napa Valley. Joe is on the record, on the Bancroft Library tapes, with this explanation for his reluctant acquisition of vineyards: "As the children become more involved, they have to have something to get their claws into."

Between my first and later visits to the Heitzes, I had moved from a satellite town of San Francisco deep into American farm country. From the vantage ground of my new home, I noted ways in which Joe and parts of the Heitz estate might fit seamlessly into heartland America—far more readily, certainly, than into Napa. The plain, creamy white farmhouse in which Joe and Alice live, and the detached cottages nearby, seemed to proclaim *homestead*.

Joe and Alice were as plainspoken as my new neighbors. Yet while my neighbors were warmly welcoming and eager to satisfy their curiosity about this foreigner dropped in their midst, Joe—and Alice, too—asked me almost no questions about myself. They seemed wary of cosmopolitanism, disenchanted with it—as if Napa had brought them one bellyful too many of it and they preferred to stick to home-cooked fare these days, thank you.

And there was another stark contrast. My farmer neighbors I found comforting and reassuring because they themselves were deeply at ease in their surroundings. But Joe and Alice struck me as being dissatisfied with theirs.

On one visit, I asked whether they liked the way Napa had evolved in their forty years in the valley.

"Oh *yes*," Alice said. "It's very exciting." She seemed to be telling me what she thought I wanted to hear.

Joe spoke in the tone of one delivering an angry jeremiad. "The people that are bitching about the way it is now are also the ones like the Davieses [of Schramsberg] that came in and made it this way. It was a nice, quiet, sleepy valley. And then people came in from Los Angeles—and people from all over the world came and . . . you know . . . they, er . . . "

He spluttered to a halt. Alice broke in nervously, "We just don't want to see . . . "

" . . . and now they're complainin' about it! And they're the ones that came!" Joe burst out.

"We just don't want subdivisions," Alice said soothingly. "We'd sooner have wineries."

"That is what we voted for—an ag-ri-cul-tur-al preserve!" her husband thundered.

For all his exaggerated chauvinism, Joe Heitz is not quite the greatest xenophobe in cosmopolitan Napa. He is, however, a peerless francophobe. At our first meeting I had asked him whether, growing up, he had been given small quantities of wine to taste, "like a little French child." He stiffened. "Don't say I was like a little French child. A little almost any other kind of child." So I had to know what he had against French children. "They have French parents."

Later, Alice told me that her and Joe's impression of the French, from fifteen to twenty years ago, was that "they weren't very nice to people." She had the usual complaint about the French lack of sympathy for foreigners unable to speak their language.

Distinctive as his own style is, Joe's refusal to acknowledge any indebtedness whatever to the French tradition is scarcely persuasive. The teacher who had most to do with his evolution as a winemaker deserves to have the last word on the subject. André Tchelistcheff told Ruth Teiser:

"I am always considering French wine culture as one of the funda-mental cultures for one single reason. Recently . . . one of the out-standing winemakers in Germany . . . said to me, 'We are known for centuries and centuries for the Rhine wines,' . . . but if you would take every German winemaker individually, and suspend him, and try to turn him, eventually he will face towards France."

I cannot imagine André's erstwhile assistant, the proudest of American sons, his family tree thick with German forebears, ever admitting as much in relation to his California classics—not, any-way, until his tannins have had a good deal longer to soften.

CHAPTER FIVE

The Mexicans

"We have trouble with gringo names, just like gringo faces, they all look alike; their language sounds like Chinese."

The Old Gringo,
CARLOS FUENTES

AFTER I FIRST MEET Leticia Reygosa I hunt for a book I bought before it became fashionable for mortal women to turn to literature about goddesses to dispel existential angst. I'm not sure what I'm looking for, precisely, only—like a frantic burrowing animal—I cannot rest until I have found Larousse's *World Mythology* and in it, a photograph of a statue of Tlazoltéotl, the goddess of unbridled sexuality and uncleanliness, in the act of giving birth. This is no symbolic "virgin" birth: Tlazoltéotl's childish body is squatting, knees apart, and between them a baby with an anxious middle-aged face is diving out, hands forward, palms down. Pain has the goddess baring her teeth; her wide-open eyes stare blankly. As I have had no child myself and am curious about childbirth, the statue fascinates me—is the most vivid artistic rendering I have seen of the blood-and-guts business that mothers I know well have described to me.

There is a coincidence in my discovery that Leticia reminds me of the Tlazoltéotl image. She cleans short-let rooms for a living and the Aztec goddess is sometimes referred to as the "eater of filth." Not that anything about Leticia herself is less than immaculate: the sparsely furnished apartment in the town of Napa that she rents with her husband, Virgilio, is so spruce and orderly that it borders on ster-

Note: Some names and identities of people in this chapter have been changed.

ile. No, it's just that Tlazoltéotl seems to stand for the stuff-of-life-clean-and-unclean, and I find it odd that the livelihood of this earthy child-woman should mesh so flawlessly with the symbolism.

As tiny as Leticia's round, short-limbed body is, and though she is just twenty-five, when she growls at her children, nine-year-old Elba and six-year-old Pedro, or chatters to them in a voice pitched high with good cheer, she is all mother—eternally, anciently. I recognize this in the way we sometimes know others most surely by the aspects of ourselves that they call into question. In her presence, I am aware of an anxious, dimly audible churning in myself about a petrification of the instincts, a fossilizing of the womb I have never used—the fear that I will turn brittle in a middle age too far removed from the pulsing chaos of life.

In a corner of Leticia's living room—clearly a sacrosanct corner, a bit like a shrine—is a stacked black stereo system and, arranged on a lace doily on top of the television set beside it, bottles of Robert Mondavi and Domaine Chandon wine, testimonials to Virgilio's work in Napa's vineyards.

I have found wine in similar solemn displays in the living rooms of other Mexican families in Napa. It is sometimes given away as gifts to visitors but almost never drunk by its owners. I have asked why not and been told time and again that Mexicans seldom drink wine. Their labors in Napa's vineyards and cellars have not led to their acquiring a taste for the fruit of their toil.

But I had glimpsed the vast cultural gulf separating Napa's Mexicans from the valley's wine-sipping gringos long before my visit to Leticia and Virgilio's home.

One hot summer afternoon I had sat sorting out notes in the estimable, francophile Model Bakery on St. Helena's Main Street. At the only other table in the shop, two sleek young matrons in Bermuda shorts whom I had watched emerge from a blue Mercedes and a white Volvo station wagon were debating—above the chatter of their children—whether they should order grilled quail sandwiches with tarragon butter at a bargain $3 each. Suddenly I remembered a call I had promised to return and dashed out into the street in search of a telephone. The closest one was in use and, in the quest for another, I came to an open doorway and an empty, dark interior beneath a sign that said "Ana's Cantina." I ducked out of the sunshine and seemed to make an Indiana Jones–ish transition between continents.

A ceiling fan turned slowly in the gloom—for me, an image long entwined with listlessness and hopelessness in punishing heat. Behind the bar, a thickset man without a neck, a large drooping mustache and a severely downturned mouth nodded when I made my request and stooped to retrieve a rotary telephone from a shelf beneath the counter. I dialed my number and he returned to polishing glasses wearily and with a look of blank despair. Who knew what his ethnic origins were, but I was reminded that the Aztecs' is among the most pessimistic of the world's mythologies: the gods in it die, too.

I was only in the cantina for a few minutes but I did not forget my astonishment at so abruptly leaving plush and cheerful St. Helena for a slice of Mexico cut adrift. I would have to return to Ana's for another visit, I knew, to see if laws of time and space could once again be perverted.

A few weeks later I saw a classified advertisement for mariachi music at Ana's in *The St. Helena Star*. Friends of mine, a couple who could be trusted to play fly-on-the-wall roles flawlessly, came with me one Saturday night after dinner. The cantina was perhaps half full when we slipped into metal chairs at a table by the door.

The same no-neck man presided over the bar serving customers. The same arthritic fan stirred the air, only now I saw that it had bulbs attached to it which shed a velvety light that flattered Ana's high, old-fashioned tongue-and-groove walls and ceiling, apparently painted cream a long time ago. There was a mural of a desert scene behind the bar—saguaro and sand—and, suspended from a ceiling at one end of the counter, an enormous television set on which Anglos in crisp checked garments silently wielded golf clubs in a tournament in, probably, Pebble Beach.

The sound waves in the room were produced by the seven-man mariachi band, their music the classic festive keening of Mexico, dominated by two trumpets carrying the same tune two notes apart. All the squat and stocky band members were dressed alike in starched white shirts, short black jackets and black trousers with outsized silver belt buckles—the lead singer's in the shape of a heart. Their expressions were grave or absent.

All but one of Ana's almost exclusively Mexican patrons— perched on the bar, playing pool at the table in the back or watching the band—were men; this was the single most alien feature of the scene. I saw starkly illustrated what I had heard—that most of Napa's Mexican workers were men who jumped the border alone, leaving their families behind.

But the eye-catching detail of the tableau vivant was the lone Mexican woman in the room. She was thirty, or perhaps a young forty, taut and sensuously lean, dressed in tight blue jeans and a black shirt and ceaselessly in motion—raising her forearm and a clenched fist in the air, shouting something in Spanish, when the band came to the end of a number, or rushing up to the lead singer to throw her arms about his neck. Now she perched briefly at a table occupied by three white young Americans—tourists, I thought— and now she stood up, her torso writhing, drumming the heels of her cowboy boots on the wooden floor in time to the beat.

She might have been made of glass, from the way all her country- men—including every member of the band—looked through and beyond her, too embarrassed to ask her to keep her distance, it seemed.

After half an hour or so the wild girl left wrapped around one of the gringos, a strapping ginger-haired man, like a boa constrictor in heat (never mind my ignorance of snake biology). The relief in her compatriots was palpable. And yet, in some peculiarly convoluted way, she had seemed to express an exaggeration of the throttled- down longings of their own woman-starved existences—something like lust by proxy.

I remembered her months later when a Spanish-speaking gringo vineyard manager warned me that any woman who approached Mexican men alone was liable to be taken for a prostitute.

That bit of advice and my two visits to Ana's persuaded me that it would not be wise for me to buttonhole vineyard workers on my own. But who would I find to go with me?

I was lucky. I discovered, through his German stepmother, an unof- ficial ambassador to Napa's Mexican community who could not have been more bizarrely right for the role. He was the thirtyish, aquiline-nosed, liquid-eyed son of a retired Iranian diplomat who had once been ambassador to Austria and the last head of protocol under the Shah. A few years before the fundamentalists came to power, Hossein Namdar's uncle Morteza—sensing the turmoil that lay ahead at home—had bought thirty acres of vineyard land in the Carneros region of Napa, an investment that was imitated by other members of the family after they fled Iran. Why the Napa Valley? "Because it's beautiful and chic and wine is nice," Hossein explained succinctly. When I expressed astonishment at Muslims growing wine grapes, his courtly and handsome father Mostapha made me a gift of a splendid edition of the *Rubáiyát of Omar Khayyám*, drawing my attention to such paeans as,

> Here with a Loaf of Bread beneath the Bough
> A Flask of Wine, a Book of Verse—and Thou
> Beside me singing in the Wilderness—

and:

> The Grape that can with Logic absolute
> The Two-and-Seventy jarring Sects confute:
> The subtle Alchemist that in a Trice
> Life's Leaden Metal into Gold transmute.

Hossein was in college, a student of religion, when he found work in the nursery and vineyards of Domaine Chandon, the Napa subsidiary of Moët & Chandon. No member of his family had ever, in living memory, undertaken manual work, but Hossein felt he needed a practical grasp of the business of grape growing to help his clan protect its investments.

It was no mean feat for him to be allowed to serve this apprenticeship. The Mexicans have a lock on the vineyard work in Napa: aside from a few Filipinos who tend a small vineyard near Calistoga, and the odd Guatemalan, no other nationality has broken in, in the postwar era. It is hard for non-Hispanics to acquire the skills involved because Spanish is virtually the only language spoken among the vines. Field hands tackle the major manual chores like planting, harvesting and pruning in small groups whose shared culture and language bar—or discourage—non-Mexicans from joining them. Actually, the culture is even tighter, because virtually all of Napa's Mexicans come from just a few predominantly agricultural states at home—Michoacán, Jalisco, Oaxaca and Guanajuato.

Hossein did not know any Spanish when he started in the fields, but believed it helped that his modest height, dark coloring and curly black hair made him look indistinguishably Mexican. Also, no matter how clearly he pronounced his name when introduced, his co-workers never failed to respond, "Ah, José!" and were puzzled by his inability to reply in their language. He learned bits of it on the job, then started taking Spanish classes a few weeks after he began and soon knew enough to discover, as he put it to me, that "the mentality of Mexicans is very similar to Iranians'. The only difference is that in Iran they worship Allah as their prophet and here, María. They are both very macho but at the same time sensitive." Soon he was singing and yelling Mexican *ranchera* music—"Yai yai yai yai!"—in work crews to which he was assigned.

Once I met Hossein and his father, some questions I had had from the start about Napa and Mexicans now acquired a burning intensity. If Mexicans did virtually all of the hard physical work in the valley, why did no Mexican own a plot of land of any significant size? When I considered this in my first forays into Napa, the explanation seemed to be that most of the foreigners who owned land were well-to-do natives of First World, European countries, and that the Mexicans simply couldn't afford to buy large vineyards at $50,000 an acre. But what about upwardly mobile Chicanos—Mexican-Americans who had been in the country for several generations?

Why had no rich Mexican from Mexico done what Hossein's family had? When Hossein completed his religious studies he enrolled as a part-time student at the University of California at Davis, working towards a degree in agricultural economics and viticulture. In partnership with one or two other investors, he and Mostapha gradually acquired shares in roughly three hundred acres of vineyards. In 1987, the Namdars enlisted a fellow student of Hossein's as winemaker and began to make Pinot Noir and Chardonnay wines in facilities rented from an established winery, under the name Pars, the old

Farsi word for Persia. They made 150 cases that year and, as their wine found more customers, expanded to three thousand cases three years later. Hossein put fifty thousand miles on his car in little over a year—most of them burned up in sales calls to restaurants and hotels in and around San Francisco. He learned a great deal from grinding gears in the many cultural shifts that marketing his wine called for. He found, for instance, that oblique, gentlemanly salesmanship does not work in America—"when you try to be subtle they think you are dumb"—and that he had to adopt a directness that in Iran would be viewed as uncouth.

Hossein had no answers to the questions about Napa's Mexicans that obsessed me. I would have to spend time with some Mexicans and ask them, he said; women would be my best guides to the community and he had exactly the right one in mind. "You can't trust Iranian men around a woman and you can't trust Mexicans either," he said with a smile in his voice.

I couldn't see his face as he said this because of the unusual circumstances of our conversation, an arrangement proposed by him that he, in his caretaker role, would certainly have advised against—as he was, after all, Iranian and male. By the time I had realized it was important that I talk to him his diary for the week ahead was already chock-full of appointments—so he had suggested we talk on a walk after dinner at his parents' home.

So there we were, strolling along an unpaved road in the foothills of the Vaca Range on a moonlit night, with only one house indistinctly visible—as if seen through veil upon veil of fine muslin. Dried grass gleamed whitely on dark hills on the horizon. Jackrabbits bolted across our path as if pursued by fiends. Two white horses grazed in a field, their manes and muscles flowing like watered silk. A peacock with its train in full, opulent display, minced by like an emissary of some Oriental potentate from centuries past. But by far the most distracting feature of this place—the Wild Horse Valley Ranch, where Napa equestrians board their animals—was its sound. Think of a chorus of out-of-tune organs—of deep, vibrant and faintly mournful sounds—produced, Hossein explained to me, by courting bullfrogs.

"It's the males that make the noise," he whispered when we stood eavesdropping in tall reeds by the edge of the pond. He mimicked the amphibian serenade and then attempted a free translation: " 'I want you! I want you!'—that's what they are saying."

I asked him to describe the woman he proposed as my guide to the Mexican community. She was called Aileen Flanagan, he said, and she worked in Domaine Chandon's nursery, where her colleagues were nearly all Mexican; she spoke fluent Spanish—and she lived with a Mexican vineyard worker by whom she had had a son, and with a revolving collection of three or four house guests from south of the border.

Then we talked about Hossein's plans for the rest of his life. He would build a small winery one day and make no more than ten thousand cases of wine. He would marry a clever woman who would gradually take over the management of the business from him. Once he handed over the reins to her he would build himself a small hut in his backyard and spend his days lying in it, thinking and reading philosophy between siestas. I burst out laughing but he insisted he was perfectly serious. "You see, I am working very hard now, but I am basically lazy," he said. "Again very similar to Mexicans—the ones that come here."

Aileen Flanagan defies many stereotypes—would seem, a priori, to be the least likely lover of a Mexican man because she is descended on both sides of her family from rednecks. Curiously, she almost looks as if she might be a Mexican albino: she has the sort of broad-shouldered, hippy, short-limbed, short-necked body most common among Mexican women. Yet to anyone who accepts the idea of beauty as a glimpse of an interior radiance, Aileen is extraordinarily attractive: intelligence makes her blue eyes crystalline; her thick dark blond hair has reddish lights in it. She has a melodious, bell-like voice that contrasts oddly with a laugh that can sound like car tires screeching to a halt.

The house that she shares with her man, Marcial, and assorted friends and relatives of his from the Old Country, is a plain gray and white rectangle. In the middle of spring you drive up to it past a fence lined by rosebushes covered in indecently large pink blossoms.

The front windows of her house look out onto tidy rows of infant coniferous trees, part of her neighbors' Christmas tree farm. The views from the rear are of a paddock where a small white horse chomps enthusiastically, and a vineyard, at the end of which the land slopes down to the Napa River.

Aileen's house, on land owned by her family, is in the Carneros district just south of the Napa Valley and southeast of the town of Sonoma—and each of these counties has a part of it. Some wines made from grapes grown here carry a Napa appellation; those from parts west are identified with Sonoma. The Spanish word *carneros* means sheep, and farmers from Portugal who once settled in the area kept huge flocks of them as well as dairy cows. There are still restful stretches of pasture in this rippling country—smooth-topped hills bleached platinum in the summer and tinted lime green in the winter—but, bit by bit, they are being converted to vineyards. The farmhouses and barns scattered here are smallish, plain, smothered in roses and, if they are not still in the hands of ordinary American farm families, look as if they are. Yet a couple of knock-your-socks-off winery headquarters buildings—including an outlandish Taittinger replica in wood of its château in France—have already been built in the district and, sadly, more of these seem certain to dominate the scene in the future.

"How long has your family owned that piece of land?" I ask Aileen as we roll away from her house in her shiny new red Toyota utility wagon which, with her powerful shoulders, she swings about like a toy.

We are on our way to one of the Robert Mondavi Winery's vineyards where Virgilio Reygosa, Leticia's husband, works as a field hand.

"Since my great-grandfather bought it in 1920," she says proudly. "This was my mother's parents' and they came from Kansas. And my dad lived in New York state and he came out to California, too."

"How many acres did your great-grandfather buy?"

"Forty-one."

"And how many have you managed to hold on to?"

"Thirty."

"Not bad! Are people always trying to buy it?"

"Yeah. Constantly. My dad gets letters every day in the mail from people who would like to put in vineyards."

Her father, like her brother, is an insurance salesman.

We discuss the miracle of this particular spring—the young willow and oak trees seem to have trapped green-gold light in their canopies—after the winter just past. December was marked by a rare freeze so severe that it killed off citrus trees and burned the leaves of even the tallest and sturdiest eucalyptus to a crisp. Then, in a seemingly endless January and February, when Pacific storms usually bring the grass on California hillsides back to life, no rain fell. As the vines at that time of year are dormant and leafless, the entire Napa landscape was an undulant donkey-brown. Day after day the vegetation blighted by cold found no chance to recover under the terrible clear blue sky. This was also the winter that America went to war with Iraq. In California, the combination of plagues made it seem as if the crack of doom lay around the corner: you woke from fearful dreams and the world outside your window looked all wrong, and then you remembered that soldiers were drawing on your tax dollars, too, to create piles of corpses in a war against a country led by a lunatic. Suddenly in late February the war ended and, within a week of the ceasefire, one storm came hard on the heels of the next: the grass grew green again.

Sitting beside Aileen, I remember from the rainless months the rude explosion of my illusions about California as a place apart, protected in its blessedness. Physically, the drought made plain California's true nature as desert. That aside, I felt as if, with inconsequential differences in degree, the place was suddenly on the same level as the India I had left—its people also hostages to fortune, its future uncertain, its parched present full of dread—and as if everything that had ever led me to see it otherwise was as substantial as the skin of a bubble.

If India seemed much closer than the seven-thousand-odd miles that separated me from it, so, too, did every other materially deprived place on earth—including the foreign country on which I am now trying to focus my imagination, Mexico. I decide not to tell Aileen any of this. She has the consummately practical person's impatience with philosophical cud-chewing, even with honest, simple-minded marveling: "Gosh, isn't everything stunningly green—doesn't it make you feel we live in paradise!" I'd exclaimed minutes ago, to which she had replied politely, in a faintly bored voice, "Uhuh. It was greener three weeks ago." She often takes it on herself to bring me down to earth.

Recently, in urging me to visit a certain vineyard manager, she warned that I should "read up a lot about grape growing before you go over there, so you won't come across as, you know, ditsy."

Still, I trust Aileen's bluntness more than the conventional Californian niceness, which can conceal a multitude of unfriendly thoughts. And she must find me at least mildly congenial because of all she freely reveals about her life with Marcial, whom I must describe. He is her age, thirty-four, a pale-skinned handsome man of medium height, slight build and brown eyes that crinkle benevolently at the corners: his hair is tied back in a short pony tail and he has a suggestive, roué's smile.

He was a soccer player in Mexico, talented enough to go professional, Aileen tells me, when he discovered he did not have enough money to build a career in the game. When he came to America eleven years ago, it was to work, make a pile of dollars and go home. In 1980, he had been employed in Domaine Chandon's vineyards for about a year when Aileen arrived there to take a job in the nursery, tending new vines. She was single and in her evenings alone often baked cookies to take into work. At Christmas, she bought and hung decorations in the sheds that were the headquarters for the vineyard crews. She would have stood out without doing any of this, being the only gringa among the workers, but the men so far from their families—and especially Marcial—were touched by her mothering. One day Marcial returned from a visit to Mexico with an embroidered shirt as a gift for her. "We basically dated for about four or five months and then we moved in together," Aileen remembers.

They had Mark, today a six-year-old with dark-lashed deep blue eyes, Aileen's exuberance and, being precocious, Marcial's lady-killing confidence. But Aileen says that even as they try to have another child, she does not want to marry Marcial because "he will not give up partying with the guys!" She goes on, in a weary, mock singsong voice, "He's not married but he really is married, and yet he still wants to go out with the single guys. They think they should party on Saturday nights together and play all day Sunday together. Just like little boys. And it's real hard to get across to them that if they have a family, they need to pay attention to their kids. And when we go to Mexico to visit it's worse—because I *lose* Marcial. I mean, I don't even know where he *is*." She pauses, surmises, flat-voiced, "Probably in some bar."

I ask her how she can stand an endless succession of long-term house guests. She gives an exasperated sigh. "Well, the only solution is for me to leave. I tell Marcial I can't take anymore—you know, when we went to Mexico, I found my house was famous everywhere we went—but he just ignores me and tells them to come anyway. So I think, well, I'm going to walk out. Problem is, it's *my* house!"

Yet there is more than even Mark and the prospect of another child to bind them together. After eleven years of doing roughly the same work in the Domaine Chandon vineyards—he has been promoted from purely manual chores like pruning and picking to driving tractors and mechanical harvesters—Marcial is ready to set up in business as an independent grape grower. "He's already planted his own small vineyard at our place and it's going to get bigger," Aileen explains approvingly.

Aileen and I have arrived at our destination in another part of the Carneros—hillier than the land around her home—a former dairy farm bought by the Robert Mondavi Winery that is gradually being embroidered with rows of vines. The sign at the entrance makes her brake, stare, and giggle.

"See, it says 'No hay' in big letters? And I thought that's, like, real thoughtful of them! They don't want people to stop and ask them if they have any hay for sale—because, you know, dairy farms are good places to get hay. But then I looked again and it's in Spanish! The sign's saying 'No Hay Trabajo Aquí. Gracias,' which means, there is no work here, thank you!"

Now we must find Virgilio when all we can see is a small prefabricated building, a large shed, a car or two, the odd tractor and no people whatsoever. In the first building, which turns out to be the vineyard manager's office, we are given a likely set of coordinates for him. We cruise over the brow of a hill.

"Ah, there he is!" Aileen exclaims.

I ask how she knows it is Virgilio in the old brown truck we can see chugging along in the middle distance, since I know he owns only an old American car.

"Because it's brown and it says, Robert Mondavi Winery," she says with patronizing glee.

I am still baffled because we are too far away to see the face of the driver and I am sure Virgilio is not the only employee who could be in a company vehicle.

But Aileen is right. We draw abreast of the cab and there is Virgilio's melancholy, walnut brown face and prematurely graying curly hair leaning out of the window; he gives us a wan smile of greeting.

He had agreed without a moment's hesitation to let me come and watch him work. After several long conversations with Mexican workers, I am beginning to wonder whether my obsession with the question of why no one Mexican is in a position of any power in Napa might be unanswerable. Certainly I don't expect my quest to end here, but it seems obscurely important that I see vineyard work close-up as I struggle with competing hypotheses. Two of these suggest that the work itself could have something to do with Mexican field hands' seeming lack of interest in upward mobility. Perhaps it is so indescribably delightful, working outdoors in beautiful country that some city dwellers pay hundreds of dollars a night to sample, that there is little incentive to leave the life on this land. Or perhaps, appearances to the contrary, the work is so physically taxing, and performing the same chore on one pretty vine after another so tedious, so soul-killing, that the men are left too drained of energy and hope for any spark of ambition to catch fire. Or perhaps, like most of us, they swing between these poles of experience which anyway have the same consequence: they stay where they are.

Aileen and Virgilio confer—in Spanish, which Aileen found she had to study at night school after her first few weeks working at Domaine Chandon. As I don't speak the language, I listen to the very different rhythms of their speech. Aileen's is staccato, hurried—her voice skips up and down the range of registers for dramatic emphasis—and she uses as punctuation a repertoire of sharp exclamations and shrieks. Virgilio fixes her face with his sleepy, gentle look and answers her softly, at an exaggeratedly leisurely pace. They know each other well, these two, because he and Leticia lived in Aileen's house for two years, and I wonder whether he might not be trying deliberately to slow her down, to keep her from overwhelming him.

It seems that Virgilio is having a most untypical day, unfortunately. We expected him to be planting vines—a job done in a team, like virtually every other job in large vineyards—but for this morning he has been assigned the one-man task of checking the drip irrigation system for glitches. The broad outline of his day: he arrived at the vineyard, as usual, at seven o'clock, turned on the pumps and then drove around to make sure that individual drip hoses installed so far are capable of producing the trickle of water that will be critical when the dry season begins. At ten o'clock he went to his car to eat the *mole tacos* that Leticia made him at six. It is now nearly eleven and he will spend the rest of his day attaching lengths of rubber hose to risers and then stringing them along the trellis wires between the posts in each row—to extend the irrigation system. At half past four he will go home.

As I want to see vines being planted, Virgilio says he will lead us to another part of the ranch. We follow him in Aileen's wagon but almost immediately come to a halt on a steep slope.

"Oh, shoot!" she groans, glaring at the motionless brown truck. "Goooooo on! He's gotta get enough momentum to get up the hill but he doesn't know how—none of these guys ever really learn how to drive properly!"

She puts the Toyota in reverse and we retreat a few yards to give Virgilio enough room to make his great push, but he fails again. They address each other in yells. She explains that he has given us directions to the planters and is returning to his irrigation work.

A three-wheeler—an all-terrain vehicle—rumbles past us and the short, cubelike man driving it briefly exchanges shouted, merry greetings with Aileen.

"Who was that?"

"That guy's called Jorge. He's done time in prison. He and his wife got into a fight and he had a gun in his hand when the cops showed up. He was put away for basically trying to kill her, which I don't think he was, really."

Now we spot the planters, about twenty-two men lined up along the spine of a hill. Aileen tells me each man is moving from left to right along his particular row. A plump, bald man with a pleasant round face who wears a clean white shirt walks up to the truck and

Aileen justifies our presence. He nods, smiles and tells us where to park.

"That's Rigoberto," Aileen says, out of earshot. "He's the plant bringer—he brings the plants to the guys and he's supervising them to see that they are doing things right. Now, he's one of those guys that's super-super-polite. But, uh—he cheats on his wife, even if he acts like God's gift to—" She cuts herself off with a sarcastic laugh.

We walk up to Rigoberto, who is standing beside a small wooden trailer that holds a mound of sawdust and a bunch of twigs in a white plastic bucket half full of water. I am told that the twigs are rootstock. Any wine-grape vine is usually made up of two plants, one of sturdy, disease-resistant stock that is allowed to put down roots in the ground: onto this is grafted the more delicate varietal vine, like Cabernet Franc or Cabernet Sauvignon, from which grapes are picked for use about five years later.

The twigs are twelve-inch segments of branches, each bearing an orange tag with this legend: "Gino's Nursery, Madera, California. Teleki 5C grade #1 rootstock." The ones in the bucket will be planted next, followed by others presently lying hidden in the sawdust, which is damp.

All of this seems straightforward enough—yet while I understand Aileen's explanation, I do not believe it. The twigs, as I examine them, are uniformly brown—there is not the tiniest streak of green in their barks. They look dead beyond all hope of resurrection. No, says Aileen, they have been sitting in a refrigerator since they were cut last October and are merely dormant. They had their roots trimmed in the nursery on the way here and, after about six weeks in the earth in moist spring weather, will begin to "push" and sprout green leaves.

We walk over to the file of men in baseball caps and baggy overalls, or loose shirts hanging over jeans, hunched over their spades, their heads and elbows bobbing up and down. Some wear several chains hung with charms and crosses around their necks. They are digging holes in the soil one foot deep at intervals of four feet. I had wondered, when I first saw them, whether the white plastic knives stuck in the ground might be offerings to some agricultural deity, but they turn out to be markers for planting holes.

The lengths of rootstock are placed in their holes so that the two leaf buds at one end of them just barely peep out above ground level. Then each plant has shoveled over it a little stupa of loose, protective soil designed to give the roots a chance to get established before the leaves work their way out to the light. It is important that the mounds not be too high, and Rigoberto patrols the line of men to ensure this. The workers often compete to see who can get to the end of a row first, and corners are cut when the rivalry gets out of hand.

Rigoberto, translated by Aileen, smilingly tells me that this land is especially fertile because of the cows that have been grazing on it over the years (I have always been told that infertile soil produces better wines, so I assume that this estate will be used to make lesser wines for the Mondavi empire). Rigoberto the philanderer says that each man plants an average of 230 vines a day. They certainly seem glumly intent on their work—have given us no more than swift, assessing glances tinged with disapproval. We might easily be unwelcome intruders into an exclusive men's club. Aileen has told me that the men gossip back and forth as they work, and grumble about managers they do not like, typically referring to them as *cabrones*—a truly terrible insult that can mean simply, billy goat, but also pimp or cuckold. They are silent in our presence.

We thank Rigoberto and leave.

"Aileen, I believe you, of course. But Rigoberto seems so decent and mild and so respectful of you. I suppose I'm being naive, but it's hard to imagine him having affairs behind his wife's back."

"Whoooah!" Aileen chuckles knowingly. "Uhuh. What did I tell you? But Rigoberto has actually been having an affair with the wife of a friend of mine. And Marcial has done it to me! He got arrested for drunk driving and so he had to go to this school for drunk driving. And he started seeing this woman he met at the school—and I was pregnant with Mark." Her voice wavers a little. "To me, it wasn't that big of a deal. But I was angry with him because he kept telling me I was stupid and that he wasn't seeing anyone else. And I *knew* he was."

"But if, as you say, ninety-five percent or more of the men have left their families at home and there are relatively few Mexican women here, who do the men have to be unfaithful with?"

"Well, most of them have one-nighters. There's no *love* in it. It's like the guys go out, they get loaded, some of them will find some-body—get a piece—some won't. The different Mexican bars each have four or six Mexican women hanging out there—just *huge* women, you know, like four {feet} by four by four!"

"Prostitutes?"

"No. A lot of them are just lonely women. I remember one time I was in this bar—even though Marcial doesn't *allow* me to go to bars—and there's this one large woman and this guy—a good-lookin', thin guy, and he's basically checkin' her out and wants to see if he wants to go home with her. And he looks at the bartender and he goes, 'Do you think I can move this piece of furniture around?' It's like, gee, if the guy talked about me that way, forget it—but, you know, these women just make a big joke out of it."

I gather that the men are not notably discriminating. The most famous habitué of Pancha's, the Mexican bar in Yountville, is a woman in her late thirties who was a man before a sex-change oper-ation. Several people, as well as Aileen, have told me stories about how the tall and blond Miss Terry, as she is known, likes to lift the tiny tank-tops she favors to show off her large, perfectly shaped sili-cone breasts. When I have asked why Miss Terry spends most evenings at Pancha's, the answer invariably given is that she likes Mexican men. They get so drunk, the legend goes, that they usually fail to notice her deep, manly voice and knobbly knees.

I ask Aileen if there is as much infidelity in Mexico.

"Yeah! In Mexico they are *allowed* to screw around. So you have some guys who will have a woman in each town."

She tells me about one of her house guests, Juan, who was a judge in a small Mexican town in which his side lost a political election.

"And in that place, losing an election means jail or exile—so he was put in jail and had to pay his way out. If he stays out of Mexico for two years, all charges against him are dropped, so he's been stay-ing with me and Marcial.

"Anyway, when he got here, this guy—a *funny* guy, with a hug-gable personality—but a real sonofabitch," she adds with a delicate snort of laughter, "he started getting all these calls from Puerto Val-larta which is, like, one hour from his city in Mexico, where his wife still lives. So I'm going, who in the hell is calling Puerto Vallarta—

and it turns out to be this little twerp calling his girlfriend! And so he's been sitting in the corner of my living room talking to her and he comes out with these things like, 'Oh, your eyes are as blue as the river'!"

We have been driving to the gate of the Mondavi ranch. We pass a plant pathologist bumping along in a tan pickup truck: a large orange dog bounding beside him on the mud track casts adoring glances his way.

There is filtered gold dust, surely, in the shimmering air, and gusts of wind like soft kisses on my skin make long waves in hillsides upholstered in tall silver-green grass. I feel a pang of regret for being so long past childhood, when I would have made myself dizzy rolling down these slopes, covering myself in sharp green scents.

Aileen points out an enormously long shed that used to house the dairy's four-legged milk factories and is now being used to store tools and materials for the expanding vineyard. How clever of the Robert Mondavi Winery to leave the dairy buildings untouched, to help preserve the unpretentious, down-home look of the Carneros, I say to Aileen. She has a fit of the giggles to let me know I am far wide of the mark.

"No. It's because it would cost money to change it," she says. "Everyone—all the wineries are on a very tight budget, and these people have put a lot of money into the vineyard already. You can see it in the irrigation system."

She stops the wagon and jumps out to show me. It seems this is the most advanced drip irrigation system anyone has in Napa—that some of its innovations have been forced on the management by the particular combination of topography and climate here. This is an unusually windy district, and when the wind blows hard it misdirects the water dribbled onto each plant by the little spouts in the rubber hose pipe running along the rows of stakes. The spouts here are specially angled to compensate for the distortions of the prevailing wind.

Soil erosion is also a hazard here when wind combines with heavy rain in the winter. So tall grasses are being allowed to grow between the rows to keep the soil in place, giving this vineyard a curious shaggy look.

We come to a bridge over a narrow creek that will take us to the gate, but Virgilio drives up to say goodbye before we can cross it.

I tell Virgilio through Aileen that I envy him being able to spend all of such a beautiful spring day in the open air. He gives me a twisted smile and Aileen rolls her eyes in sympathy. She tells me he has submitted an application to work in the Mondavi winery.

"What, work in the gloom as a cellar-rat, or shut indoors, anyway, when he could be out here?"

"He won't really miss this, he says. It pays a lot better in the winery—$11.40 an hour, and he's getting, like, $9.05 an hour now. The work is harder but it's easier in that it's less hours. They work nine hours a day here and in the winery they are treated as regular people, not as agricultural workers—most of them work eight hours a day, five days a week. They work only forty hours a week before they get overtime. But as an agricultural worker you have to work ten hours a day for six days before you get any overtime.

"In the winery the work is more secure. Like, right now, if you're lucky, you are still planting and then you get to sucker—that means cutting off some of the new shoots the vines are putting out—so there's three or four months' work there. Then usually June, July, there's nothing, so there are layoffs. Then in August the harvest starts and so it's like another two months' work. Then you get laid off again. Whenever it rains, you get laid off. And in the meantime, you've still got to pay all your living expenses. That's why you often find eleven guys sharing a two-bedroom apartment with most of them sleeping on the floor."

"And by contrast, layoffs at wineries are rare?"

"The wineries are pretty good. They do have some layoff times, but they usually tell their people beforehand because they plan them. Like they'll say, over Christmas you'll be laid off two weeks. And what's also good is, in the winery you're kind of going at the same pace all the time. Whereas here, well, you gotta go fast because you gotta finish the pruning in time. And then you get laid off. And then you gotta go fast because you gotta do the planting because there's a limited time you can plant. And it keeps going like that."

Virgilio stands by patiently trying to decipher all she is telling me—because most of her long answers to my questions are her own, not translations of his.

"But is the Napa Valley itself everything he hoped it would be when he left Mexico—I mean, in opportunities and choices, for instance?"

He listens to the question in Spanish and answers impassively.

"He says yeah, it's okay, it's fine, when there is work. But without work . . ."

We say goodbye to Virgilio. Just before we turn into the road someone gives a great lusty yell from behind a full-size pickup truck.

"Oh, Ai-leeeen!"

"Hola! Adiós!" she belts back.

"Who was that!"

"Who *knows*?" says Aileen. "I'm a woman and there's not that many women in the agricultural field and I speak Spanish. So they all know me and people I've never seen in my life will, like, come up to me in the supermarket and want me to help them decide what to buy. And it's like, do I *know* you? But I always end up helping them, because I know what it's like for them—because most of them can't read English and they don't understand that a generic brand of a cough medicine can be exactly the same thing as a much more expensive one with a certain label."

I was afraid—before I began to get to know some of Napa's Mexicans—that I might find myself obliged to write a nonfictional pastiche of *The Grapes of Wrath*. But labor unions have almost no grist for their mills in the Napa Valley. The uncertainty about employment that Virgilio so dislikes he also accepts as intrinsic to agricultural work, and the wage he earns in the Napa Valley is far higher than the $3.80 an hour he made picking tobacco in Virginia in 1983, or the $6 to $7 an hour that friends of his in Silicon Valley make assembling and testing batteries. At Mondavi, as at other large Napa wineries, the health and other benefits for all employees are excellent. His boss does not stand over him—gives him goals and leaves it up to him to decide how he will meet them, and Virgilio likes this. Like most Mexicans I spoke to in Napa, he sees the presence of the unions as close to pointless. At some wineries, the workers told me about new immigrants being allowed, with a nod and a wink from the management, to sleep in their battered cars in company parking lots at night and take showers in company bathrooms—until they could afford rent somewhere.

But if no material for a Steinbeckian saga presented itself, once I was deep into my investigations it was a Hispanic *Peyton Place* I had to resist writing. Tales of sexual peccadilloes popped up in virtually every context.

Soon enough, they enter the conversation here, for instance, in Chuck E Cheese's Pizza Time Theatre in the blue-collar town of Fairfield roughly a half hour east of Napa—which I am visiting one Saturday night with Aileen, Marcial, Leticia, Virgilio and their children, as well as two of Aileen's semi-permanent house guests and three men staying with the Reygosas.

At Chuck E Cheese you play video and slot-machine games with large plastic toys; between games you crunch pizza and swig fizzy soft drinks or beer. In a corner of the dining section is a stage on which four mechanical hounds dressed in bell-bottomed trousers jerk mimetically at toy instruments beside a sign identifying them as *The Beagles*: for a token deposited in a slot by wide-eyed small children, "She loves you, yeah, yeah, yeah" and other recordings of a certain 1960s pop group blast forth from a hidden tape player.

I am the typical single adult in this sort of place—it's as if, like the Tin Man in *The Wizard of Oz*, I need to go looking for a heart, because I share none of the excitement around me. I dislike harsh fluorescent lighting and I detest games of chance that devour tokens worth a quarter faster than I can blink, but to Leticia Reygosa, this is as close to heaven as she gets in America. Her face has the same blissful glow as her children's as she darts between games in tiny pink sneakers tied with black phosphorescent laces. For her sake, I strain to work up a measure of enthusiasm: I turn a miserly $2 into tokens (she and Aileen have each converted $20 bills) and try my luck at the Last Chance Saloon where, for one token, a plastic gun gives you three chances to knock down elderly Western characters who peer out of the saloon's windows and balcony. Prize tickets sputter out of a slot and I hand mine to an incredulous Leticia, who has accumulated a thick wad of them in a jeans pocket: on another day, when the gift shop is open, she will exchange them for overpriced T-shirts, toys and candy.

We adults leave the children in the game room and at the food counter take delivery of two enormous pizzas and a jug of beer. In my jeans and fading red jacket, with my dark coloring, I might be part-Mexican: I notice that the teenage gringos serving us are faintly wary of our group, not half as cheerily eager to please as they are with their Anglo customers.

No table is large enough to hold us all, so that the women and Virgilio and I sit at one, leaving Marcial and the other men to arrange themselves around another.

How did Leticia and Virgilio decide to come to America and at what age, I ask. Was it an ambition that one or both of them had as children?

Aileen translates.

"Noooooh!" Leticia exclaims loudly.

She came at eighteen and Virgilio at twenty-two, and they came because of *"problemas"*—they had decided that their three-year-old marriage was on the rocks. It would be easier to separate and survive independently in America than in Morelos, where they lived with Virgilio's parents. Leticia, who had lost her mother at four and been brought up by an aunt, had no family to turn to for support after a divorce. She had been taking in washing and working on Virgilio's brother's rose farm, tying bundles of seventy-five flowers, and this work could not produce enough income to support her and Elba, born a few months after the wedding.

"But what was wrong with the marriage?"

Leticia says something to Aileen in a low, gravelly voice that makes Virgilio stare blankly into space.

"She says he was going out with other women and she caught him!" Aileen gives an unconvincing, neighing laugh to relieve the tension at the table.

It took them six months to beg from relatives the $300 they needed to hire a *coyote* or professional smuggler to get them across the border. Then it took them a day to find a *coyote* in one of the seediest parts of Tijuana, and he led them on a hike through the "Liberty Mountains" (actually the Coastal Range) from seven o'clock in the evening to five o'clock the next morning, when they arrived in America. I ask many questions to try to discover what the experience was like but their answers are monosyllabic and their faces frozen expressionless. Leticia will only say that they were terrified of the Border Patrol's helicopters and horses.

They went to Los Angeles to stay with distant relatives, but neither of them could find work: Virgilio, who had been a roofer and field hand at home, had been hoping to find a job as a carpenter. Shortly after their arrival Leticia discovered she was pregnant. Since they had no home of their own, she had to return to Virgilio's family in Mexico—and to Elba, whom they had left in her grandmother's care. The question of their splitting up became academic.

Virgilio, still hunting for employment in Los Angeles, heard that he could count on being taken on to help with the harvest in Napa. He discovered he would have a place to stay there, too—because of *problemas* between Aileen and Marcial that had led to Marcial being thrown out of the house on the Flanagan estate. Virgilio, like Marcial, came from Miahuatlán, and so was invited to join him in the apartment he was sharing with ten other men.

Here the Reygosas' story is interrupted because they excuse themselves to check on the children in the game room. Aileen and I, left to ourselves, can't help overhear a frizzy-haired blonde at the next table complain shrilly to a hefty black man: "It's her whole behavior I can't stand! If she's upset about something he does, she can't say she is—she just has this really sick laugh like, 'heh, heh, heh'!"

"Oh no," I murmur to Aileen. "More *problemas!*"

"Yeah! And Leticia couldn't tell you the whole story about her and Virgilio. When they had just had their first baby, she found he had another woman—in the same town! She was driving around looking for somebody in the back of a pickup truck of a family member. And she passed by this house and he was outside it, with this chick—so she *saw*—and they were kissing. So she went home and took her frying pan to bed with her and then when he showed up, she smacked the hell out of him!"

"Did he have to be taken to hospital?"

"No. And then his father came in and he knew she'd caught him and he beat the shish-ka-bollies out of him!"

When Virgilio and Leticia return, I learn that she had to stay in Mexico for four unhappy years, fighting with her mother-in-law, before she left to find Virgilio. He had crossed the border once or twice to see her and the children, but he was often laid off and did not send her money for months at a time, or reply to her many letters. Through a network of women gossiping over the telephone lines she had learned, too, that Virgilio—having fallen into the pattern common among Napa's Mexican men—was drinking his way through his money and certainly not leading a monk's existence.

"If you're a Mexican man and you don't send money home and you fool around with other women, you can count on having your wife land on your doorstep, sooner or later," Aileen tells me in a rapid aside.

So Leticia hired another *coyote* and, from Los Angeles, took the Greyhound bus to Napa to confront Virgilio. Two years later, a woman *coyote* spirited their children across the border.

Now their life together is more stable than it has ever been. When Virgilio leaves for the vineyard, he drops Leticia off at the Sterling Suites, the short-let apartment complex where she cleans fourteen rooms a day, five days a week—including weekends—and has to finish each room by vacuuming a star into the carpet. She earns $4.80 an hour.

Is Virgilio glad not to be lonely any more, I ask him through Aileen. An exchange between her and the Reygosas is marked by squeals of laughter from the women and Leticia pounds her husband's knee with a fist.

"Oh, do explain," I say.

"He's telling you that he's feeling a lot more confident these days about taking her out with him and she's, like, 'Uhuh. Right. Sure!' Poor Virgilio, he's building himself a grave!"

Somehow Virgilio continues to smile good-humoredly. The children return, hungry, from the game room, and he takes them away to get drinks.

Aileen and Leticia rattle away in Spanish. Suddenly I remember a question from a few days ago.

"What was that word you two were using to refer to men the other day—something you said meant 'dummy'?"

"Oh, *mensos*."

"How strange—it sounds like 'men.' "

"Hahahah! Can't be an accident!"

She explains what I have said to Leticia, who replies with guttural glee, "Yannnnh!"

"So it's *hombres mensos*," I say, haltingly.

"*Hombres mensos—todos!*" pronounces Leticia warmly.

"She says, *all* of them are!" laughs Aileen. "When I first got to know the Mexican community, I kept hearing this from the women—that the men are no good—and I heard it so often it made me wonder how people ever get together to populate the planet!"

The affection between Leticia and Virgilio is unspoken—and they hardly ever look at each other—but it is strongly apparent all the same. Every now and then Aileen and Marcial exchange looks lit with flashes of amusement and electric appreciation of each other. And when Leticia heard I was not married or even quasi-married like Aileen, she made a soft deprecating sound and her face turned momentarily sad—then sadder still when I said I had no children.

When Virgilio returns and Pedro and Elba and Mark are tugging at slices of pizza, I ask what aspirations the Reygosas have for their future in America.

Aileen turns the question into Spanish and there is a slightly stunned silence. It seems I have been insensitive, because I hear a reproving note in Aileen's dulcet tones. "Survival," she says dryly.

"Yes, but what do they have to say to the question?"

There is a brief discussion.

"Yeah, Leticia says they wanna pay the rent, which is $500 a month. It's just basic survival."

But then, later in the evening, I gather that Virgilio is going to night school four days a week. He is taking a course in practical mechanics that is given in Spanish once a week—he can earn more money by turning his hand to the odd equipment repair job—and on three nights he studies English. The existence of Napa's Mexicans is so hermetic that it takes a special effort to learn English: Spanish is spoken at work and in certain grocery stores—including one I saw in Rutherford, La Luna, that has a large rack given over to magazines from Mexico—and at home, where dials are turned to Spanish-language radio and television stations.

Leticia is getting too tired cleaning rooms, she says. She would rather be exhausting herself as a seasonal worker in a vineyard making twice her present hourly rate. Though the fields are still an almost exclusively male preserve, seven women were recently taken on for picking at the Mondavi vineyards where Virgilio works.

Their hopes are vested in their children having all they lacked, Aileen says, so they are constantly urging Pedro and Elba to study. I ask the dimpled, ever-smiling Pedro what he wants to be when he grows up and he says, *"Bombero!"*—a fireman. Elba, duskily slender and graceful in flowered culottes Aileen gave her for Christmas, will not confess her ambition. Aileen says she will have many choices open to her because she is doing well in school.

"What do the Reygosas think of those Napa Mexican families of which I have been told in which the children are studying to be lawyers?"

"They view them as gringos, not Mexicans."

"Why?"

"Well, a lot of the children in those families will talk to you in English, French—anything but Spanish."

In other words, they are seen as having made a second, truer, and more final migration than their parents, crossing over to the parallel world.

I spend part of an evening with one of the families on the other side of the divide, known in the Mexican community as *arribistas*—or, loosely, climbers.

Armando Ceja is one of a class of people that appear, from their very pores, to be custom-built for success. He is acutely sensitive to the impression he makes and so camouflages his luminous self-confidence with self-deprecating humor. He has huge dark eyes sharply tilted at the corners and alive with curiosity and the desire to please. The arrangement of the stone-cut planes and angles of his face reminds me of an Abyssinian cat sculpture. At thirty, his thatch of straight black hair has just begun to go gray at the temples—a testimonial either to his genes or to the stresses that accompany high ambition.

Here at last is the Mexican rags-to-riches story I have been looking for in Napa, I tell myself, sinking deep into a soft leather sofa in the new, vaguely colonial house in which Armando lives with his wife, Martha, and two children. If it weren't for that thought, I should be uncomfortable here. This lower floor of the house—the kitchen-dining-living room—is as pristine and impersonal as a decorators' showroom. There is not so much as a child's toy or photograph or a newspaper or piece of mail on any of the brushed or gleaming surfaces to identify its owners—even though the Cejas have lived for over a year in this small housing development just off the highway, at the northern edge of the town of Napa.

Nor does the house contain any of those hallmarks of Napa Mexican households—a crush of bodies sharing the bills, or long-term guests from the south. I remark on this to Armando.

"That's true," is all he will say at first. Later I ask why not.

"I think in our family we tend to help people move along," he says. "I mean, I have a big house and if anyone needed a place to stay for a week, two weeks . . . but I would encourage them to move out after that. We have a busy day and a hectic schedule and time for ourselves is limited. We did have Martha's cousin staying with us, but she was taking care of the kids and helping with the house."

This is far from all that is unusual about Armando and his family. His parents and nine brothers and sisters jointly own a fifteen-acre vineyard in the Carneros that is now worth over three quarters of a million dollars. The acquisition of this piece of land—in 1981, at around $8,000 a bare acre—was an unusual and impressive feat for a family in which the head of the household was an ordinary vineyard laborer and then a worker in a steel mill. Still more remarkably, these are the occupations of Armando's nine siblings: a middle-class housewife (she does not have to work); field-service engineer; drafting engineer; diesel mechanic; biochemist; student of electrical engineering; junior college student; (a second) student of electrical engineering; and a fifteen-year-old high school freshman. Few of Napa's Mexicans have earned high school diplomas.

Armando himself has his own vineyard management company that occasionally employs his father, Pablo, who is semi-retired, and a seasonally fluctuating workforce of between eight and seventy-five other men. His chief customer is Domaine Chandon. He spends most of a typical working day driving between the vineyards of different clients, talking on the telephone in his pickup truck and issuing instructions to his crews. He says he completed most of the bachelor of science program in viticulture and oenology at the University of California at Davis but did not earn his degree because his father was unexpectedly laid off at Kaiser Steel in nearby Vallejo, and Armando had to drop out of college to help pay the family's bills.

Davis is not easy to get into, I murmur. "I had the grades to get in only very tightly," he says, charmingly rueful. "Having English as a second language makes it a little difficult. But Davis is one of the best experiences I ever had."

I am asking him how his parents persuaded ten children to keep their noses in their books when there is a scratching metallic sound at the front door.

"Oh, that must be Martha," Armando says. It is a little after five o'clock and she has finished her day's work as a dental hygienist. I have been curious about Martha ever since I was told that Armando once had a reputation as one of Napa's greatest ladies' men; that he kept her waiting—engaged to him—for nine years after they met at seventeen.

A small, thin, narrow-boned girl with long dark hair, smooth pale skin and a madonna-like expression enters with a baby boy and a rosy-cheeked little girl, their daughter, Belén.

After introductions have been made, Armando answers my question.

"I have to say it's because of my mother, Juanita. She really encouraged us all to better ourselves. She's fearless—she gets this from my grandmother who brought up her children herself after my grandfather died young, in a very rough environment in Mexico. My mother's mother was probably only five feet tall—green eyes, very much of the French-Spanish class. My mother's brothers are also very well off in Mexico. They have all worked very hard—my mother, too—and been blessed with the fruit of their labors. A lot of people work very hard but aren't blessed or don't have the luck."

I look at Martha. "Yes, their mother is a wonderful woman," she says in a low, uninflected voice. "And it's an extremely close family."

We discuss the family's—and Armando's—future in Napa wine. At present, two large Napa wineries, Domaine Chandon and Domaine Carneros (the Californian offshoot of Taittinger, the French champagne firm), buy most of the grapes from the Ceja vineyard.

Family members make a small quantity of wine for their own use—usually no more than two barrels. A taste for wine is developing in some Mexicans, Armando says, even though wine has a hard time holding its own in meals of heavily spiced foods. Yes, he says, he is toying with the idea of renting part of someone else's winery to have wine made under his supervision and to test-market it. "I'm enjoying what I'm doing now and I'm going to give it another year and then—who knows?" he says expansively, quite the young-man-in-a-hurry. Later he gives me a bottle of the family's four-year-old Cabernet Franc to try and I find it smooth and agreeable—perhaps too much so to age well.

Finally, reluctantly, I broach the subject I must. I tell Martha and Armando that it is my understanding that one can be Mexican or Anglo—but not both, and that Mexicans that embrace the American cult of success are given up as lost by most members of the community.

For the first time, I see Armando acutely discomfitted. He exchanges a fleeting glance with Martha, who stares at me and nods dumbly.

"I think that I, uh—" Armando pauses and continues reluctantly, vague and a bit confused, "I have a lot of relationships with the Mexican people and a lot of good American friends. So the connection with the culture here in the people—in the community—is still strong or stronger."

His voice lacks conviction, whatever precisely he means to say.

Eventually I meet his mother, Juanita. We chat sitting beside the swimming pool of her recently renovated house on the perfectly groomed family vineyard. She is a lean woman, plainly dressed in slacks and a T-shirt, and through her glasses, her eyes express pride, a sense of humor and a cool, discriminating intelligence. I am a little surprised, because I had expected her to be a cuddly maternal sort.

She hardly speaks any English, and Armando is obliged to interpret for us. I ask him whether she deliberately chose not to learn the language so as to ensure that her children did not lose their Spanish.

He nods, grinning broadly. "I think so. That's real common among the older ladies—although things are changing now."

A devout Catholic, she attributes her children's success entirely to divine munificence. No, it was not difficult bringing up ten children: she wishes she had been given twice as many.

I find that Juanita's home, too, has the same new-looking furniture and showroom stiffness as Armando and Martha's—even though there are personal touches here, like the wooden plaque into which are carved the names of the Ceja parents and all ten children. When Armando and I walk over to the other—newly built—house on the estate to say hello to Amelia, his brother Pedro's wife, I discover yet another decor clone. Only in Amelia's living room there is also a handsome wine rack about six feet tall and three feet wide, filled with bottles. I am relieved when I come upon it because, with this single object, the room is removed from the Anglo aesthetic to which everything else so rigidly conforms.

Tiny, green-eyed Amelia is the only aggressively chauvinistic Mexican I have met in Napa. "I think you are asking the right questions," she says feelingly, a little taken aback. "I think it's very wrong that there is no big winery owned by Mexican people when this valley would not exist without us!"

She embarrasses her brother-in-law. "Oh Amelia, she talks a lot. She's dynamite, though the package she comes in is small," says Armando, affectionately dismissive, as we walk away through her flourishing rose garden.

Long before I made my first contacts with the Mexican community I had begun to introduce questions about it—its preoccupations, its yearnings—into conversations with Napa's rich and famous inhabitants. Some of the things these people said I later repeated to the Mexicans I got to know, and my reports were met mostly with bafflement or amused incredulity.

Only one man in Napa's wine elite was able to offer me at least a partially accurate outline of the Mexican workers' experience of the valley.

I believe he got it mostly right because Spanish is also the mother tongue of both Agustín Huneeus and his wife, Valeria, who are wealthy expatriates from Chile. A Dutch ancestor settled in Chile early in the eighteenth century, and Huneeuses became part of Chile's ruling class; the urbane and patrician Agustín was obliged to become an exile when Allende's Marxist government took over. For some years he ran the wine business of Seagram, the multinational drinks conglomerate, which he left to become part-owner and chief executive of Napa's Franciscan Winery at the invitation of the Eckes family, wealthy Germans based in Germany, who had bought the winery from its founder.

The day we first meet in Agustín's salmon pink stucco and wrought-iron house on a special tourist haunt—the steep, twisty stretch of San Francisco's Lombard Street—I have to wait for a television crew to release him before we can talk. He is being interviewed for a business program on investment in wine and yet, all too inevitably, its producer is anxious to have him spell out for viewers—in the goggle-box's equivalent of billboard type—the connection between wine and culture.

I watch the crew do three takes of a slender, tweed-jacketed and gray-haired but boyish-faced Agustín holding a cello and patiently repeating for the cameras, "So this is what my *real* hobby is all about—the cello, which used to belong to my father. It's a Gagliano, actually, an eighteenth-century Italian cello. Pablo Casals once owned it. A marvelous instrument as you can see—look at the woodwork. Unfortunately the cello is such a demanding instrument and I find it hard to keep up with. For the last six months, for example, I haven't had a chance to play . . . "

And on to the message he himself is most anxious to get across: " . . . You see, people think the wine business is a very romantic, easygoing business, but it's *very* time-consuming."

Eventually we are alone in Agustín's luxurious paneled study seated in high-backed medieval-looking chairs upholstered in burgundy brocade.

Napa's Mexicans, he tells me, are separated from its other inhabitants by barriers of language, economics and culture. They live like an entirely different species sharing the same territory. He predicts that I will find the experience of getting to know them interesting, but without any connection to the rest of the valley. The Mexicans have their own stores, they go to different (Spanish) church services; they even see a different set of doctors—at the Clinic Olé in Yountville. They don't question the system here or feel any resentment towards it, or even think about it, he says quietly.

All of this I later find to be true.

But, at our second meeting—he goes on, "Anyway, among people from Latin America, you see, you have a very class-conscious culture. At Franciscan, we have a certain way of dealing with our workers—there's a slightly patriarchal overlay to it. For example they take flowers to Valeria. Anglos don't understand that, to the Mexicans, the relationship is more than just being paid for a job—they want to feel part of things. And they want to feel that the owner is the *patrón*, which is different from a boss—it's like a king and his subjects. They don't like the way American owners walk around in dirty overalls—even though the Americans are doing this to try to be friendly. To them, the king is the king. He has the same authority as a boss but is governed by a different set of rules.

"Social mobility is not even a question for them—it's as if you were to yearn to breathe underwater. The class structure is related to heritage—so even if a worker makes a million dollars, he's still just a rich peasant. The ones that climb the social ladder with money are never secure; they are miserable. The workers in Napa just become little moneymaking machines, sending most of what they earn to their families in Mexico, where they return one day to retire."

He says this matter-of-factly, in the same silky, even tones in which he describes his fiercely egalitarian marketing strategy: he sells his wines for far less than most Napa vintages of equivalent (fine) quality because he believes that this is the only certain way to persuade more Americans to make room for wine in their lives.

Months later I ask Marcial, through Aileen, whether he agrees with Agustín about missing cultural and emotional ties to his employers—whether he misses taking flowers to the wife of the *patrón*. Marcial looks sincerely puzzled and slowly shakes his head. Aileen sniffs and laughs in a short bark. She says, "I think they are too grateful to be able to eat and have a roof over their heads here to think of anything like that!"

One day I am introduced to Ramón, the foreman at Schramsberg, whose days are spent turning hundreds of bottles of champagne a precise few inches in their racks—a job called riddling—in cold, artificially lit stone cellars. André Tchelistcheff had told me that unlike the puritanical Anglos, Napa's Mexicans understand the value of leisure;

they know how to live life as a song, and indeed literally sing their way through their chores. Was it music that made his fifteen years at Schramsberg at this job tolerable, I ask. "Oh, yes, we all sing," he says, a little sadly. "But mostly I make plans that come to nothing!"

On another day I am at the Robert Mondavi Winery at harvest time for a ceremony in which the berobed bishop of Yountville solemnly blesses a silver bowl of grapes at the commencement of the crush. Sampling the wine at the gracious buffet lunch afterwards, I chat with the chef, a striking blonde in a tailored suit and a smart green felt hat she says she bought at Harrods.

"There's a south-of-the-border theme to this meal," she tells me brightly. "Because, you see, we are honoring our Mexican workers today."

I look around and indeed see on silver platters avocados and olives and tomatoes and tortillas and chicken wings coated with a spicy-looking red sauce. And I feel a thrill of anticipation, imagining the intermingling of diamonds in the rough and smooth that is about to begin.

"So where are they then? Perhaps we can go and say hello."

"Who?" She looks perplexed.

"Well, the Mexican workers."

A shade passes across her perfectly symmetrical features, which color slightly.

"Oh, *they* aren't here," she says. "They are working. It's the harvest, you see."

CHAPTER SIX

La Perspective Française

By the fifteenth century all the cultivable land within easy access from Bordeaux was under vines. Indeed the history of the Bordeaux *vignoble* [winegrowing district] is one of advance as the forest retreated in the face of the vines, and then of decline in the nearer suburbs, as the town itself spread; but this came later, in the nineteenth and twentieth centuries.

The Wines of Bordeaux,
EDMUND PENNING-ROWSELL

I AM NERVOUS and dressed in black in Yountville, waiting for possibly the most famous man in wine the world over, a man who is said to be coldly and deliberately obscure when displeased—or simply when he feels like it. It is lunchtime in an Italian restaurant apparently decorated to persuade its patrons that, entering it, they step into a Hockney. The pastel swirls depicting fruits and vegetables on the walls and the white-on-white airiness of the place, called Piatti, are unseasonal. The views are of the low hills beyond Yountville—a strip of restaurants, gift shops and agreeably plain wooden houses at the valley's heart, besieged on all sides by vines—and the slopes of these hillocks have turned from summery gold to khaki and gray. The harvest is over. Yellow leaves on the vines and on the graceful walnut trees and petals of blowsy roses wait to be clawed off by the winter's first big storm.

There is poignancy in this landscape veiled in a faint mist of pearl gray, but there is a certain perversity about it, too: winter always seems aberrant in holiday destinations. It strikes me, though, that this scene is exactly right for a meeting with a Frenchman. Think about it: the clichés about the French are inconsistent. Gastronomy and a special talent for seduction and lovemaking are associated with the French. Frenchness is a sort of stylish earthiness and a cherishing of a peasant past. But fussy precision, excessive rationality, cynicism and the chilly exclusion of outsiders are French, too. Frenchness is stern traditionalism as well as the futurist extravaganzas that are Charles de Gaulle Airport and the Centre Pompidou, which have no precise counterparts in the future's own country, America.

But, naturally, the expert opinion I have been keenest to have, trying to estimate the value of the Napa Valley and its accomplishments, is that of someone French—preferably someone associated with the great châteaux.

Now here is my host, Christian Moueix, *régisseur* (technical director) of Château Pétrus, a tiny Bordeaux château—which, depending on how you view the sale of three-year-old wine for $480 a bottle (the 1990 vintage, in 1994), makes some of the best or most overpriced wine in the world. I haven't seen him in the flesh before but, even if I hadn't been examining photographs of him yesterday, I'd guess that the dark-haired, bespectacled man in the impeccably tailored, sharp-creased tweed jacket was asking the maître d' to be led to me. He acknowledges me with a brief tilt of the head, a graceful little wave and a wide smile: he is so tall and thin and erect that he seems not to walk towards me so much as faintly sway, like a fir tree in high winds. I'm not sure why, but I am immediately reminded of André Maurois's observation that, "in France, if a man does not carry his head like the Blessed Sacrament, he may be regarded as an amusing character, but he is not respected."

"Your face looks different in the pictures I have seen," I tell him when he sits down. He says that is because he owns many pairs of spectacles with frames that vary enough to transform his looks. "I like anonymity," says this man who has been photographed for and written about in *Time*. "I travel under different names and I like to change my appearance." He explains that he is dressed to fly to France later in the day, that in the past he has come to lunch at Piatti straight from the vineyard, in jeans and muddy boots.

It has been a while since I was so close to quite so meticulously groomed a man. His slender hands look manicured and his black hair is swept back in a sort of bouffant. Yet his is a completely command-ing presence and you sense a diamond-hard will behind the soft, caressing manner.

He orders carpaccio for his first course. I have spent enough time with fanatical European gourmets to understand the calculation behind this selection. The simplest items on the menu are the wisest choice where culinary skills are less than reliably superb. Our shiny-eyed young waiter sets down a plate on which transparent slivers of pink beef in olive oil sport a dashing zigzag pattern of piped mus-tard, cubes of hard white cheese and a munificent scattering of capers. Christian freezes and stares, as if confronted with a prop in a chamber of horrors.

"Oh *no!*" he murmurs incredulously.

"What's the matter?"

"Mustard on carpaccio. Mustard is *never* served with carpaccio. You have a little olive oil and pepper. But not *mustard!* You see? This is America." He shrugs, raising his hands in the air. "Mustard. Just to make a pretty pattern!"

"Well, let's send it back then," I suggest, deciding that a show of support is required of me.

"Oh, I never send things back in restaurants. No!"

"Why not? You won't embarrass me if you do. I have sometimes sent things back in California and I find restaurants here don't mind—if you explain the problem politely."

The showcase for resplendently white teeth that is our waiter reappears.

"Is everything to your liking, sir?"

Christian says, with an air of infinite sweetness and reasonable-ness, "Has your chef changed here? You see, you didn't have mustard on the carpaccio before. You used to do it beautifully, with just a lit-tle olive oil."

"Well, it's been some months now, sir, since we changed our chef. But would you like me to get you another one—without mustard?"

"If you don't mind—*please!*"

A plate of minimalist carpaccio arrives. Christian tucks a napkin into his collar. The meal proceeds.

I know that in his early twenties, he studied oenology and viticulture at the University of California at Davis for two years. So I ask him what it was like, learning about winemaking in a country in which wine is an alien substance—in what was (is) still a Puritan culture.

I encounter the notorious Moueix penchant for oblique answers. He tells me about the winery called Dominus that is to be built in Napa for a joint venture between himself and two American partners (see Chapter 7). The Chinese-American architect I. M. Pei, whom he considers a genius—"one of the few I've ever met"—had agreed to design the building. He told I. M. Pei he was free to do as he liked but that he, Christian, would express only one broad preference: "I told I.M. the only thing I am interested to see in that country, in your building, is the meeting of the Christian Spanish culture, coming up from the south, with the local Indian culture. That's all."

You mean, that's the only part of American history that interests you, I say.

"Yes. I think the Indians were probably more sophisticated than the people who live here today."

Which demands this obvious question: why bother with making wine in California?

His answer is an anecdote designed to mystify. "An English friend of mine with an outstanding palate who lives in London said, 'Christian, why do you want to waste your time making wine in California?' I said, because you know, John, I like challenges. And he said, 'Do you know what I think of California wines? If you go to New York and you sit in a bar at five o'clock in the evening, in fifteen minutes the person you are sitting next to has told you his whole life story and you are bored to tears. That's California wines for me.'"

I ask about his ambitions for the Dominus wines, whose style, he says, is still evolving. I broach this subject more than once in the course of the lunch. Once, his answer is this: "I want to have the product which will have harmony, and which would express the American culture at its best."

Remembering his story about his English friend I say, "Ah. Then, perhaps you should make an incredibly forward wine that is open and friendly and with so little complexity that it is completely finished in two years!"

His face takes on a prim, schoolmasterly look and his tone turns admonitory: "I think you know very well that there is a lot more to American culture than that!"

The role of Frenchmen and the French tradition of winemaking in the evolution of the Napa Valley has been decidedly curious. The best-known red wine of quality made in California today is the Cabernet Sauvignon; Chardonnay, its wildly popular equivalent in white wines, is also made from the fruit of elite vines of French origin.

Fine French wines have always represented the pinnacle, the standard to which ambitious people making wine everywhere else have aspired. This was why in California, over the decades, acreages given over to the varietals used to make the great wines of France gradually outstripped land given over to the multitude of other types—Palomino, Alicante Bouschet, Aramon, Carignan, Riesling, Green Hungarian, Burger—as more Napa winegrowers chased after glory.

Even so, for most of the twentieth century, the best California wines—including those sometimes judged superior to top French wines in blind tastings, from the late 1970s onwards—bore little resemblance to the pantheon of French "classed growths." Even with French grape varietals as ingredients, the Californian style of winemaking—especially in Cabernets—was much less like anything French than like the chunkier rugged Italian wines. Comparisons can mislead but it is safe to say that the big, tannic and more alcoholic Cabernets from Napa are much closer to wines made in Barbaresco and Gattinara from Nebbiolo grapes, described by Hugh Johnson as "dark and powerful, tannic and tremendous."

Partly this is because the classic winegrowing regions of France do not get the many hours of sunshine that the Napa Valley and much of Italian wine country do. Heat causes grapes to make more sugar, which becomes alcohol through fermentation, so more heat tends to make heavier and—at their least attractive—fleshier, flat-tasting wines.

But there is a better explanation for the lack of wines made in the French style in Napa—indeed in all of America—until roughly the last quarter of this century. It is that Frenchmen (and -women) do not travel well. For the majority of Chauvin's countrymen, the charms of anywhere else—however enticingly exotic—are no match for those of *la belle France*. The French were hardly a presence at all in Napa's early days: they remain scarce to this day.

Under this scowling September sun, my wilting morale is hardly helped by my sprightly companion. Blinding light sheers off the huge outdoor stainless steel fermentation tanks at Clos du Val and Bernard Portet has a spring in his step, marching me around them, explaining that the grinding and clanking above which he is shouting at me is the sound of Pinot Noir being crushed.

He has a rather American superabundance of energy, a skeptical and self-deprecating manner, and a technophile's passion for dimensions. Clos du Val makes between 55,000 and 60,000 cases of wine a year, he tells me. The fermentation tanks have a collective capacity of 160,000 to 170,000 gallons. The various kinds of wine, red and white, are aged in 2,500 oak barrels imported from France—a modest collection compared with Robert Mondavi's store of 10,000 to 12,000 barrels, he says. Clos du Val's grapes are grown on 160 acres of the vineyards that surround the winery in this, the Stag's Leap district of Napa, and on another 100-odd acres southwest of here in the foggy Carneros region.

Bernard is beginning to remind me of a tour bus in which I was once imprisoned on a trip to Communist Moscow, on which a recorded voice recited the heights of all the national monuments en route, the quantity of water employed to keep the fountains at the university going; numbers of elevators and their passenger capacities in important buildings.

I see a chance to distract him from his statistical sermon as we enter a room resembling a small aircraft hangar in which barrels smudged with sinister red stains are piled high. "I never see wine barrels without feeling there should be a monk or a peasant running around among them—they make such an archaic image," I say.

"Yes," says Bernard, flashing me a grin but adding swiftly, "we don't varnish our barrels. You may have seen some barrels that look brand-new all the time but here, every time we push the bung back in, a little bit of wine flows out and paints the barrel. Right now we are getting ready to fill some of our 2,500 barrels with Chardonnay juice."

My little maneuver failed: I cannot get him off the Official Tour. He is plainly a technocrat in the peculiarly French mold, even if nothing about his looks would suggest this. He is extremely handsome in the classically Gallic, dashing anteater fashion, tall and lean, and there is a healthy gloss on his nut brown skin. His hard brown eyes usually express a knowingness and caution, but they blaze with good humor when he smiles.

I sense that he wants me to admire his array of mechanized winemaking aids, so I ask whether he would have quite as much sparkling new equipment to work with in a French château as he does at Clos du Val. He says he visited another winery of almost the same size yesterday that had a lot more. "See, here in the United States, more money is available and technology is prevailing. Okay. Whereas in France, it's more tradition. In France it takes much longer for an oenologist to get approval for a $50,000 piece of equipment."

After this exchange he seizes every opportunity to show how he does things differently from his Napa neighbors. The main Clos du Val building, for instance, is no grandiose, bogus château; nor, indeed, is it architecturally noteworthy in any way. It is a "tilt-up" structure whose supports and prefabricated walls were simply winched into place. "Mostly it's *totally* functional!" Bernard says proudly. "My boys are really happy to work inside the winery. You see how much room we have between the tanks and that sort of thing? There's no risk of accident!"

His disdain for ornamentation would do a Shaker credit. On our way from the cellar to the tasting room, we take a brief outdoor detour and I admire the brilliant red roses on bushes tied to the end stakes of the Clos du Val vine rows. Bernard shrugs. It's a common Bordeaux practice and it has been imported here at the behest of "Monsieur Goelet, my principal." That is how Bernard refers to his employer—the half-French, half-American businessman and art collector, John Goelet, who owns Clos du Val, lives in Manhattan and leaves virtually all important decisions about the winery's running to Bernard. I admire the magnolia trees and the Italian cypresses lining the driveway, the copse of weeping willows standing knee-deep in vines, the ivy snaking up the tilt-up walls and the short, boxy hedge of rosemary at the building's perimeter.

Bernard reluctantly admits that he is responsible for the garden. He confesses he is worried about the Virginia creeper climbing one wall. It is supposed to be covered in red leaves at this time of year but the leaves have inexplicably been dropping off before they change color "just like the Merlot vines," he says, frowning a little, striving to reason his way out of his distress. "It's probably because of three inches of rain we had last week. That's a lot at harvest time."

So far as Bernard knows, he was the only Frenchman in Napa wine in 1972, when he was twenty-eight. He himself does not even hint at this but, then, he was also the best-qualified arrival on the scene of all time. His father, André, was *régisseur* at Château Lafite-Rothschild for over twenty years.

When the branch of the Rothschild family that owned Lafite offered André a job in 1955, when Bernard was ten years old, he moved his wife and children to the Médoc from Cognac, where Portets had tended vines since 1710. The living off the ancestral fifty acres was too modest to support its many inheritors. Bernard, when he had completed his studies in viticulture and agronomy at the elite schools of agronomy at Toulouse and Montpellier, approached the owners of Lafite for a job and was told to go off and get some experience first. "So I did, and I never went back," he says, unable to disguise faint but distinct satisfaction at having repaid in kind what he perceived as a sort of snub.

A mutual friend, a Bordelais (wholesale) wine merchant, introduced him to John Goelet—whose mother had family connections with the Bordeaux *négociants*—who dispatched him on a mission to scout around for promising locations for winegrowing in the New World. At the end of his odyssey Bernard narrowed the list down to Chile, "where the political situation was not appropriate," the Napa Valley "for Cabernet," and Australia, where John Goelet also bought land and created a winery called Taltarni that would eventually be run by Bernard's brother Dominique.

The original Goelet plan called for Bernard's odyssey to end with his serving as a consulting winemaker to these foreign estates, based in France, "where M. Goelet was developing a château." Bernard stopped off in California in 1971—to help the staff he had selected for Clos du Val with the first harvest—on his way back to France from Australia. Then he got word that the plan for a French château for the Goelet empire had fallen through and he stayed in Napa—temporarily, he thought.

Helia, a girl Bernard had met in Chile and later married, came over from France to join him in May of 1972 and their first child, Olivier, was born in November, but he still resisted the idea of making a home in Napa. In about their second year in California he firmly informed M. Goelet that they would all return to France when Olivier was eight years old. A family friend remembers the lawn chairs being carried in to dinner at the Portets' for a great many years—of being told it made no sense for them to invest in real furniture when they knew they were leaving.

But by Olivier's birthday in 1980, "I was so enthused about building up Clos du Val that I did not even think of returning to France! My wife was so respectful about my development here that she did not want to tell anything!"

With credentials as rare as Bernard's, it might seem as if the job of creating an avid following for Clos du Val's wines would have required hardly any effort. Actually—paradoxically—it was the long, drawn-out struggle to win acceptance for Clos du Val's markedly different, French, style of winemaking that kept Bernard from going home.

We are in Clos du Val's tasting room, whose utilitarian style reminds me of an upscale motel lobby. I first met Bernard seated next to him at a dinner party at which he gave me his card and invited me to visit him. To express his pleasure at my appearing today, he has opened nearly a dozen bottles of wine of various vintages and varietals for me to taste. I protest that my palate is not sufficiently educated to warrant such abundant hospitality, that I am not a "wine writer," after all.

Pointless embarrassment is a feeling to which I am easy prey, and it only intensifies with the first wine we taste, of which Bernard is especially proud. It is a Sémillon bottled the previous year—one of the traditional white wines of Bordeaux that is rarely made in California.

"Here's a wine which is very delicate—full of melon, peachy and figgy flavors," Bernard says. "And it's soft, not quite as aggressive as Chardonnay in its taste."

I am all but speechless and mumble noncommittally, because to me, the wine seems thin and sour—what I would expect the blood of a shrew like *Great Expectations*'s Mrs. Gargery to taste like to a high-living vampire. It is a relief to be instructed by Bernard to spit out rather than swallow it, like a professional taster.

We proceed to the next bottle, a Chardonnay from Clos du Val's Carneros vineyard that is more ingratiating than the Sémillon: it does have a certain perfumed warmth about it, but less of this than most other expensive California Chardonnays I have drunk. I ask Bernard for a formal oenologist's description of the wine, and his answers demonstrate Clos du Val's contribution to the maturing of Napa winemaking—one that is more than a little baffling to an amateur wine drinker.

"The wine is still tight," he says. "What I like is the austerity of it—the California people don't like it because it is not enough fat. But I like that austerity because it ages very nicely. And also the wine is well anchored and stays long in the mouth—and the fruit hangs in there very nicely. And it's refreshing—so it's not going to overpower the food too much. None of the Clos du Val wines are very aggressive." He notes my skeptical expression and smiles. "You don't have to agree with me!"

"Well, the acidity is a little excessive for me."

"Yeah, but that acidity will carry a wine for many years. That acidity is also the austerity that people don't like in California."

"What exactly happens when the wines age, then?"

"They get fat." He means that they become smoother; lose their rough edges.

"So why is it better if they get fat later than sooner?"

"Well, it's a difference of philosophy. Here in California—well, you know Californians, they want to enjoy everything right now. Nobody has any patience. But I have to make wines that are going to develop [other facets of flavor and aroma] with age. It's a waste for me to make wine that's going to be a real charmer right now and in three years totally fat and aged and uninteresting. It would be failing to my ideal of optimum quality."

"So then yours are indistinguishable from French wines of the same types?"

"Clos du Val's wines are *California* wines. They have the *power* of California wines. But they have the *style* of French wines. The type of wine is independent of the winemaker. So if it's Cabernet Sauvignon, the soil, the climate and the varietal are the three things that are going to be giving you the type of the wine. Then the winemaker, if he is free to do what he wants and is not compelled by marketing strategies [to make what the market is believed to want], he gives it his own style. And I was raised in France with the French philosophy and, good or bad, it gives a style and a character to the wines of Clos du Val.

"People in the Napa Valley keep saying, we make our wine like Burgundy, we make our wine like Bordeaux, but you've got to go there and see how different it is from what these people say!"

For the first few years, Clos du Val's wines could not garner the slightest of public testimonials to the appearance on the Napa scene of a new purveyor of notable wines: it failed to win a single medal at any of the numerous competitions—blind tastings—held at state and county fairs. Although wine connoisseurs do not set much store by these prizes, they do, nonetheless, tell something of some lowest common denominator of perceptions of the quality of a wine and make it easier to sell. When even the best-educated and most sophisticated members of society are unsure of their tastes in wine, advertisements like "gold medal winner, Los Angeles County Fair" are useful for moving bottles off liquor store shelves.

Californian experts—the judges at those early competitive tastings—tended to complain that the Clos du Val wines were elegant but "stylistically weak" and "lacking fruit," or the tiny explosions of grape flavors that Californian wines traditionally delivered. Because their alcohol content tended to be lower, they also lacked the "kick" of rivals made in the indigenous tradition—which typically tasted intensely of the single variety of grape from which they were made. By contrast, in Clos du Val's wines, the characteristics of the varietal are usually muted by blending in judicious quantities of other wines. It is a dilution dictated by the harmony and balance that are paramount in the French tradition. Interpretations of this tradition can be strikingly different, but the practice of blending was something that clearly distinguished French from Napa wines when Bernard first came to Napa.

There is an edginess, an icy hauteur, that Bernard's deliberately matter-of-fact manner cannot conceal when he speaks of the American competitive tastings—so much more important than in France, where the reputations of the best wines were established, seemingly for all time, over a hundred years ago. "All those fairs, all those blind tastings, all those judgments, all those people. And in those fairs they [the judges] taste a hundred wines a day! If you make a wine that's well balanced but softer, that's not going to win any gold medals. For me, blind tastings are a plague."

Probably the Clos du Val wines were further handicapped by Bernard's having grown up as the son of Château Lafite's *régisseur*, tasting that château's wines in its cellars under his father's tutelage from his early youth. Connoisseurs always say that in Bordeaux, the Lafite style has traditionally represented delicacy and finesse and makes a striking contrast with Château Latour, which is all gutsy bountifulness. So, even by French standards, the tradition that shaped Bernard's taste in wine was an extreme of understatement.

I consider all of this in the Clos du Val tasting room, standing beside Bernard and spitting mouthfuls of his wine into the sink. I ask, how has Clos du Val managed to stay in business for nearly two decades and win praise and fame for its wines? Bernard's face lights up in a Maurice Chevalier smile. At first, only a few of the better wine writers—fewer of them on the American West Coast than in the Northeast, where French wines were (and often are) still preferred to anything Californian—understood and liked his wines.

The other great boon, he says, came from reactions similar to one I had only a few minutes ago. I was tasting his year-old Cabernet Sauvignon—not due for release to the market for another eighteen months. At last we had got to a Clos du Val wine I could wax warmly enthusiastic about: after being underwhelmed by three or four of Bernard's wines I had begun to fear that the fault might lie with me—for failing to eat breakfast that morning and worrying about the ailing transmission of my car.

But the instant I tasted it, the Clos du Val Cabernet struck even my untutored taste buds as different from any other California wine of the same varietal. Despite Bernard's warning that the wine was rough and immature, it had a surprising mellowness and subtlety. I wanted to wallow in the sensations it produced—the way the eye delights in running over the colors and shapes in a Matisse again and again. The famous California Cabernets I had met until then were more like Picassos—say, *Guernica*—in which technical virtuosity and powerful, unexpected dislocations and juxtapositions inspire respect but no affection. The difference is explained by the Merlot added to this wine—just under a tenth or so in this particular vintage.

It was the smoother, rounder character that this one Clos du Val wine—the Cabernet—acquired by blending that won the winery its first fans. These wines sold briskly in restaurants because they did not overwhelm food but flattered it; they were mellow younger, were relatively inexpensive, and would-be wine snobs who understood that they had to learn to love Cabernet to be taken seriously were thrilled to discover one apparently willing to help them acquire that taste.

When the French swap stories about the *gaucheries* of Americans making wine, one popular theme concerns the transatlantic visitor to the château who insists on knowing precisely what percentages of different wines make up its blends. Bernard allows himself a brief tirade on this subject and other contentious issues in the great transcontinental divide. "The one thing that bothers the Americans is that they go to France and the French don't tell you percentages of things! And I say, who cares, as long as the wine is good!

"Some people believe in formulas in winemaking. I don't. For me, the taste comes first and the statistics of the lab come second. But there are people that start with statistics and go from there to build the wine they want. So whether winemaking is art or craft or whatever—it's certainly not scientific. There's too much left to hazard for it to be scientific at all.

"If you were blending seventy-five percent Cabernet, twenty-five percent of Merlot and this blend was too soft—because the Merlot brings softness—then the reason of logic would say that eighty/twenty would be better. Okay. But actually, what you might find is that seventy-five/twenty-five is good, eighty/twenty is a disaster and eighty-five/fifteen is the best. And why that? There is no logic in blending, you know. No logic!

"The right balance in a blend depends on the grapes, depends on the vintage, depends on the way wines were made from those grapes—so many things!

"People who are trying to bring winemaking to a formula, however complex a formula, are totally wrong in my view. You can use the formulas to make a good, sound wine—it's like you can build a good body with formulas. But what you really want to do in winemaking is put the soul inside the body. And you can't do that in scientific terms, so I'm a bit at odds with the University of Davis as far as this is concerned. *Very* much at odds! They are nice people, there, but our philosophies of winemaking are very different.

"You have a Dr. Noble at Davis who made a study of Bordeaux showing statistically that she could not prove that a St.-Estèphe is much different from a St.-Julien from a St.-Emilion. Now you can see how friendly people must have been to such an opinion in France!"

There is indeed little about Napa or American wine that engenders friendly feelings in the French—although, over time, they become less secure in their prejudices. Each half of a married couple I visit one day demonstrates a different phase in this evolution: she is further along than he after their ten years of traveling to Napa.

Strolling into the drawing room of Francis and Françoise DeWavrin-Woltner's home, I suppress a smile. It is a smile of recognition. This is the kind of house foreigners choose when they want to be in America but not actually be here, chiefly to do something, accomplish some end they are unable to at home. The first house I myself chose to rent in America was a close cousin of the DeWavrin-Woltners', which is reached by an alarmingly narrow road bordered by forlorn, wraithlike digger pines that shoots abruptly off the Silverado Trail and twists up a steep slope. The views from the plate glass walls of the house at the top are of the family's Mediterranean Garden of Eden pressing up close and shutting out the rest of boisterous, discomfiting America. That is the whole point of this setting.

The furniture and the geometric Mondrianesque prints on the walls recall Paris—or perhaps it is Françoise with her short, short black hair that does this, a matter of a certain studied, mannequin-like sinuousness in the way she maneuvers her large-boned svelte figure around a room.

Francis like his wife is unusually tall. He flings himself out of and into chairs in which he sprawls like an overgrown spider. He might be a particularly distracted Oxford don in his tortoiseshell spectacles, capaciously baggy trousers and patched-elbows cardigan, but the clever eyes and smoke-blackened teeth—bared both to express amusement and ferocious disagreement—are straight out of a Left Bank café.

Françoise tap-taps her way in her modest high heels between the living room and kitchen, preparing our lunch. "Don't move!" she almost snaps, when I rise to my feet with a diffident offer to "help carry things."

"Françoise don't like help in the kitchen!" Francis warns. "When I was cooking anything, I was cooking badly! When she was requesting from me to make the washing, I make it badly! So she said, better if you don't touch anything in the kitchen!"

But, a far cry from the otherwise subservient sort of my-kitchen-my-domain wife, she insists on keeping up her end of the conversation even as she cooks. And better than that: the DeWavrin-Woltners' conversational style involves talking over each other's sentences. They compete in daredevil bluntness.

Hard by their house lies Château Boswell, a stone structure clearly built as a shrine to Rumpelstiltskin by the owner—a dentist named Richard Boswell. He comes up when Françoise and I are discussing the curious American faith in the idea of remaking oneself and one's life at will. "At age fifity," she says incredulously, "he decided to stop being Richard Boswell and he wants everyone to call him Arty. I told him, 'I re-*fuse* to call you that! I am going to call you Richard.' "

Francis does no better at suffering pretensions. Like every other famous French name in that business, Taittinger, the champagne firm and dynasty, bought vineyard land in California and commissioned a headquarters building in Napa's Carneros region—an exact carpentered replica of its stone château in Reims. It looks like an oversized stage set and dominates the beatific, undulant Carneros landscape for miles. At a lunch party for Taittinger's California champagne, Béatrice Taittinger was reckless enough to ask Francis what he thought of the building. "I told her, 'It is like a mink coat in the summertime! In New York in the winter, fine! But a building like this in Cal-i-for-*nia*?' "

We sit down to eat in the dining room full of shiny, dark and faintly oppressive furniture. The first course is a salad of crisp lettuce, hearts of palm and baby shrimp, lifted above the quotidian by home-made mayonnaise of surpassing delicacy. The wine served with it is a Château Woltner St. Thomas Vineyard Chardonnay that is, quite simply, exquisite: yes, it is sharp and lean where the California Chardonnays I have grown to love have a positively Rubenesque fleshiness. But it also has a depth and generosity all its own—a mysterious floweriness and spiciness—and passes my own simpleminded test for a great wine: one sip produces at least three distinct waves of taste sensations, whereas a merely good wine produces just one.

I ask whether they find the life they lead here very different from that in Paris or in Bordeaux where, until 1983, Françoise's family owned La Mission-Haut-Brion, a château of the first rank.

"I would say that we live here more a summer life and more a winter life in Paris," Francis replies. "You can stay here in the winter if you want to, but you have to like hunting and fishing! We don't hunt. We don't fish."

"So your Paris life is full of fascinating friends and wonderful long conversations about all sorts of things," I murmur.

"The same life we have here in the summertime, when there are many visitors," he says, "we have in Paris in—"

"It's *never* the same!" exclaims Françoise, cutting him off.

"No, not the same life," he concedes reflectively.

"Because," she continues, "the fact is, the life in a big city—it's anonymous. Totally anonymous. You have an enormous choice of people. When you are fed up with a circle, you can find another circle."

"You know, women here," Francis says with something like a faint sneer. "They have their bridge evening without their husband. They have their hiking day when they go hike in the mountains . . . "

He means that they and the routines of their parochial, pampered lives bore him.

"But they have that everywhere, Francis!" his wife protests. "You know, something I said to many friends when I first came here is, it's very closed—like Bordeaux life."

"In what sense, closed?" I venture.

"It's the same thing," she says. "You see your friends; small circle. You live in your pretty houses and a vineyard and you all have the same interest."

"Same thing! If you are living in St.-Emilion, you see always the people of St.-Emilion," he adds glumly.

"In Bordeaux, people have the most beautiful climate. They have the sea. They have the mountains. But when you are with them they talk about wine and the wine they taste in California, because they do travel, but they travel for wine," Françoise concludes with a Frenchwoman's deprecating moue.

"The problem in the Napa Valley is very easy thing: the crowd is not enough quality!" exclaims Francis. "You meet someone like X [famous American winemaker] and he's only wine. I'm fed up of wine. Especially when his wines are not good And he has a lot of talent compared to many others. The others are really *duulll*—aaagh!" he gasps, like someone being strangled in a melodrama.

She says, her tone gently admonitory, "You have the same thing in Bordeaux, Francis. It's people that are wine, wine, wine."

He says, "The people that are in Bordeaux with talent, they go to Paris on the train. They don't want to be buried in the countryside."

She says, "I'll tell you one thing. Bordeaux is unlivable."

I ask why.

"Because that! You have wine people."

Francis changes the subject to what is plainly a bigger bone of contention between them.

"You know, here, in the wintertime, when you see that rain—*uwum*, uwum, *uwum* . . . " he says in a sonorous, droning voice.

"For me, it's not the rain—" interjects Françoise.

"—*Uwum!*" booms Francis. "I will be un*able* to spend a winter here. That's what I know."

"For me, that's no problem," she says vehemently.

"You can do it, Françoise," he snaps. "I cannot do it. At least when I am in Paris I can just take the bus and go and spend an afternoon in the Louvre."

She nods, conceding him a point.

"The pleasant thing is to go down your building and to walk in a street—and see people," she says. "You don't know them, you don't care, but . . . "

" . . . The spectacle of the street! The show of the street!" he says exultantly.

I say, but people in the streets look so sad in Europe—and they really do seem depressed more often than they are here. How can the DeWavrins not be affected by that, even if conversations there are much more interesting, routinely, than they are here?

"That's why we like to come back here," Francis acknowledges with an air of exaggerated reasonableness. "But sometimes we are fed up with people that are too nice and too innocent!"

"They are nice. They are *nice!*" protests Françoise, smiling frantically.

"They *play* to be innocent. I'll soon be happy to see the sad people with bad temper in France! You say the people in Europe are sad, but they've got brains. They can talk of many things!"

Françoise, looking my way, suddenly shouts a warning. "No! You have to be careful—because with that, you will never cut!"

I have been so mesmerized by their conversational duet—my eyes meeting Françoise's tiny hazel orbs, brimming over with warmth now, and now Francis's, beaming ironic amusement—that I have absently lifted the first knife I have found, by touch. It is a fish knife, but the plate Françoise has set before me is occupied by a steak and boiled potatoes. The Woltners exchange a significant glance and I wonder whether the decorative knife might also be a test-the-barbarian routine with which they amuse themselves. But Françoise says, innocently enough, "It's my fault! I just put that for the look! Isn't that stupid? It's not for use!"

I praise the steak, crisp on the outside, pink and succulent on the inside, and topped by a little heap of onions sautéed dark brown. She added the onions, she says, "to make something that gave it a small taste . . . that's typical of Bordeaux." She insists she is no cook—that she only learned rudimentary skills at thirty-five, over twenty-five years ago, when with Francis, then an executive with the multinational Glaxo, she began to live part-time in Brussels "and we found maids but no good cook."

The wine that has been opened and breathing on the table, waiting for this course, is a La Mission-Haut-Brion of the 1978 vintage. It truly is a remarkable collection of flavors—so hard, at first taste, that it is like drinking gravel dust but then, spreading across one's palate, acquires a mysterious smoothness and fullness that invite another sip. I wonder how much of this wine the Woltners managed to rescue from the sale of the château but do not ask, fearing that they could find the question offensive.

Instead I repeat what I asked Christian Moueix: does it not feel like wasted effort, making wine in a country without France's ancient gastronomic traditions, where even the bread is never quite as good?

"But you know, it's come here, the change!" she says. "When I first came from France, I used to bring pans to cook—and many things. Now it's better than in France—you find everything you need."

"It's cheaper! Croissants are better and better every year, too," he adds.

Yes, I say, but very few Americans share the intensity of the French interest in food—or the intimate understanding of what is and isn't good. "And I imagine this means that most of your friends here are French—yes?"

"No!" Francis protests, appalled. "The French here—we don't communicate with them. Oh no! Oh no!"

"We have no French friends," she adds. "You know, I always say for fun that when I want to see French people, I have four months per year in France—when I have fifty-two million people at my own disposition, when I can have my choice."

"The French people who come here, they come to make money!" Francis explains. "They don't come for the pleasure of living in this country! I have never met any rich French people in this country. None of my friends take vacations in America!"

I ask what he thinks of the winemaking efforts of the French in Napa.

"In my opinion they are giving an image—they use the fact that they are French and they are just doing wine in the worst way that can be imagined."

"Really?"

"Sure. Really. Everywhere, there are people that are greedy. Most of the French people are coming over here because the cost of living was not too expensive and they were feeling that with the reputation of being French they will be able to have a product they will market at more money than an American."

I ask what he thinks of the French engaged in joint ventures with Americans in the valley—Christian Moueix's involvement with Dominus and the joint founding of Opus One by the Rothschilds and the Robert Mondavi Winery.

"It is good wine," he says. "But I don't believe in people that sell their name. Why they are not owning their own vineyard? Why they are not owning their own winery? Philippe Rothschild sold his name! What was the beginning of Opus One? It was the selection of different juices in a winery by Robert Mondavi. It is a franchise business!"

"Well you are a very honest man," I tell him. "You say exactly what you think!"

"I'm a *very* honest! We are dedicated to make wine *from a property*. We just mature our own vineyard."

The explanation Francis DeWavrin-Woltner gives most readily for his and Françoise's grabbing a stake in the Napa Valley is that they like the weather in California. If you insist that that cannot possibly be the only reason, Francis will say that in the six years in which he ran La Mission-Haut-Brion for Françoise's family—between 1977 and 1983—he grew to like the wine business enough to mind that Françoise was only one of six partners in the château and that estate duties would wipe out most of what she stood to inherit of it. Vineyard land in California was cheaper—on average, at least three times cheaper than in Bordeaux. It was clear that while Françoise's share of the family fortune was too small to convert into another estate in prime French wine country, a transatlantic investment would buy real value for their money.

To the 180 acres they bought high on a mountain on the northeastern perimeter of the Napa Valley, Francis and Françoise brought the most exacting standards for developing a winegrowing estate. The idea, from the start, was to make a small quantity of superb wine, and to be guided strictly by French viticultural and oenological philosophy and traditions in doing this.

Central to these is the idea of being true to the peculiarities of *le terroir*, the particular soil in which the particular vines grow—as if the ultimate goal, in making wine, were a distillation of essence of earth. Château Woltner produces just five thousand cases of wine in most years and a mere three thousand cases in others. Francis finds absurdly American the definition of a "small" winery—for the Internal Revenue Service's purposes—as one that makes less than 100,000 cases of wine a year: "For me, a small winery is below twenty thousand cases. After that, you become an industry. In Bordeaux the combined production of the top châteaux [in a year] is less than 250,000 cases."

Most American wine is made by monstrous producers like E&J Gallo, Francis observes, and bigness to him equals hopeless mediocrity. Anyone trained in the French tradition makes this point, sooner or later. The bulk of French wine, too, is *vin ordinaire* made by hulking great wineries—wine that even honest Frenchmen will concede is usually inferior to California-made table wine—but the famous makers of French wine have been run on the less-is-more principle for long enough to dignify all of French wine with their reputation for superiority. In any case, Francis, like his fellow Frenchmen, firmly believes that the larger a winery becomes, the further it retreats from the ideal of expressing a measure of earth, so to speak; the more it has to resort to artifice to find customers. And—the ultimate horror—it is not uncommon for large producers of California wine to add grapes that are not *Vitis vinifera* or wine grapes to their blends, to save money.

None of these are in Napa Valley, of course, but even most of Napa's "boutique" or "premium" wineries offend Francis in their approach to making wine. For a start, to him and all the other French people I met in Napa, the term "winemaker" is a shocking conceit. With a withering look, Christian Moueix had interrupted me in midsentence: "I have great difficulty with the idea of a winemaker. Just that term suggests an attitude . . ." An attitude? I asked whether he meant that wine really makes itself. "Yes. Partly. You put grapes and juice in a container and by natural forces you have a product, which is of course better if it has some handling. In France we say *oenologiste*, people who have the science of wine. It's a much smarter word, you know, it's a question of culture. You don't *make* wine—wine is an intellectual process, in some ways."

Francis, in a letter about Château Woltner's origins that he wrote me before we met, included this passage, seemingly written by a henchman of the Académie Française:

"As I told you on the phone, we don't like the terms 'winery' and 'winemaker.' In French, we like to be referred to as a *'vigneron,'* which in English means 'grape grower,' and *'maître de chai,'* which means 'cellar master.' "

Later, I inadvertently slipped and asked Francis if he directed the winemaking at Château Woltner and the result was a small explosion: "We don't *make* winemaking! We direct the philosophy of the property!" Official stationery is printed "Château Woltner Cellar."

Francis says he cannot take seriously boutique wineries that blend in grapes from other estates—even if the imported grapes happen to be of the finest quality—or that enjoy showing off their gleaming laboratories. "Why do you have a laboratory?" he asked rhetorically, with a small snigger. "Because you are a chemist! We want the taste of the real grapes, the vineyard, not the chemist!"

Château Woltner only makes Chardonnay. Of the land Francis and Françoise bought on Howell Mountain—a twenty-minute drive from the valley floor—the fifty-five acres they cleared and planted to vineyards are divided into four estates with different microclimates. The grapes from each of these go into four separate "estate-designated" wines. The most intense and extraordinary of these, labeled Titus Vineyard, is named for a family dog. Another parcel is called St. Thomas, both for the doubting Thomas of the Bible and family friends in France; a third, Frédérique, has the same name as Francis and Françoise's daughter—after Frédéric Woltner, Françoise's paternal grandfather, an émigré from Latvia and a successful wine broker who bought La Mission-Haut-Brion in 1919.

Davis-trained American wine industry consultants studied the soils of what would later become Château Woltner's vineyards and advised Francis and Françoise that the site could yield exceptionally fine Chardonnays. In 1980, when this analysis led them to buy the land, the Howell Mountain region of Napa was beginning to be known for robust red wines: it was unknown in connection with white wines.

It cost the Woltners $7 million to acquire and develop the land and restore the nineteenth-century three-story stone "cellar" that came with it: seven-foot-high fences were built to keep out the deer, small forests of trees were felled, and six tons of dynamite were exploded to clear boulders. Putting in the vineyard cost three times as much as it would have on the valley floor.

There is no question that the Woltners could have chosen easier rows to hoe: the American wine pundit Robert Parker was warranted in describing Château Woltner as "one of the most interesting, courageous and some might say foolish vineyard operations" in a 1989 issue of his newsletter, *The Wine Advocate*.

But what Francis and Françoise wanted in the *terroir* for their wines was the viticultural equivalent of a very great natural beauty (never mind if she was shockingly difficult). Ask them whether they use French oak (barrels) in aging their wines and Francis says—in his usual fashion, each word enunciated so precisely, with so much fervor and so many gestures involving his entire body, that he might be struggling to communicate with an extraterrestrial—"Totally. But we don't have *new* French oak. A lot of people here are so proud to tell you, 'We use only new French oak!' And that's too much makeup. We use older barrels and we get the minimum of oak's taste from the barrel. Because if you have to use brand-new French oak, it means that your wines don't have enough qualities in themselves."

The serpentine uphill drive to the Woltner land on Howell Mountain begins exasperatingly. I am running late and, judging by the map and what I am learning of this road, at Château Woltner I shall be a good three quarters of an hour late for my next appointment, on the Napa flats.

I begin to notice how this Vaca (which means, simply, cow) Range has the same live oaks, scrub oaks, digger pines, madrona and Douglas fir trees as the Mayacamas to Napa's west, but—because it gets far less rain—you see less greenery here and more rocky protrusions, sheer stone faces and stretches of rolling high desert. The contrasts between the two ranges suggest seeing a man at twenty-five and then at thirty-five, when he has paid a price for his ration of maturity in handfuls of his hair.

They usher in different states of mind, these ranges. On certain days in the valley, in the mornings and sometimes at dusk—in an otherwise cloudless sky—there are vaporous whitecaps on the Mayacamas, emissaries of the ocean beyond them. To drive or walk in them is sometimes to catch faintly briny whiffs of fresh air and always to feel the presence of that watery immensity, commanding respect for the powers of sorcery, dreams and enchantment in this world—to experience transcendent California. Whereas the Vacas screen from view the practical agrarian heartland of California, wrought out of desert, and, beyond it, the endlessness of the continent, reducing all our species to mortal specks of matter: no more than that. Winding my way up these slopes with France on my mind suddenly conjures up Jean Baudrillard, the left-wing French philosopher who, in his idiosyncratic *America* (1988), indirectly uses his politics to justify his profound contempt for modern American civilization:

> . . . for us the whole of America is a desert. Culture exists there in a wild state: it sacrifices all intellect, all aesthetics in a process of literal transcription into the real. Doubtless the original decentring into virgin territory gave it this wildness, though it certainly acquired it without the agreement of the Indians whom it destroyed. . . .

Naturally he is no less dismissive of the business of the Napa Valley:

> When I see Americans, particularly American intellectuals, casting a nostalgic eye towards Europe, its history, its metaphysics, its cuisine, and its past, I tell myself that this is just a case of unhappy transference. History and Marxism are like fine wines and haute cuisine: they do not really cross the ocean. . . . If, for us, society is a carnivorous flower, history for them is an exotic one. Its fragrance is no more convincing than the bouquet of California wines (in spite of all the efforts being expended to make us believe otherwise).

Such opinions, as extreme as they seem, must have been held even more passionately a century ago. Yet around 1877, two Bordelais, A. B. Brun and Jean Chaix, began to plant eighty acres on the site of the Woltner estate, at close to two thousand feet above sea level. Little is known about these gentlemen or their motives for setting off for California to found the winery they called Nouveau Médoc.

Even though it has long been a tenet of European wine country lore that hillside vineyards yield the best wines, Brun and Chaix's choice of this particular location in the Vacas, in the age of the stagecoach and buggy, seems mildly masochistic to me as I approach my destination. It is easy to see why Robert Louis Stevenson wrote of a journey along one of the county's "unfenced, abominable mountain roads" in that era: "As we continued to ascend, the wind fell upon us with increasing strength. It was a wonder how the two stout horses managed to pull us up that steep incline and still face the athletic opposition of the wind, or how their great eyes were able to endure the dust."

I see that Howell Mountain is actually flat-topped, a sort of hilly plateau: did Brun and Chaix like this spot because it made them feel as if they were at the top of the New World, did it encourage overweening ambition in them? I turn off the main road onto a rough dirt drive generously studded with large, sharp stones (a deterrent to casual, uninvited visitors?). The Woltner vines, immaculate and seemingly precision-pruned, begin on an incline. I park my truck by a ramshackle metal outbuilding and begin the brisk climb up the track that skirts the vineyard to my right. I might be walking directly into the horizon—for the path, from this angle, ends in brilliant blue sky graced with a single, wispy May cloud. To my left, stunted, round-leafed manzanita bushes—hardy natives, these—stretch away in a sort of dwarf forest. The vines are something of a wonder in this still only partially civilized setting.

Unaided by the sophisticated soil tests that confirmed the site's outstanding potential for winegrowing for the Woltners, Brun and Chaix evidently reached a similar conclusion (and were rewarded when their wines won prizes at the 1889 World Exposition in Paris). They surely noted the cool breezes that blow in from San Francisco Bay on the afternoons of hot days—bringing the temperature down far enough to make this spot an excellent one even for white wines. It was only in the last decades of this century that most Californian winegrowers learned enough to plant fewer white-grape vines on the valley floor, where many more uninterrupted, furnacelike summer days lead grapes to manufacture more sugar—too much for white wines, which are more reliant on acidic "bite" for character than are reds.

Despite these advantages, and even if all of Brun and Chaix's reasons for climbing quite this far from the valley floor must forever remain speculative, why did Francis and Françoise decide to take on the location's inconveniences—the many that persist in the age of the tractor and four-wheel-drive pickup? Their answers go no further than recitations of viticultural logic. But there is fierce glee and pride in Francis's accounts of the battles that had to be fought with the environment to establish vineyards in it, and to restore the exquisite, plain stone Nouveau Médoc winery that Prohibition took out of commission—that then did no more than gather cobwebs and dust for over sixty years.

One day, in reply to a question I have asked about his family, Francis sends me a rambling genealogical report that describes the DeWavrins as one of Flanders's most illustrious, almost across the entire span of the Middle Ages: "The Wavrin were warriors, and warriors on a grand scale: they were chevaliers of their times, sheathed in iron, who lived for nothing but war, just as proudly leading charger or palfrey, wielding stake, lance or sword, laying about them recklessly, prodigally shedding the blood of others and even more of their own."

I decide that he was merely obeying genetic promptings when he chose to grapple with the resurrection of Nouveau Médoc.

Over the years, Napa notables, including Robert Mondavi, considered taking on that task and decided it would be too difficult to recover the enormous expense it would entail. Indeed, once the DeWavrins had wine to sell, this posed as much of a challenge as any of the more unlikely feats of Alexandre Dumas's musketeers.

Francis launched Château Woltner's first wine with a price tag of $54 for a single bottle. He is indignant about the wine-buying public's reaction. "When we started, nobody wanted to buy our wine! People were very, very bad with us, telling us, 'At this price we buy Burgundy, not California wine!' That's what we were hearing, whether it was a French chef, a French owner of a restaurant, whether it was an American chef, an American owner of a restaurant! Then the people came to visit our property and they understand that the wines cannot exist if they are not very expensive, because . . . [Francis mimics a drowning man gasping for air] if I sell them *cheap*, you are going to visit me in jail and bring me oranges! If the market will pay for this wine $80 a bottle, I will sell it for $80. And I expect to arrive to that one day," he says with a touch of defiance.

Robert Parker—for many years the reigning monarch among

American wine critics and notorious in Napa for his conviction that virtually no California wines approach the quality of France's greatest—has waxed and waned in his enthusiasm for the Woltner wines. Still, he stuck his neck out on their behalf in 1989, even comparing one of them to Burgundy's finest:

> . . . the prices for the . . . wines appalled many people. Nevertheless, anyone who takes the time to visit this estate will see that the tiny yields of one and a half tons per acre, the high quality, new French oak barrels that are used [clearly, *he* skipped Francis's lecture on the evils of new oak], and the commitment to do something special are all very real. . . . It would appear that it's simply a matter of time before Woltner establishes itself as one of California's best Chardonnay producers. . . . The best 1986 is the Titus, which is also prohibitively expensive. It's rich, with a style not unlike a good premier cru from Puligny-Montrachet.

But bit by bit, Château Woltner began to find a following among the super-rich, the class of patron that the Woltners knew from their Château La Mission-Haut-Brion days—although not the identical clientele, because La Mission sold only Cabernet Sauvignon and Merlot wines, and Chardonnay is the base for a wine that belongs not to Bordeaux but to Burgundy. "It's very funny," Françoise told me at my first lunch at their house. "In my family we had the experience that when you have a big crisis, a recession, the wine that sells the best is the top quality and most expensive. Why? Because you always have rich people! When we come here, I knew only the business of top luxury wines. I don't know anything about the two million cases of inexpensive table wine. It's another trade, another job and other people."

A little taken aback, I wondered if I only imagined that France had a Marie Antoinette who was packed off to the guillotine for expressing a similar perspective on things. But then I sense that the remarks were made in the spirit of *épater les bourgeois* that she and Francis so clearly relish. After all, twenty-two-year-old Frédérique, the graceful and bookish child of their marriage—a second for both—is being educated at nearby Sonoma State University in the deadly earnest profession of business management, which carries no snobbish cachet whatever.

Still, I do not doubt that the hold France has on this family has to do with the mystique conferred by its connections with the *noblesse de bouchon* and with the ancient lineage of Wavrin—distinctions that are virtually meaningless in America. And then, like Jean Baudrillard, Francis and Françoise doubt that their distinctive cultural traditions can cross the great pond without being drastically diluted.

"When Françoise was four years old, she was getting always a small glass of wine from her father at the dining table," Francis told me proudly. "She has drunk more good wine between five and twenty years of age than Joe Heitz during his whole life! He was believing that you have to establish your taste young—so he was taking a bottle of La Mission, of Mouton, of Lafite, a bottle of Pauillac, and he was having miniature glasses for Françoise and her brother to drink."

All the other French people I met in Napa also emphasized how unremarkable it was for them to sip wine at meals as children, and that being taught to drink it correctly as soon as they could use a knife and fork had prevented them from turning into souses. Bernard Portet said, "The only negative I've had in my life as far as wine is concerned" occurred when he was about nine years old. His grandfather scolded his younger brother Dominique for drinking his wine before his soup, disobeying the family rule of never drinking on an empty stomach. "I remember my grandfather saying that if you drink wine before your soup, your teeth fall out!"

One day, after several months of failed attempts to arrange a rendezvous, Bernard introduces me to his wife, Helia. The Portets are my hosts at lunch at Petri's, a tiny restaurant on the outskirts of the town of Napa—housed in something like an English stone country cottage that they once considered buying for a house. Helia seems far too elegant and exotic for a cottage: her linen blouse and skirt, wide red leather belt and gold shoes flatter her bronzed skin and hawkishly beautiful face.

She tells me that although the American way of life has a great many flaws—viewed from the perspective of her upbringing or Bernard's, which had many Latin traditions in common—criticism of America is now all but forbidden in the Portet household. Nineteen-year-old Olivier, the oldest of their three children, strenuously objects to it, pointing out that he and his sisters, Nathalie and Paula, are American, too. This is not a little ironic because Bernard and Helia deliberately chose a somewhat isolated house in the Vaca foothills "because it is very difficult to pass on your culture to your children if you live in a *neighborhood*," Helia says. "Small neighbor children are always knocking on your door, asking to be let in."

"Here everybody comes from different backgrounds, so there are no rules. So there is no culture," Bernard says, safely out of earshot of his children. "And there is no humor! In France there is a sense of humor which varies from north to south, but it's cynicism, irony, which makes life enjoyable. Here it's like the only thing in life is to make money. Who cares about that? You know, you don't take money to Paradise!"

I try to imagine him arguing with Francis DeWavrin-Woltner about whether the quest for pots of gold is more important to Napa's Americans than to its resident Frenchmen.

Still, it is easy to get Bernard and Helia to talk about what they like about America and the Napa Valley—the other side of the tortuous ambivalence that every part-time or full-time expatriate expresses. For instance, Bernard worries about the disappearance of the one quality of the Napa scene he has most prized: its egalitarianism. "There is some social snobbery setting in, it's beginning to be a little bit like Bordeaux, and I can't stand that. It was *much* less structured here in 1972, much more free-flowing. When you have bigger numbers, you have to have a lot more structure." He praises American generosity, friendliness and the willingness of Napa wineries to exchange ideas and even come to each other's aid in crises—inconceivable among the Bordeaux châteaux, he says.

He also graciously confirms that American innovations have influenced many winegrowing practices in France—when I list the ones I know of for him. There are the more familiar reverse imports like automated, temperature-controlled fermentation in stainless steel tanks (not American inventions, these, but practices widely adopted and perfected sooner on this side of the Atlantic). Then there are such surprising, little-known innovations as Christian Moueix's adoption of crop thinning—removing roughly half the fruit on the vines at midsummer or so, a measure proven by the boffins at Davis to concentrate flavors in the remaining grapes (so making for wines with many more facets). I tell Bernard that I have read that Christian did this over the protests of his father, Jean-Pierre Moueix, the head of the family business, who eventually had to admit that crop thinning had done wonders for the quality of Pétrus; that the once heretical practice had since been widely imitated in Bordeaux. Bernard smiles and nods.

Embarrassing American influences are at work also in Bordeaux architecture, tourism and town planning. I mention to Bernard that I have been reading about a 1988 exhibition called "Châteaux Bordeaux" at the Centre Pompidou in Paris—that its catalogue suggests that the Napa Valley is being viewed as a model for environmental planning, modern architecture (in spectacular designs for new châteaux) and the controlled encouragement of tourism in Bordeaux.

But now Bernard, listening carefully, has a skeptical glint in his eye. He doubts that the traditional Bordeaux hauteur and exclusivity—the châteaux have historically opened their doors only to important and illustrious folk—can easily be altered to a hail-fellow-well-met, tourist-getting style. "You cannot easily change the characteristics of a breed, you know. The French people—if it takes ten hours of knowing you before they become hospitable—it's not because they have opened their winery to you that they are going to be any better."

In Napa the *Vitis vinifera* has forced many French and Americans into a far more intimate relationship with each other than either would wish. The many facets of their mutual antipathy, when you encounter them, preserve the valley from blandness.

Despite my own occasional ambivalence about America, the hairs on the back of my neck often rise in protest, listening to the excoriation the French in Napa heap on our large-hearted host country. But any lasting indignance is usually checked by instances of the equally extreme intolerance of Americans for French ways.

There is, for instance, André Tchelistcheff's retelling of Joe Heitz's account of his first visit to a France he found insufferably pretentious. "He hated it. He hated every man in the wine industry of France and he came back and said, 'You know, André, I thought I was going to

separate from my wife,' he was in such a foul mood. 'They are so stupid—they are not normal people. They are built entirely different
than we are! They are not formulating life as simple things that are
going on, a physical reaction. They are something *out of* life—the
way they eat, dress, everything.' "

But this I must set against the tremor of *quelle horreur!* that ran
through Christian Moueix when I said, innocently enough, "Unlike
Bernard Portet, you would never buy a house here, I suppose?"

"Oh, please, *never* say never!" he exclaimed, spreading his hands,
palms up, some way above the table—a look of superstitious dread
on his narrow face. "It would be very difficult for me. *Yes!*"

CHAPTER SEVEN

In Remembrance
of a Lost Napa Château

Last night I dreamt I went to Manderley again.
Rebecca,
DAPHNE DU MAURIER

So was I once myself a swinger of birches
And so I dream of going back to be.
"Birches,"
ROBERT FROST

NOSTALGIA'S IS A LYRICAL VOICE. In all the time I spent with Robin Daniel Lail, who once expected to inherit a Napa estate and a winery built in the early 1880s, called Inglenook, the refrain that ran through what she said and did not say might have been: So was I once a girl in a great house in the valley/And so I dream of going back to be.

The man who ran the one winery that, in the middle years of this century, most closely resembled the great French châteaux in the standards it set for its winemaking—and was once the greatest name in American wine—failed to hold his inheritance together for his daughters for reasons that constitute Napa's greatest irony.

On the one hand, John Daniel was too high-mindedly European. He detested self-promotion. He fought compromises in the interest of profitability freely made by equally illustrious but less idealistic Napa notables, including even Georges de Latour. This is certainly

André Tchelistcheff's opinion: he sees John Daniel as the single, out-and-out exception to the opportunism of Napa's rich and famous in his fifty years in the valley. And he sees Inglenook in the Daniel era—between 1935 and 1963—as the only Californian winemaking enterprise then dedicated, to the exclusion of all else, to quality.

But the other element in John Daniel's undoing was a manifestation of American puritanism in the bosom of his own family. John's wife, Betty, was a Mormon. A "word of wisdom" or dietary law of the Church of Latter-Day Saints counsels against tea, coffee and tobacco—and all alcoholic substances. In public, she was teetotal; in private, she knocked back not wine but whiskey. After eighteen years of enduring his wife's active dislike of his occupation in a marriage anyway rife with discord, John Daniel sold Inglenook to a conglomerate in 1964.

Much of Robin Daniel Lail's life has been spent trying—at times deliberately, at others, unconsciously—to salvage something of what had seemed to her a birthright traded without her consent. And it is revealing of life in Napa, the cultural crossroads, that nearly thirty years after her father sold Inglenook, conflicts between Old and New World values made for one of the most trying passages in her own struggle.

The Inglenook story also exposes a facet of Napa society. The combination of a head of household with exemplary high standards in all things and a magnificent ancestral setting should have made John Daniel's Napa's first family—by a modern application of the oldest of Old World logic, the Greek conception of an aristocracy as government by those of superior character.

But by the end of my many visits to the valley for this book, I concluded that the place has no elite—lacks even a convincing nouveau elite of any kind, for all that its stunning facades, great gates at the end of mysterious long drives and formal gardens betray of elitist aspirations. Mostly this is because too much of the valley's history as part of the United States has been in turbulent modern times to allow an upper crust to set and solidify.

So far as wishes for some such top tier go, a final, monumental irony in the Inglenook story is that for all John Daniel's famous refinement, the tastefully spectacular estate he inherited was created by Napa's first great parvenu, a Finnish seaman and fur trader called Captain Gustav Niebaum. The aristocratic yearnings that the Inglenook winery and house embody are especially curious because Finland never had a monarch or nobility—was peopled by nomadic Finno-Ugrian tribes who settled down to become a nation of sturdy, mystical peasants. They have no history or written records and scarcely anything in the way of traditions of their past: Finnish literature only dates from 1835.

Robin Lail, growing up in the house Gustav built, a big white house like a dream in lace, like a wedding cake, knew nothing of Inglenook's incongruities. I imagine her at seven, sometimes seeing herself the way playmates at her school in nearby St. Helena surely did now and then, as a fairytale princess—complete with golden tresses—going home to a castle. I imagine her gazing out of an upper-story window at row after row of mutely subservient vines stretching away from the house towards the valley's center, or out of a west-facing window overlooking the recondite, forested slopes of the Mayacamas, taking for granted that the great sweep of foreground in every direction of the compass belonged to her and her family, believing it always would.

Deep in a dense forest at the foot of the Vaca Range, in the glade that is the site of the Meadowood Resort, my truck slides into the car park full of deluxe chassis gleaming in the dappled light. I turn off the engine beside a sign remarkable in the countryside:

NOTICE

Oak Trees Drip Sap

Not Responsible For Any Auto Damage

This is a reminder that Meadowood is the sort of get-away-from-it-all place to which people bring with them virtually every preoccupation and anxiety of their everyday lives. It is the kind of retreat in which you glimpse tense bodies in tennis clothes clustered around slide projectors through the windows of conference rooms and, in the restaurants, catch fragments of edgy wheeler-dealer talk: "What's your time frame for this?"; "quantum"; "strategize."

The many-tiered, multi-gabled Meadowood buildings, which only date to 1985, are meant to evoke Old World grandeur in the Victorian style, but authenticity has been sacrificed for the Californian architectural ideal of bringing the outdoors indoors: the dormer windows are disproportionately huge and there are far too many of them. Still, against the dark green of the woods and lawns, these cool gray and white structures do delight the eye.

Robin is a partner in the firm of San Francisco developers that established the resort and soon after its opening she managed it for a while. These days the place is a second home for her: she is at play here nearly every fine summer week, practicing croquet, or organizing tournaments—and these, I have gathered, are serious business.

Not long ago, I sat beside one of the English courts as Robin won one match after another in the Domaine Mumm Croquet Classic, partly sponsored by the Californian offshoot of the famous champagne house. A crochet-clad public relations lady, though she plied me with bubbly, was determined that the gravity of the occasion should not escape me and handed me a press release. "The purpose of the gathering is not exclusively for the tasting of wine, as is often the custom in Napa Valley," the document lectured prissily, but ". . . a stylish competitive event on the leading edge of the sport of croquet." This woman and almost every other organizer of the tournament, and a croquet player from faraway New Zealand, variously informed me, in hushed tones, that Robin—the chairwoman of the event—was the "granddaughter" or "grand-niece" or "great-granddaughter" of Gustav Niebaum.

In the Fairway Grill, the less formal of Meadowood's two dining spots, Robin sits writing energetically at a table strewn with papers. She is quite the American businesswoman today in a tailored, drop-shouldered red dress with black piping and small earrings styled as loops of gold rope. On the croquet court, she had cut a graceful, Amazonian figure—tall, blue-eyed, long-limbed, her cap of short blond hair blazing in the August sun as she strode from hoop to hoop; in breaks in the game, a teenage boy rushed up to her with a lit cigarette. Her changes of mood were mercurial. One moment she stood slouched and frowning in concentration, an intimidating presence, but in the next, a player walking past her clearly said something teasing because there was suddenly a beseeching, little-girl look in her eyes as she smiled up at him, tilting her head.

She tidies her papers away. Then she lights up and the inhalation of nicotine punctuates her sentences.

"My family history begins with Niebaum. It begins with Captain Gustav Niebaum, who was a fascinating man and *not* my blood relation. Whose origins are somewhat obscure. But he grew up in Finland and went to sea."

It strikes me as odd that someone not consanguine, a relative by marriage, should be identified as her family's genesis, but I decide I must let her tell her story her way. I ask whether Niebaum was a Finnish or Swedish Finn: the name sounds Swedish to me.

She says, Finnish, "to the best of my knowledge. You know we have been unable, after some very diligent work, to find out much about his early life."

She tells me about an episode in the search for Captain Niebaum's beginnings that casts her father—by all accounts, conservative, sensitive, compassionate, understated and thrifty—in a most unexpected light.

In 1956, when Robin was sixteen, John Daniel took his family on a European tour. They went to Helsinki, where the publisher of a leading newspaper had been trying to assist their investigations.

"Daddy had found a man named Niebaum—through much poking and prodding and so forth—who claimed to be a descendant of Gustav." She pauses; laughs long and smokily before she can continue. "So he went to lunch with him and they had many, many aquavits and much lobster. It was the only time in my life that I ever saw my father high!"

No new facts about Niebaum were unearthed on the trip.

Months after this conversation with Robin I will find, in a history of the Napa Valley by William Heintz, that Niebaum, the son of "an official with the local police," was born in Helsinki on August 30, 1842. At the Finland Nautical Institute he earned his master's papers at the age of nineteen. He went to sea in command of a cargo ship, buying at Alaskan ports chiefly seal furs, which fetched high prices in Europe. In 1868, the year after the United States bought Alaska from Russia, Niebaum went into partnership with a group of American businessmen—some of them Alaskan contacts—to found the Alaska Commercial Company based in San Francisco. The firm is said to have been outrageously successful, paying the United States government more in rights than the $7 million paid for Alaska itself.

This version of the Niebaum story is less impressionistic than Robin's—which is more like a family's recounting of its story for its members' sake than for public dissemination. She tells me Niebaum was trained at a Finnish naval academy. So he'd left the navy when he started the Alaska Commercial Company? "No, no, no. He was still involved with the navy." What navy, I find myself wondering, since I know that Finland did not free itself from its Russian yoke until this century. I find it hard to understand a naval officer being allowed to command a ship at nineteen—let alone run a trading business on the side, as she suggests.

She does rather better at speculating on why—having turned immensely wealthy, he changed the spelling of his name from the original "Nybom," and established a house in San Francisco—Gustav Niebaum chose to go into the wine business. The facts are these: in the course of his many voyages to European ports, he acquired a yen for fine living and a love of wine, which was not traditional Finnish tipple. True, purely commercial logic might have been inducement enough. In the 1870s, the phylloxera disease had been laying waste to European vineyards, slashing transatlantic wine production and creating a gap for New World wine producers to fill. Since the promise of California wine had begun to be widely appreciated in this decade, land planted to vines grew exponentially. Napa land prices soared in a sort of green gold rush.

Other remarkable characters had begun the work of deliberately shaping Napa into wine country. The Napa chapters in the lives of two pioneers came after others in personal histories so eventful and extraordinary that I offer only these shrunken versions of them:

George Yount, born in North Carolina in 1794, had been a soldier, hunter, trapper and carpenter—in which capacity he worked on the Sonoma house of General Mariano Vallejo, an administrator of Mexico's Alta California. In 1836, as a reward for other commissions he undertook for the general, he was granted twelve thousand acres of the Napa Valley—having been baptized a Catholic, Jorge Concepción Yount, as an essential precondition for taking possession of the land. He made wine from Napa's first *Vitis vinifera* grapes, which were harvested on his ranch: they were of the déclassé Mission variety, "an early-maturing, dark-skinned bag of sweet juice; no more," in Hugh Johnson's unflattering estimation.

Another energetic early settler, Charles Krug, was born in Prussia in 1825 and became an American citizen in 1852. In 1860, fourteen years after the Bear Flag Revolt—in which twenty-four Americans ended Mexican rule in California—he planted grapes on land north of St. Helena that was part of his brand-new wife's dowry, having established vineyards twice before, in San Mateo and Sonoma counties. In earlier phases of his life he had been a failed revolutionary (in Prussia), an Oakland newspaper editor and a clerk at the government mint in San Francisco. His was the first wine made in Napa that experts deemed worthy of the name, and he effectively founded commercial winemaking in the valley.

Three other Germans drove progress in this era. Jacob Beringer, who had worked in the wine industry in his native Mainz, as an importer in New York, and as a cellar foreman for Charles Krug, founded his own Napa winery with his brother Frederick in 1877.

Jacob Schram, a Rhinelander, planted vines on weekdays in the mid-1860s and plied his trade as a barber on weekends. His wine found its way to San Francisco hotels and, later, to London.

But Gustav Niebaum—when he bought three parcels of land near Rutherford in 1879, aged thirty-seven—was the original predecessor of the immensely wealthy foreigners like Donald Hess and Jan Shrem who would make "second careers" for themselves in Napa in high style about a century later. Like these latter-day versions of himself, Niebaum did not give up his original occupation but merely cut back on the time he allotted to the Alaska Commercial Company.

I ask Robin what, in her view, explains Gustav's and the contemporary foreigners' common ambition to create "the jewel of the wine business," as she puts it. Why wine?

"I strongly believe what is only a generic statement: leaders want to leave a mark," she says, her eyes lighting up. I have the sense that she doesn't speak as a wholly detached observer: she is also explaining what brought her back to Napa years after the sale of Inglenook, when she thought she had left it forever. "Wine is a business of enormous culture. I often think about why it is so addictive, and why do people become so embedded, and what keeps bringing them deeper and deeper and deeper.

"If you have stature within the industry there isn't a door, really, that's closed to you. People of great interest and import are interested to see you when you are traveling in their country. And then they come to see you in yours.

"So it's a fantastic international communications tool. And that becomes more and more the case daily as the wine industry becomes more globalized. So there is a fluidity that, I think, has a siren call all its own.

"And you know, the wine business is also a business in which a man can pursue business and the quality of life simultaneously.

"Then, last and not least: as students, we all read about the magnetism of the soil, the land, for man."

Gustav Niebaum did well in responding to its pull. Aided by his linguistic skills—he spoke five languages by some accounts, seven by others—he read widely to educate himself about viticulture and winemaking. According to Robin, he traveled to France and Germany to study the design of châteaux and *chais*, and brought back cuttings of vines. The Exposition Universelle in Paris in 1889 was a fantasy made real for Niebaum and indeed for all dreamers of a glorious future for Napa wines. "Of the 34 medals or awards given to California entries for wines of various sorts, the Napa Valley won 20," Hugh Johnson wrote in his world history of wine, *Vintage*. The Inglenook wines won the silver medal given for "purity and excellence."

Niebaum's extreme obsession with cleanliness, purity and neatness is the aspect of the man most frequently remarked on in tellings of his story. In directing the making of Inglenook's wines, it served him somewhat in the way the ordering instincts of an artist must impose themselves on creative *ferment*—a word that does, after all, connote unrest, agitation and disorder. He is sometimes credited with bringing science to Napa winemaking—but only in the sense that hygiene is fundamental to the controlled fermentation on which modern winemaking is based.

An enormous special feature on Inglenook in *The San Francisco Examiner* of April 6, 1890, described "concrete floors . . . [that] give

no foothold for dirt and cobwebs, and furnish no spot for the production of poisonous germs. . . . Brazen door sills and brass taps,
pumps and brass-bound buckets take a good deal of work to keep
clean . . . but the slightest stain reveals that someone is breaking the
rule of scrupulous cleanliness." Once Niebaum's grapes were picked,
the reporter continued, awestruck, "a score of workmen armed with
shears turn the branches over and cut out every berry that is green,
over-ripe or in any way damaged." No one else in Napa was remotely
as fussy at the time (later, Joe Heitz would become Niebaum's spiritual descendant in this respect).

"I'm not sure he was a very nice man!" Robin says. She gives her
signature laugh—a low gurgle. "He was certainly a man with a lot
of fetishes. He had the long roadway from his home to the highway
swept every morning by Chinese coolies."

Compulsive neatness is not a trait I myself find endearing but, in
William Heintz's meticulously researched history, I discover that
Niebaum had redeeming eccentricities and interests. At a time of
blatant anti-Semitism, his closest friends were Jewish: he sold most
of his wine through a distributor who was a Jew and, though in fact
a Lutheran, answered in the affirmative when asked if he, too, was
Jewish. Heintz also maintains that scholars are indebted to Niebaum
for his translations—published in academic journals—of accounts of
explorations by Norsemen of the northeast coast of America. His collection of totem poles and other objects fashioned by Indians of the
far north eventually became part of the anthropological collection of
the University of California at Berkeley. In Gustav's day, Indian arti-
facts were generally considered beneath attention.

Still, all in all, what is known of Niebaum adds up to more enigma
than man. I have found no record of what specific kind and style of
wine he most admired. The list of wines made at Inglenook in his
day is evenly divided between red and white, French and German
styles. The unidentified *Examiner* writer only quoted Niebaum as
saying he wanted "to produce the finest wines, to equal and excel the
finest vintages of Europe." Conceivably, Niebaum went into details
that went over the reporter's head: the Médoc is twice referred to in
the spread as "Modoc," the name of an American Indian tribe, and
Rhenish wines as "Rhonish."

Certainly the good captain was built on a heroic scale—he was well over six feet tall, and large-boned—and he had a Scottish draftsman draw up plans for a winery to match. The main Inglenook building is not merely imposing like the massive, medieval-looking Greystone Cellars nearby, but graceful too. It has a red-tiled roof, a central tower, cupolas and a Virginia creeper–covered facade—the whole effect a sort of streamlining and scaling down of the Gothic look.

In a curlicued style long lost to American journalism, the *Examiner* article waxed delirious about the setting to which this architecture had to do justice:

> Those who only know our California scenery by a dash over the Sierras and a ride through the dusty plains of the San Joaquin can have no conception of the beauties of this magnificent estate. . . . Behind the tree-bowered "nook," from which the place takes its name, rises a chain of mountains. A tall cascade leaps down their side and goes to swell the stream that ripples through the floor of the valley. To the north, Mount St. Helena, a few miles away, rears its head 4,000 feet above the sea and stands like a gallant sentinel overlooking an earthly paradise. . . .

Great blocks of stone were used to build the Inglenook winery and cellars. Oak is the principal material used in the gemlike tasting room just past the front entrance: by day, light filters softly through its single stained-glass window, enhancing its mysterious intimacy. It is easy, in this room, to imagine as a physical presence the Captain Niebaum of sepia-tinted photographs—a stern-looking, powerful-bodied figure who, in old age, had a flowing white beard and something about his eyes that suggests breadth of vision and largeness of spirit—in spite of his preoccupation with details and decorum.

The tasting room's heavy oak table and carved oak chairs specially imported from Germany, the antique wine cups and German steins—like everything Niebaum commissioned or chose—speak of solidity and permanence, as if built to say: *forever*.

Usually, creations on this scale are justified not merely as monuments to a man's accomplishments but as means of securing the future of succeeding generations of a family and keeping it together. But there was no issue from the marriage of Gustav Niebaum and

Suzanne Shingleberger—a woman of German stock who had been a neighbor of one of Gustav's business partners in San Francisco.

Indeed, if the founding of a great Niebaum dynasty was a dream of his, two grand plans of Gustav's came unraveled in his marriage. The other was "to build a state-of-the-art sailing ship and circumnavigate for the rest of his days, taking Suzanne with him," Robin tells me, warmth and keen amusement in her voice, as if she enjoys retelling his story. "Unfortunately she suffered from *mal de mer*. So he moved to plan B and went into the wine business."

If the Niebaums had succeeded in producing a male heir who inherited his father's enterprise and overweening ambition, the result could conceivably have been a clan like the Rockefellers lording it over the Napa Valley.

Instead, wines made under his direction had to serve as Gustav Niebaum's messages to posterity. He would have been gratified by the receptions they got. In his 1984 biography of Robert Mondavi, the late Cyril Ray, an éminence grise of English wine writing, cited Inglenook wines of the 1887 and 1892 vintages as proof that, contrary to European prejudice, Californian wines have the same capacity for aging as the great clarets of Bordeaux. He observes that a fellow connoisseur, Michael Broadbent—the Christie's auctioneer—suggested in a 1982 speech in San Francisco that twenty years was about the limit for California wines' capacity for development. Yet, says Ray, this same critic knew better. He quotes tasting notes made by Broadbent about an 1892 Inglenook Cabernet Sauvignon wine, which described it as having "good body; long, relatively soft finish—considerable vinosity and character."

I find it curious, though, that there is nowhere any mention of what the distinctive characteristics of Captain Niebaum's wines were—in the way the unusual softness of wines made at Beaulieu by André Tchelistcheff is always remarked on. Gustav Niebaum died in 1908, aged sixty-four. In the last decade of his life he appears to have lost faith in the idea of establishing California's place among the supreme winemaking regions of the world—or perhaps he simply got bored.

"After his winery's first fifteen to twenty years, he sort of drifted away from the intensity he had at first and things began to peter out a little bit," Robin tells me. "Of course there was the phylloxera epidemic that eventually got here, too, and I don't know what effect that had on him. And my impression is that in the last years of his life he was not well."

The brevity of human life is perhaps sadder for visionaries than for everyone else. Gustav's original optimism about Napa wine's prospects would be borne out when his wife's great-grand-niece Robin used the scant remains of his legacy to establish a joint venture with one of the most famous names in French winemaking. But that happened much, much later—seventy-four years after his death.

The foundation for a winemaking dynasty that Gustav laid but failed to build on passed into the care of Robin's grandfather John Daniel III—then was handed over to John Daniel, Jr., Robin's father.

Three things strike me most forcibly about John Daniel, Jr.'s, stewardship of Inglenook.

The first has to do with him personally. His connection with the winery began with a dutiful quashing of his life's ambition; its continuation was marked by much unhappiness, stoically borne; and it ended in cruel disappointment.

Second. He was famous less in Napa for what he did than for what he chose not to do. No startling innovations of any sort are associated with his management of Inglenook. He devoted himself, above all, to carrying on traditions begun by Gustav Niebaum, striving for perfection, and counting chiefly on intrinsic quality to sell the wine.

Third. The scrupulousness and integrity that distinguished everything he did were so extreme that anyone who started out poor and lived by his principles would also have died poor. His own career in wine might easily have been the basis for the darkly humorous Napa joke that to make a small fortune in wine you have to start with a large one.

Tragedy in two successive generations of John Daniel's family led to his being brought up by his great-aunt Suzanne Niebaum, née Shingleberger, a stern, straightlaced and strong-willed woman.

Following their orphaning, Suzanne's niece Leah and nephew Louis went to live with her and Gustav Niebaum.

Leah married Robin's grandfather, John Daniel III, whose granddaughter describes him as "the single most handsome man I have *ever* seen," and as a spendthrift and womanizer. Leah died young, of either diphtheria or a broken heart, or both.

When Robin was twenty-nine and going through her father's papers in the months before his death, she found a cold-blooded agreement between her grandfather, John III, and her great-grand-aunt Suzanne. It gave her the right to rear his and Leah's children, John Jr. and (her namesake) Suzanne, provided that she and Gustav willed Inglenook to them.

After Gustav Niebaum died in 1908, the running of the winery had been overseen by John III. Though it produced no revenues during the fourteen years of Prohibition, the family continued to pay for the upkeep of the vineyards.

John Daniel, Jr., had been trained as an engineer at Stanford, longing all the while for a career flying airplanes. It was in keeping with the extreme dutifulness—martyrdom, some would say—he exhibited throughout his life that when Prohibition ended in 1933, he obeyed his father's order that he leave the family construction business in San Francisco and go north to revive Inglenook—though he had no particular interest in wine and knew nothing of winemaking.

The hands-on management of the winery was done by an experienced winemaker called Carl Bundschu, the descendant of one Charles Bundschu who had founded a famous Sonoma County winery with another German in 1858. John Daniel educated his palate on the job and gradually learned enough to understand what would have to be done for the Inglenook wines to return to the exceptionally high standards established by Gustav Niebaum. Later, he replaced Bundschu with another German, George Deuer, and continued his pursuit of that goal.

Robin tells a story from her childhood about her father trying on for a lark the old dress clothes of Gustav, stored in an attic. The men were about the same height, "but the sleeves of the tuxedo were *much* longer than Daddy's—they were thirty-four inches long!"

Certainly Gustav's reach exceeded his grand-nephew's, yet there's no denying that John Daniel accomplished an extraordinary work of restoration. And in the uncanny way in which wines mirror the character of their makers—or, in this case, the director of their fashioning—there is much of Daniel in a 1992 evaluation of Inglenook wines made during his tenure and after it, in the same style.

Of the prestige Inglenook wine, the Reserve Cask Cabernet, *The New York Times* wine critic Frank Prial said: "If there is a word that describes the Inglenook style it is understatement. These are intense, deeply flavored wines, but they are not forward, aggressive or obvious, descriptions that apply—with no negative implications . . . to California cabernets in general."

André Tchelistcheff remembers that in years in which the harvest failed to yield wines that met Daniel's "exquisite standards," he ordered that they be disposed of to competitors at bargain prices. There was no Inglenook label for those years, and no revenues. "We, Beaulieu," André told an interviewer, ". . . never was able to eliminate a vintage. . . . So he was the leading man." Beaulieu liberally compensated for shortages in its grape supplies with purchases from other growers. At Inglenook, again, in the loftiest French tradition, Daniel only allowed wine to be made of grapes from his own estate.

Beaulieu's French owners had retained ties of fealty to France; Georges de Latour's daughter had even acquired a large estate there, through her marriage. John Daniel, as an American, cared passionately and unequivocally about raising the profile of Napa winemaking to meet the most exacting criteria anywhere. He led the fight for "varietal labeling" in California—felt it was important for the industry's credibility that wineries be legally bound to state the types of grapes from which wines were made.

Robert Mondavi worked with him in the 1950s to set the stage for the Napa Valley (legal) appellation. He remembers that Daniel "wanted Inglenook to be a jewel and would not upset that by even entertaining wine tastings and things like that if he thought it was really pushing too much."

If a pattern in many of today's family-run wineries had held true, John Daniel's leeriness of promotion might have been compensated for by an expansive, extroverted wife. The dedicated wine wife cooks gourmet fare designed to show off the family wines' fruit, oak or lack thereof, tannins hard or soft, and so on. Coyly, she effuses her own personal enthusiasm for them; warmly congratulates guests on their discrimination when they offer praise.

But John's wife, Betty—née Naylor, whom he had married the same year he was dispatched to Inglenook—was an extroverted beauty who affected a religious disdain for the work of a wine wife. Old-timers remember her disapproval casting a pall over both the enjoyment and discussion of wine. She was worse than no help to John: her ill-concealed affairs with other men have been recorded in soap-operatic detail elsewhere (see *Napa* by James Conaway). (Not only did John not divorce her but he remarried her some time after she divorced him to run away with a lover.)

According to Robin, when John Daniel astonished Napa and members of his family by selling Inglenook to a company called Allied Grape Growers (later, United Vintners), it was chiefly because of "religious conflict in the household." There was never any question of her or her older sister, Marky (Marcia), being groomed to take over from their father. "It would have caused havoc. We were raised as Mormons and my mother did not allow us to discuss the wine business at all. We were allowed to smell the wines but never to taste them."

A brief account of the depressing story of Betty Daniel is unavoidable: a woman severely at odds with herself, she supplies the core of the explanation for her daughters' being left with so little of what Gustav wrought. Mormonism notwithstanding, she had been reared for a life as a cosmopolitan socialite. "As a child, she'd played polo in Europe and then dated several crown princes and so forth, and studied opera here until, at the age of eighteen, she started smoking and her teacher picked it up immediately and threw her out," Robin told me.

Betty failed to make a home in the world for herself through her marriage to John Daniel. She neither took any pleasure in matters domestic nor had a career. She was a strict and often harsh parent but inattentive, and frequently absent. She might have patiently worked her way into the graces of the high-caste San Francisco society to which her husband belonged but was too proud or bored by it to make the effort. And yet she disliked the role of country wife, even as mistress of Inglenook—or rather, given her aversion to the wine business, especially as mistress of Inglenook. Her affairs and heavy drinking were the result of what might have been diagnosed before our Age of Psychology—and not unreasonably—as simply not having enough to do.

For over ten years before John Daniel's death in 1970, "she did less and less, until finally she just sat in her bed all the time," Robin remembered. A reminiscing Napa old-timer said she recalled the Daniel family eating at the Miramonte restaurant near St. Helena every night, for years, because Betty neither cooked nor hired anyone for the job.

Still, Betty's inadequacies and opposition were not entirely responsible for the sale of Inglenook. In making that decision, John Daniel's hand was forced also by the losses the winery had made, year after year after year. They didn't allow for the replacement of geriatric equipment. And, Robin remembers, "the winemaker was getting elderly. He and my father tried training a string of apprentices but as soon as they could get their wobbly young legs under them, they went off somewhere else. Because my father, through and through a Scot, was conservative in his pay scales."

The loss of Inglenook turned Robin's universe topsy-turvy. She was twenty-four at the time. "Tradition was so important to my father that he had said, from the beginning, 'All of this will be yours.' And I assumed that it would. And I believed I would be wealthy—not violently wealthy, but well-to-do—never questioned this, the idea of a smooth continuum. After the sale, I saw Inglenook as a closed chapter in my life: it was clear that it had been the best there was. But I was left with a very strange feeling."

If Robin was left saddened and disoriented, her father was infinitely more so. When he died six years later, aged sixty-three, circumstantial evidence strongly suggested that he took his own life.

All I know about Jon Lail, driving to his office on Highway 29, is that he is an architect and Robin's husband. The expectation lurking in the back of my mind is of a taciturn, impeccable WASP Brahmin, who will have me chattering frantically to fill in gaping conversational canyons.

Imagine, then, the shock of finding in the modest, boxlike offices of James Nolan Construction a handsome, faintly ironic cowboy with small sad blue eyes and a sun-lined face. No, he doesn't wear the hat or Western boots—just a cotton shirt of many colors and blue jeans. And no, it isn't even the prints on the walls of cowboys on horseback galloping up a storm that suggest a place-warp—as if I am not in

Napa but back in the sagebrush country where I now live. It's the look-you-dead-in-the-eye frankness of his gaze; what he says; how he says it. He's the talkative kind of Westerner, glad after days riding alone in wide open spaces of a chance to unburden himself of his thoughts—someone rather disappointed with the modern world.

For this is a cowboy-turned-architect whose specialization is the restoration of "Victorian" buildings, and designing new ones in that idiom: "If somebody wants a contemporary structure, I tell them to get someone else." The dramatic Clos Pegase building in Napa, and other sensational creations of the architect Michael Graves, he dismisses, without rancor, as "very modern. Very contemporary. Very ugly."

We zip away to lunch at Meadowood in his dusty black baby Mercedes (a mate for Robin's black Porsche). He says he really did grow up partly on a family ranch in Colorado, "and they kept saying, all the years I was working on it, 'This will always be yours.' " The rest of his upbringing was in Denver, where the banking business of his mother's socially prominent family struggled to recover from the blows dealt it by the Depression. The Denver portion of Jon's childhood was spent in a house that had a six-car garage but no cars. When Jon was eighteen, the ranch became a casualty of the family's financial woes: it was sold.

Sic transit gloria mundi as the chief lesson of early adulthood, I suggest, is something he and Robin share. He agrees, but chivalrously insists that Robin's losing Inglenook was much harder. He didn't linger in Denver to try to recover anything of his heritage. When he got out of college, he was dismayed to discover that classmates who were as talented as he—or more so—got only a few job offers. He, on the other hand, "filled in ten applications and got ten offers," owing to his family's renown. He left for San Francisco: "I really needed to find out if I could make it on my own, as opposed to living off an old family."

We are seated at our table in the Fairway Grill, where Jon orders mineral water to go with a spinach salad.

He and Robin met in San Francisco. They were twenty-five years old and lived two floors apart in the same building in Pacific Heights. Each recognized in the other a blond, blue-eyed and athletic quasi-twin: they played tennis together; Jon had been a reserve for the

Olympic ski team. Only a year had gone by since Inglenook's sale, and the trauma was still with Robin. She had been to Stanford where she studied international relations and French and then, through a connection of her father's, had got a job at the Bank of America.

Their marriage disappointed Robin's mother. Jon flashes me a mischievous grin. "I think she always envisaged Robin marrying a gentleman from England or New York—you know, the right family and background, and definitely *not* a cowboy from Colorado."

A note of hero worship enters his voice when he speaks of his father-in-law. "He was a superb person. You want to use the term 'conservator of the keys' for him."

It was clear that there was no heir apparent to manage the 1,900-odd acres of vineyards that remained after the sale of Inglenook. Marky had married one Jim Smith, who was far less interested in the then somnolent wine business than in making a fortune in outdoor signs and in real estate development—and they had settled in Washington, in the far northwest. Because of this and a fascination with wine that grew out of his admiration for John Daniel, Jon—having won Robin's approval for the idea—was about to propose becoming his assistant when his father-in-law died.

Not long after that, the question of who would run the estate became largely academic. Perhaps because Robin's mother derived an emotional charge and an enhanced sense of freedom from the death of her husband, she rose from her bed and, at fifty-eight, set about revolutionizing her life. She made an abortive move to New Zealand to start afresh, but before she left, sold Niebaum's dream house and, Jon says, "1,700 acres of the ranch for $1,000 an acre when the going price was $10,000. She got the money and gave it away to the priests." He is still acutely disgusted, twenty years later.

The next twist in the tale I have already heard from Robin. When her father sold the winery she had been horrified, but, as if frozen in a nightmare, voiced no protest, did nothing. When her mother began to "unlace all this tradition," Robin said, she found her voice and at last began to speak up. As one of the executors of the estate, she tried to stop the sale. She had to fight both her mother and her co-executors in the trust department of the Bank of America, "who saw me as grasping, greedy and disgruntled. But I set my jaw in iron." She succeeded in having Napanook—a 124-acre parcel of vineyards near Yountville—set aside from the sale of the family vineyards for herself and Marky.

The year was 1970. For the first time since the final decades of the nineteenth century, the Napa wine business was seeing notable infusions of new capital—both on a titanic scale, through the acquisition by the Heublein conglomerate of both Inglenook (which it took over from United Vintners) and Beaulieu, and, rather less noticeably, by entrepreneurs with high hopes, like Robert Mondavi, Jack and Jamie Davies of Schramsberg, and Joe Heitz. Robin, too, might have started her own winery. The Napanook land, whose harvests were being sold to other wineries, might have supplied the base. Jon was keen on the idea—actually, wanted them to leave the suburb of San Francisco where they were living at the time to resettle in Napa and work their way into the wine business. But, Robin argued passionately whenever the subject was broached, "You *can't* go home again."

At thirty, a determination not to retrace her tracks was central to her tentative plan for her life—along with the belief that, at all costs, she must not follow the self-thwarting course of her mother's. Yet even considered solely on its own merits, the valley did not seem promising as a place in which she might build a career. Contrary to what outsiders like myself imagine at first, Napa wine is not a segment of American business in which women have a natural equality with, let alone advantages over, men.

True, the selling of wine draws heavily on the traditional feminine arts of making people feel welcome and at ease. In Napa, offices sometimes have flouncy chintz furnishings and look like drawing rooms: in small, family-run wineries they literally are. An excess of Napa, for me, is marked by too many days of meals with perfectly chosen wines and food too artfully arranged on plates, too many exquisite arrangements of massed rare flowers—too many thoughtful touches of this and that; far too many furbelows.

But time and again, women in the valley told me that most of the prominent, middle-aged-plus men in Napa tend to have had earlier careers as doctors or lawyers or corporate tycoons and simply imported their prejudices about women's capabilities into their second careers. So, yes, there are lots of women winemakers and tasters and promoters these days, but only a couple of relentlessly ambitious women at the head of wineries, both of them running successful businesses for absentee owners.

In my early explorations of Napa, I had looked forward to discovering an updated version of the traditional farm's division of fully complementary labor and responsibility between a man and a woman. But I was disappointed. There were indeed some husbands and wives who worked as partners—Jack and Jamie Davies at Schramsberg, for instance—but the better I got to know the place, the more often I found couples grappling for a compromise between the husbands' wish that their wives be involved as little as possible and the women's that they be allowed to do more.

That the top stratum in Napa wine is almost entirely male is, actually, consistent with what we know of the history of wine and the sexes—for all that winemaking would seem to be a branch of the domestic arts. Hugh Johnson's *Vintage* shows women and wine (a subject for which there is no index entry) linked in a scant few folkloric and early historical contexts.

For instance: at first, only women were admitted to the Greek Bacchanalia. Far back into history, *Vintage* suggests, "the cult of Dionysus had been regarded as disreputable or worse; an excuse for underdogs of society, women and slaves, to kick over the traces."

A token few women were allowed to sit on the margins of the discussions at a Greek symposium, which originally meant, simply, "drinking together."

Johnson unearths one instance in which women were charged with possibly significant responsibility related to wine. He interprets some lines of Hammurabi's code to mean that in Babylon, wine sellers were expected to be women, adding: "But it was hardly because the calling was a humble one." Sadly, his gallant pass at consoling his women readers fails because of his other quotation from the same code: "If a priestess or nun who is not resident in a convent open a wine shop or enter a wine shop for a drink, they shall burn that woman."

Toss all those references together and you have a familiar pattern of illogic in which women were constrained by the paradox of being placed on pedestals on which they were obliged to stay—or risk disgrace. Or they were allowed to play peripheral roles—or none.

There were no "career women" on pedestals or prominent in the Napa wine business in any other way in 1970, when Jon Lail was pressing for a return to the valley. "Women," Robin told me, "were for typing and did some public relations work. Or women were tour guides."

But, having firmly ruled Napa out of consideration, she was still at a loss as to what she should do for an occupation. Her father had impressed on her the idea that "if you have gifts, you have to give back to the world"; she told me she had a strong sense of mission "to do something significant on the face of the planet from the age of five." Only she had no idea of what that would be.

At the Bank of America, where was employed when she met Jon, she became the first female officer in the international division—but still felt that, being a woman, she would never be given work fully commensurate with her abilities. She resigned and took a job that involved chiefly documentation with a small rice milling and export-ing company. She took a job as office manager for *The Saturday Review*. She saw herself as doing no more than making her contribu-tion to the household kitty. She had begun to think obsessively about some means by which she might "help fight world hunger" when she got pregnant with her first child and stopped working.

There was Napanook, of course, and in the back of her head, the idea that "I had to do something to regenerate this family tradition." But, through the curious shifting of psychological burdens that fre-quently occurs within marriages, it was Jon who became consumed by the notion of working in Napa as a step towards establishing a winery of their own. Eventually he prevailed and succeeded in returning his wife to her roots.

Jon looks rueful, stirring his cup of decaffeinated coffee. "She came back, and she no longer had the big house and she lived, in essence, with me—on the wrong side of town, in a low-income area. What do you do? It's a nice house, but not quite the home she grew up in." I think of his and Robin's rustic St. Helena street of old houses halfway through gentrification—the Lail place a sturdy, turn-of-the-century structure immaculate in its coats of white and gray paint. Inside, from a fleeting visit, I remember only the distractingly large, carved, antique dining room chairs as relics of Robin's palmier past.

At the suggestion of Robert Mondavi, who had been a friend of John Daniel's, Jon worked as a salesman for an importer of French wine in between architectural assignments. "He suggested this because he thought I had the rest of my life to learn about California wine, and because he felt that Californians really did not have adequate knowledge of European winemaking and wines." His next job in wine was a sizable step up as vice president and general manager of a small and successful new winery. Yet other jobs in wine followed: in all of them, he continued to take on architectural commissions from time to time.

I am puzzled, I tell Jon: by the early 1970s, people who had no formal training in winemaking and—to begin with—none of the necessary resources had thriving little wineries going. Why didn't he and Robin immediately embark on using Napanook towards the same end?

He frowns, smiling, like a cowboy squinting into the glare beneath his hat brim. The land, he says, produced virtually no income. "If you're struggling to pay the rent and put the kids through school, you can't just do what you want." When I had asked Robin the same question, she agreed that she could have borrowed money for a winery but did not feel sufficiently competent to draw up the necessary financial projections.

It's hard enough, I tell Jon, to conceive of a Colorado cowboy developing a grand passion for frog-water. Why, in making such slow progress with his wish to develop Napanook, did he persist with wine at all? "I think *because* of my ranching background," he says thoughtfully. "In ranching or farming, there are very few things you can be involved in and turn into a product and then actually have that small window that allows it to be a world-class product. Any other business you could be involved in, it would take multimillions of dollars to do the same thing."

But in the end the work of metamorphosing the Napanook grapes into wine of international renown fell into other hands—and through a Napa job that Robin, and not Jon, took. Still trying to stay away from wine, she took a position as executive director of a volunteer placement center and action group where she drove herself so hard, collecting funds and inventing successful new programs, that she began to give herself chest pains. So she took a job less weighted with responsibility—as Robert Mondavi's administrative assistant.

She was back in the wine business. Not just that: each day, she was observing an energetic and hyperenthusiastic winery owner at work. In August of 1981, near the end of her fifth year as amanuensis-at-large, a letter from Christian Moueix to Robert Mondavi crossed her desk. It said he was on his way to Australia to look for a New World wine investment, that he had ruled out Napa because land prices were too high. He wanted Robert Mondavi to tell him all about Australian wine country.

It occurred to Robin to suggest that Christian consider a joint venture in Napa—like Opus One, the collaboration between Robert Mondavi and the late Baron Philippe de Rothschild of Château Mouton-Rothschild in Bordeaux. She knew of a certain 124-acre vineyard whose owners were at a loss as to how they should go about shaping it for the grand destiny they knew awaited it: perhaps, in a partnership with Christian, perfectly complementary needs might be met? Robert Mondavi warmly endorsed the idea and proposed it to Christian.

As it seemed to Robin: "This prospect of a joint venture did offer the chance to start where the family tradition had left off and go forward."

By December of 1981, when Christian came to California to inspect Napanook, Robin had left the Mondavi winery and gone to work as assistant to the head of Pacific Union—the real estate and property development company that bought and created the Meadowood resort (and in which she would eventually become a principal).

Near the end of my lunch with Jon, he tells me that a year or two before the deal was struck with Christian, he and Robin had been to France on a quest for a partner for a joint venture. He ends his account of the search for the best use for Napanook with a laconic recitation of how Christian Moueix and Robin came together. He pauses. Then he says, about Christian: "You know, he's a genius type, but have you ever seen his labels for the [partnership's] wine? He's got his own picture on it. The label for each new vintage has a picture of Christian done by a different artist."

Later I discover how Jon explains to himself his and Robin's failure to save Napanook for a strictly Daniel-Lail family venture.

One Saturday afternoon I am dawdling over a tropical fruit salad at

Doidge's, an espresso place on St. Helena's Main Street, when I notice Jon in tennis shorts collecting a Styrofoam cup and a paper bag of something at the counter. He walks over to say he is on his way to his office: "Thought I'd better get something to eat because I've no idea what's happening at home tonight," he says, shrugging smilingly.

"You know, about those questions you were asking," he says. "The tradition with successful people is for one of them to stand behind the other. But with Robin and I, it's fifty-fifty. It's more of a partnership. And you can only have one leader."

He strolls away with a little wave of his paper bag. I slice into a segment of papaya, doubting that I've met his equal for plainspoken, all-American likability anywhere in Napa. Like his wife, only even more so, he harbors no obvious pretensions.

There's no question of whom the balance of power favors—overwhelmingly—in the alliance between Christian and Robin and her sister, Marky (the silent partner). It leaps off the pages of the original joint-venture proposal in Christian's precise and spiky handwriting—a document he drafted soon after his first inspection of a muddy, rainswept Napanook in December of 1981.

One page of the proposal reads as follows:

MRS LAIL'S WORK

—as soon as possible register the mark Napanook
—by next spring (summer) choose one expert for estimating at a reasonable price the value of the land and of the facilities (cost of expert shared)
—ask the manager of Moët & Chandon for the possibility of buying the acres (5?) above Napanook—ask him for the possibility of cutting the trees (oaks). Put in the balance the use he makes from your private road. . . .

True, it was far easier for Robin to get these things done than for Christian, five thousand miles away in the Bordeaux town of Libourne. But any impression that the important decisions about the venture's modus operandi might have been made democratically is summarily dispelled by the first page, entitled "Philosophy of

Napanook," which sets down steps to be taken towards the goal of producing "a top wine." In a departure from the Californian convention, it would not be labeled as a varietal (such as a Cabernet Sauvignon, Merlot, Chenin Blanc, etc.) but, as in the French tradition, would simply bear the name of its estate. As they get more and more specific, the details of the plan reach for the realm of the nonsensory, the immaterial: "The wine would have the mystery (or the mysticism) of a top wine, *uncomparable* to the wines of California. . . . Napanook is a *magic name*—People would one day ask for Napanook and not for a Cabernet Sauvignon so & so. . . . *No visitors but the real professional* would be allowed to enter the winery" (his emphasis and parentheses in all cases). The manufacture of mysterious allure is a well-known specialty of Christian's. In 1986, *Time*, in reporting that older vintages of Pétrus were sometimes fetching over $1,000 a bottle, said, "Wine experts praise Pétrus's full-bodied flavor, but not one can adequately explain the new mystique."

In a straightforward fashion, the proposal goes on to spell out the exchange of benefits Christian anticipates through the alliance:

—The John Daniel inheritors could save through a produce of top quality the great memory of their father.

—For Christian Moueix it would be a challenge after producing one of the top wines of France to try to produce a top wine in California.

In the document, he also lays out a five-year timetable for vineyard management, blending, bottling and marketing. It suggests that he will contribute in cash an amount equal to Robin and Marky's half of the capitalization—which is to be the value of the 67.1 acres of Napanook chosen by Christian to produce the raw material—*less* the cost of Christian's "skill, advices, management, concepts, trips" and the year-long training at Pétrus of a vineyard manager. He reckons the sum of these contributions at $1 million, with this most timid addendum:

—you may estimate that I am not worth 1 million dollars—

(It is in fact very difficult to estimate—If an oil man can say "I am worth x millions or billions dollars"—how much are worth Leonard Bernstein, Graham Greene or a lively painter—sorry not to be modest in those comparisons).

Neither Christian nor Robin would tell me what the financial terms eventually agreed on were—other than to say that Christian owns roughly half the venture and Robin and Marky the other half. The arrangement is probably a close approximation of Christian's original proposal. Most other details of the alliance's operation certainly are—although the wine was not, in the end, called Napanook but Dominus.

"It's a combination of names," Christian explained, "including *domanus* or domain in Latin—estate—and *dominus*, lord, or lord of the place. I worked on the name for many, many nights." In a tribute to Robin's father—perhaps to balance Christian's portrait, in solitary splendor, on the Dominus labels—the partnership was named the John Daniel Society.

Christian's original plan had called for the first release of Dominus wine in 1987. Later, the timetable was changed, so that the wine writers of the world first tasted it—the 1984 vintage—in the spring of 1988 when it went on sale at $40 a bottle or $450 a case. Some of them were not impressed. Nicholas Ponomareff, writing in *California Grapevine*, said, a month after his initial review, "We are increasingly disappointed with this first release." He described his impression: a "tight, leathery aroma with a hint of sawdust . . . harsh finish."

But the few critical voices were drowned out by the raves. Even in distant London, the *Sunday Times* commented: "tremendously concentrated, packed with rich fruit and spicy oak, but it is a magnificent wine."

The Dominus vintages have continued to sell quietly and Robin told me in 1990 that the joint venture was profitable. But in 1994, no John Daniel Society winery had yet been built: in 1986, Christian had assured a reporter that the building would be complete within five years, but the deadline passed and the society continued to make its wine at a contract winery called Rombauer.

The winery remained unbuilt because of a deadlock—the result of striking differences between Christian's and Robin's philosophical perspectives on the society's management and image.

"Robin told me yesterday—and we get along very well," Christian said, seemingly sincere, " 'Christian, our wine is taking on an elitist image. We must correct this.' I say, are we making wine for the masses or for the few people who understand wine? She said, 'Christian, we should be mar-ket-*eeng*!' And I say, Robin, what for? She says, 'I want my wine to be in California!' I say, you know I can sell as much as I want on the East Coast—California is not ready for it."

Since California constitutes the biggest market for premium California wine, Robin's position is a reasonable one. But Christian believes that the wine connoisseurs on the East Coast are far better able to appreciate the subtlety and refined complexity of the Dominus wines.

"This wine won't be recognized in California before ten years," he told me, explaining that California wine drinkers lack an "intellectual understanding" of what he is trying to do with his wine (which does rather contradict his insistence that wine drinking should be a matter of pleasure, not intellectual analysis (see Chapter 3).

He had, he said, "a spiritual goal and an intellectual goal. It's a long-term view, to give another side to California wine, to prove that better wines can be made than have been made here. But my goal is so long in perspective that it goes beyond the American approach: 'I want a re-turn! I want a re-turn!' Americans don't have goals except for making money—which is a very exciting goal, for sure!" he concluded, sotto voce.

Although alone with Christian for this diatribe, I felt I sympathized with Robin's point of view every bit as intensely as I did with his—as if I had sat down to a meal with a quarreling couple, each half of which was a friend. And yet their stances are deeply ironic. He is in Napa to express himself, for the creative freedom California offers him—yet for all his railing against money-grubbing, asked to be paid a steep $1 million for his contribution to a fledgling venture in which he was, after all, a *partner*. Robin and her sister, Marky, want the collaboration to generate enough funds to allow a restoration of their lost inheritance. But they also want to satisfy the highest aesthetic standards—want the venture to be worthy of their father's name: which is why they chose Christian, first described to me by Robin as "a male version of a bluestocking; meticulous."

Of the many contradictions, one especially fascinates me. If Christian believed he was making wine for cognoscenti only, I asked, why had he been so determined to have the society's winery designed by I. M. Pei, in the teeth of fierce opposition from Robin? Why did he want a postmodern architectural wonder for tourists to gawk at?

I thought he might silently explode. He laid down his fork and there was a long moment of utter silence. "For many reasons, some of them private," he said. "But when you are lucky to have a *genius* interested in a small venture like ours—after all, it is a pea-*nut*!—because he loves wine and he likes the idea of, at last! something modern being done in the approach of wine and wine consumption, you should never miss an opportunity like that. Never!"

The debate about the winery's architecture had been going on for years, and is a perfect specimen of the tangles Americans in Napa get into when they work with the French. "You are talking about cultural differences," Robin explained. "In France, one is surrounded by antique buildings and architectural styles of great beauty and renown. And in the United States, you are surrounded a good deal more by modern architecture. So, oddly enough, when one looks at putting up a structure, you go in opposite directions. Christian wants to do something for the twenty-first century—which is consistent with his interest in modern art, which, as you know, he collects."

I knew there had been a meeting earlier in the week at which the Dominus partners had debated the architectural question. Who won, I asked. "Christian," she said simply, making it clear that she did not want to discuss the specifics. "We're moving towards the twenty-first century."

Not until I talked to Jon Lail did I discover what really lay behind Robin and Marky's objections to the I. M. Pei building. Jon had a position of his own: "Aren't we trying to produce a wine that speaks for itself so that the building should be very . . ."

"Understated?" I suggested.

"Yes. Understated. Everything should be understated. Part of life out there is sort of ringing the bell the American way—especially the people who have recently come into money, who sort of have to tell everybody where they are, you know. Which is the problem we're having with Christian in the winery. We think the winery should be so nonnoticeable that you don't even know it's there. He wants a *statement*.

"America doesn't have any tradition—that's the biggest problem this country has. But in France or Germany, the people of my generation or younger have been raised with the tradition and don't want it.

"The design that was done for Dominus by I. M. Pei was done in 1988, but it's already out of style! Postmodern is passé. Unfortunately, we haven't been around long enough in this generation to know which styles are the real keepies!"

Dominus has neither ended Robin's quest for her true vocation nor made up for the loss of Inglenook. Because she nearly always lets Christian have his way, she feels as if she has failed to discover her life's purpose as a partner in the John Daniel Society; nor has she found it in the project management job and various spinoffs of this at the Pacific Union Company. She wonders what the final answer will turn out to be and jollies herself along with the reminder that some people are old before they find their way: "Cervantes didn't start writing until he was sixty-six. There's time."

But she is satisfied that in hanging on to Napanook and finding Christian for a partner in its development she has done as well as she could have by her family tradition—perhaps too well. Christian is every inch the perfectionist her father and Gustav Niebaum were. In one recent vintage, Christian told me, he supervised the fermentation of the equivalent of ten thousand cases of wine but decided to retain only three thousand cases' worth and dispose of the rest at a loss. "Who cares?" he'd asked rhetorically. "Still, my wine for that year will express an *idée*, a *caractère*, because I discarded the weaker vats."

Hardly encouraging for his collaborators looking forward to a more generous income stream but, without Dominus, all that would remain of Gustav Niebaum's and John Daniel's pursuit of glory would be, in a cellar here or there, a few bottles of old or extremely old wine—and the still exquisite Inglenook building, now serving rather different ends.

In a particularly disastrous phase in the 1960s, the quality and reputation of Inglenook's wines plunged under its corporate owners. In recent years, they have improved—yet in contrast to the elitist Niebaum and Daniel aims, the style of the new Inglenook is emphatically populist.

I took the official winery tour one day. A tubby tour guide with a rat-a-tat-tat patter trotted us around vast fermentation tanks and up and down cellar stairs. Then he led our group of ten shorts-and-T-shirt-clad would-be oenophiles into the visitors' tasting room—blessedly cool on a viciously hot day, between Gustav's thick stone walls—where he worked hard to put us at our ease:

"Now the first thing I want to start with is that, in wine tasting, there's nothing *wrong*, basically speaking. If you wanna have a light filet of sole or a nice salmon steak with a heavy, full-bodied red wine like a Cabernet or Charbono, be my guest!

"You know, you pull into the Sardine Factory in Monterey for a nice dinner and the sommelier comes in and shows you the wine list. And there's the Inglenook '41 Cab for $3,000—or for $4,000. And you say, okay, special occasion, let's have a bottle of that. And he brings it and you smell it and you say, 'Wait a minute, I want that on ice!' Be my guest! Now there are a lotta reasons why you *wouldn't* do it that way, but if it's *your* $4,000, *fine*. Wanna use a straw? That's fine, too."

Only some of us giggle.

CHAPTER EIGHT

Martini Country: Italian-Americans

Now the continent of Europe, of which you have heard, consists of two parts, the one of which is more pleasant than the other. . . . I was on my way from the North, where things were cold and dead, to the blue and voluptuous South.

"The Dreamers,"
Isak Dinesen

The Germans and French are major contributors to the California heritage. The French brought their marvelous flair for wine, for making the soil come alive, and the Germans their usual efficiency and perfection. But no influence has been stronger than that of the Italians. . . . The Italians have a great love affair with the soil and a marvelous enjoyment of life. . . . [They] bring a buoyant joy to winemaking. . . .

The Treasury of American Wines,
Nathan Chroman

And so later in my life when I was exposed to all the cliches of lovable Italians, singing Italians, happy-go-lucky Italians, I wondered where the hell the moviemakers and storywriters got all their ideas from.

The Immigrant Experience,
Mario Puzo

WHEN MUSHROOMS CROP UP in a second conversation with a Martini, I decide that if Martinis went in for pomp and heraldry—and they emphatically do not—a family crest centered on a mushroom would be far more fitting than the obvious bunch of grapes. Mushrooms grow close to the surface of the earth. Full-grown Martinis, though most of them loom at least six feet tall, might be caricatures of the idea of sons and daughters of the soil. Most mushrooms are colored in shy, subtle hues. Proud as they are to own the Italian-American family winery with a longer history than any other still in business in Napa, most Martinis seem as if they would be happiest in camouflage.

First, Michael Martini mentions mushrooms in a tale of culinary tragedy set in the early 1970s. When his three years in the air force during the Vietnam War ended, he faced a decision about whether he would follow his bossy elder sister, Carolyn, into the business started by his grandfather Louis in 1933. He knew he would quarrel with her: they always had. He wasn't sure he wanted to give his life to wine. So he postponed sealing his fate by fleeing to northwestern Nevada to pursue a brief, eccentric career as a hippie buckaroo.

I grapple with the idea of a Mike with a reddish blond beard flowing down his chest, doing whatever good hippies did and occasionally rounding up a stray cow or two for a local rancher. I ask if he suffered any culture shock in the experience. So he tells me about a great big farewell "spaghetti feed" on the California side of the Nevada border at the end of his year up there. He spent hours picking wild mushrooms, he says, and then he carefully balanced the ingredients of his grandfather's Genoese recipe to make a vast quantity of mushroom sauce. "But the cowboys couldn't understand not having meat in my sauce," he remembers ruefully. "So they bought all this hamburger and just threw it in!"

Driving away from a restaurant in a light drizzle one day, Mike's father, Louis, and I are trying to guess what other ingredients went into the exemplary mushroom risotto we had for lunch. Louis confesses he is handicapped as a culinary detective because he does not cook. "I think the cook threw everything but the kitchen sink into it," he says after careful consideration.

"My wife makes a very good mushroom risotto—a little darker than the one we had at lunch," he says so simply that no one would dream of accusing him of boasting. "She uses a lot of mushrooms but a small percentage of the dried porcini type that have a tremendous amount of flavor. Because they are quite expensive—they cost fifty bucks a pound! It's true that dried mushroom stored in jars goes quite a long ways, but still. What she does is, she takes the part she cleans—I guess when you clean mushrooms, a certain amount of the mushroom you throw away. She takes all of that and grinds it up and adds it to the juice that she puts into the risotto, and so it has a very intensive mushroom flavor."

It is not every day that I receive tips on saving money in my kitchen from a multimillionaire, but that hardly explains the delight surging through me. No. It's this: after three years of visiting Napa, I feel as if I have at last had spontaneous proof of the Italian peasant origins of at least one family in the valley.

In the literature promoting tourism in the Napa Valley, in the guides to visiting wineries and in text frames in the many lavish picture books about the place, you repeatedly read about its Italianate way of life.

That this is a characterization based on imaginative exaggeration began to occur to me early on, when I noticed that most of the vines in Napa are French varieties. Only in the late 1980s—roughly a hundred years after the first Italian immigrants arrived in Napa— did classic Italian grapevines like Nebbiolo, Trebbiano, Sangiovese and Malvasia begin significantly to interrupt unbroken expanses of such familiar French kinds as Cabernet Sauvignon, Pinot Noir, Merlot and Chardonnay. The Italian immigrants had never made a fuss about needing Italian grapes for their winemaking but had made do with whatever they could lay their hands on.

I can't say I am often reminded of Italy in Napa, even if the valley's landscape is disconcertingly like parts of southern Europe. One December I was briefly in the Algarve within weeks of my first visit to California, staring at topography, trees and a lustrously mild sky that might have been anywhere in the Coastal Range to which the Napa Valley belongs. In Portugal I realized what California lacked: from the balcony of my hotel room, I watched a black-robed peasant woman with a bundle on her head drift down a narrow road; smoke rising wispily from a fire in the dense foliage halfway to the horizon; an old man peeling an orange creaking by in a horse-drawn cart, slowly, like the passage of time itself, over there.

These sights of human links to the land, bearers of its imprint, revealed something of its nature in a way no native people did on the Napa Valley's behalf. A woman who died in 1976 was the last of the Wappo Indians who inhabited the place before the white men came: few residents of Napa at any time in this century have ever met one or learned anything of their lore.

Because more Italians and Italian Swiss settled Napa than natives of any other European winegrowing country, Italian-Americans have come to stand in as its "original" inhabitants. From the 1880s onwards, swarms of newcomers from northern Italy began to displace the Chinese as laborers in the valley's vineyards. The more ambitious of them saved their wages and soon were able to go into business for themselves. Italian and Italian Swiss immigrants built stone-and-wood wineries in a miniature winegrowing boom in the first fifteen years of this century.

If you are taken out to a meal by anyone in Napa who is not poor and has discerning taste buds, you will very likely eat in a restaurant with an Italian name. Two or three of the finest establishments in the valley specialize in *cucina* but, unlike the restaurants in San Francisco's North Beach fifty miles south, they are new—were started within the last decade. None of them were established by Napa-born-and-bred Italian-Americans. They have less to do with the valley's history than with an American love affair, for perhaps the last two decades, with the Italian aesthetic sensibility.

The one pure vestige of immigrant Italian Napa is a small grocery called the Napa Valley Olive Oil Manufactory that I found I could not telephone—because it has no listing in the Napa directory. Fortunately, I had shopped there and bought a bottle of the sound and remarkably inexpensive oil that, on examination, said, "Packed by G. Guidi." There were two telephone numbers for a Guglielmo Guidi in the book. A call to one of them yielded the voice of a middle-aged Italian woman speaking just enough English to direct me to another number and a younger female voice that informed me that "Guidi died many years ago."

The second voice belonged to Leonora Particelli, whose father, Oswaldo, came over from the Old Country by way of Brazil in 1960, and in 1963, with his brother Nelso (now Nelson), bought the shop from Guidi, who had started it somewhere between 1910 and 1920. Leonora said Guidi was in his sixties at the time and had no heirs or relatives to take it over.

On one of my shopping expeditions there, Leonora's burly thirty-one-year-old brother Ray proudly explained to me that his parents spoke no English—that they hadn't needed to learn the language because, for years, the grocery had almost exclusively served members of Napa's Italian community. But then, he said with sardonic glee, "Italian food became gourmet!" Walls papered with customers' business cards testify to the shop's popularity with scores of people who could not have grown up knowing what pesto was.

The Particellis enjoy playing hide-and-seek with the public. No sign for the shop is visible at the end of the street of nondescript suburban houses in St. Helena, and its screen door is all but concealed by the orange trees in its front yard. It is a windowless cavelike room in which salamis and boxes of De Cecco pasta and anchovies and tubes of onion and garlic paste and biscotti are piled higgledy-piggledy—and, yes, Ray Particelli assured me, it looked much as Guidi left it. "It was never meant to look 'charming.' But now, that's what people tell us. It's almost *fashionable*," he said wonderingly. He was anxious for me to understand that the store was started and kept going because it was one of the few ways of making a living open to Guidi and Nelso and Oswaldo and his wife, Ferruccia (in Italy, Oswaldo had made coal by burning wood, earning in one week less than a seventh of his wages for a day's work in America). "It was not a 'concept' thought up by some marketing consultant," he added loftily. "You know, like some Irish guy opening up a Mexican place because Mexican food is in."

It took several trips to Napa for me to relinquish the hope of discovering other places as embedded in the valley's Italian-settler past. I must admit that at the very beginning, I cherished an even more extravagant fantasy of finding rustic piazzas strewn with tiny tables at which local people gossiped and sipped espresso and stared into space, and smoke-filled, hole-in-the-wall trattorias serving simple and delicious meals—their patrons holding shouted conversations above the din in an Italian dialect, as if oblivious of no longer being in Italy.

In any case, in Napa—as in the rest of America—the Italians who arrived at the end of the last century and roughly the first half of this one sought to lose as many outward signs of their identity as fast as possible. At one winery, I met Julie Prince, a woman in her late forties who left the province of Ancona for Napa in the mid-1950s. She told me the first thing that struck her was how thoroughly Americanized the Italians of the Napa Valley seemed. So she immediately changed her name from Juliana to Julie: "You only ever said you were Italian sotto voce."

Still, in the privacy of their homes, Napa's Italian immigrants kept their culinary skills honed and sipped wine with their meals. The upholding of these traditions helped preserve the one human institution Italians value above all others: the family.

Later, her parents will assure me that Carolyn Martini's job as president of the Louis M. Martini Winery would never have had her grandfather's sanction. The founder of the business was, to the core, a Latin male chauvinist. He held big celebrations for the births of his grandsons, Mike and Peter, but was merely pleased when Carolyn and her sister, Patty, put in an appearance.

It takes me a while to get over my bemusement at finding a woman at the head of an Italian-American family enterprise—even if she is the eldest child of the family. But Carolyn would be remarkable anywhere.

This is a woman with a swagger. At forty-four, she has let her head of curly hair go entirely gray. She has a glowing pink complexion younger than her years and a tall, well-proportioned figure. She is draped in a long-sleeved calf-length peach silk dress over which she wears a waistcoat made of rabbit skins, the gift of a hunter friend. "Jackrabbits?" I ask. "Nah. Just plain bunny rabbits," she says. Her hands in her waistcoat pockets through most of our conversation exaggerate the swagger effect—although, whenever she grows vehement, she squeezes the garment's sides together like a child cuddling a favorite toy.

I don't ask, but feel sure she isn't got up like this every day. Thanksgiving is the day after tomorrow and, all over the valley, wineries have been shutting down for early celebrations. Silk and fur could hardly be customary clothing for the occupant of this functional, boxy office where—despite gloomy dark veneer walls—a surprising variety of indoor plants apparently thrive abundantly. "Oh, freesias!" I exclaim, staring at a pot two feet away. "Fakes," says Carolyn, pleased. The one window, looking out onto the car park, faces north—"so real plants get long and straggly," she explains.

I can imagine the shudder Carolyn's office would earn from owners of showpiece wineries: at one I visited earlier in the day, a spritelike florist in black harem pants stood arranging an armful of fresh-cut pink orchids. But those would be out of place here in the rust red, cubelike Martini building, just south of St. Helena, of which the writer John McPhee has noted: "Its architectural statement is upper-middle prime rib." Other winery owners tell visitors about agonies of indecision over choosing architects for their building's design: Carolyn's father, Louis, reminisces about being a teenager in 1933, hauling the hollow red tiles in which the building is covered all the way from Port Costa, nearly two hours away, ten tons at a time.

About the winery building, I say, "How have you resisted commissioning an architectural spectacle—you know, going Napa-spectacular?"

"Costs money," she says dryly.

"But would you—if you could afford to?"

"Mm-mm," she says, shaking her head. "You've got to maintain a *life*-style to pull that off. None of us can maintain a life-style, so—!" She gives a deep guffaw. "There's no point!"

"You mean, you don't like the idea of putting yourselves on display in a building that's an *objet d'art?*"

"Yeah. *Yeah!* You know—sorta like, if you want to make an impression on the customer, then everything you do and say has to be kind of in unison. You can't pretend to be something you're not. And if you're kind of a funky, down-home, basic, old-style Napa winery, then you're probably better off being that and playing off of that than trying to glitz it up. Because you're *never* gonna pull it off."

I've got her on a soap box, I see, and dare not interrupt.

"We're not real high-energy people. We don't like to travel or party or do any of that kind of thing. We're sort of private and really don't want to live that lifestyle. And if you don't want to put in the time or the energy for it, you have to buy it—get other people to do it for you. Well, it doesn't make sense to us, so it's not where we put our money!"

Now and then the Martini winery is mentioned in the wine press as a prime candidate for acquisition. For years it grew painfully slowly when other establishments streaked ahead. It's the smallest of the valley's large wineries, making less than 200,000 cases a year: the Sutter Home Winery across the street makes over four million, the Robert Mondavi Winery turns out roughly three million and the Charles Krug Winery around 700,000 cases. Moneymen in San Francisco speak of the Martini enterprise as one that has, until recently, been about as closely in touch with its time as Rip van Winkle. Martini is still one of the best-known names in American wine. But in the 1980s, it was all but eclipsed by others on which much promotional zeal had been expended. A wine country investment broker to whom I once mentioned the Martinis sighed exasperatedly: "That family seems to forget that there are thousands of people working for competitors lying awake at night, thinking of ways to get their brands more attention."

Pushing the pockets of her vest out as far as they will go, Carolyn explains her family's dichotomous classification of people in the wine business: they are either "production" or "marketing" types. She slips easily into management newspeak. "We have a very production-oriented mind-set. We don't know public relations and sales and marketing. We don't understand it. We don't do it well. What makes us feel good is seeing the grapes grow and seeing the wine being produced, the cases roll off the line, and seeing the trucks ship."

She sticks her jaw out and concedes, without any prompting from me, that this family bias has led to some expensive mistakes. She says the biggest of these was made in the late 1960s and early 1970s when the Martinis opted not to join other Napa producers of wine— including the many new wineries—in raising prices. It was then that the valley's potential as a winegrowing region for the ages had begun to be glimpsed by some connoisseurs who had once scorned all domestic winemaking efforts, and—in what the Martinis would deem a perfect example of the Mad Hatter logic of marketing theory and practice—the higher prices actually helped to reinforce the flattering new perception.

Martini logic dictates a decidedly different course: if a product is well made and reasonably priced, people will buy it, and that's all there should be to marketing. When Carolyn's father took charge of the winery in 1960, that was his working philosophy. "Dad thought that if you didn't need the cash, why not give the customer a break." But the younger Louis Martini failed to foresee the consequences of this eccentric restraint. Rivals earning fatter profits soon had more money to invest in expansion and modernization—and in the charlatanism known as marketing that, incredibly enough, helped them to steal Martini customers. They were introducing the American public to subtler, more sophisticated wines than the sturdy, straightforward sort for which Martini was known.

"So in the late 1960s, your father thought that the people like Joe Heitz—just barely started in business and charging stratospheric prices—had simply gone nuts?" I ask.

"Yes. Except what they did worked," Carolyn says with a dismal chuckle.

But from the late 1980s, the family saw that to stop competitors from replacing Martini wines with others on customers' dining tables, it would have to reverse itself—and spend money on updating and upgrading the style and quality of its wines, and of their packaging and promotion. By then, though, the price and quality slot above the Martini wines—into which the winery was trying belatedly to hoist itself—was vastly overcrowded. "We didn't raise prices when we could have, and now that there's so much competition, we can't raise them all that fast," Carolyn says.

Now I understand why my mentioning the Martinis anywhere in the Napa Valley has unfailingly produced an outpouring of tender concern for the winery's—and family's—future. Such pig-headed unworldliness in practical and highly intelligent people is a thing of wonder and mystery.

Carolyn says she knew the winery needed rejuvenation when she returned from some years of working as a librarian in New Jersey to become her father's assistant. But, "I had no authority." Then, as for most of the winery's history, family members were too removed from the clamor of the marketplace to have more than superficial impressions of the changing tastes of wine buyers. The winery had never distributed its wines itself but through an agent it shared with Wente Bros., a concern in the Livermore Valley east of San Francisco. The disagreeable job of marketing was someone else's headache.

I express astonishment at this delegation of responsibility, which has been continued despite radical changes in other facets of the winery's management in the 1980s. Time and again, other winery owners had emphasized to me that a company stands or falls on the strength of its ability to promote and sell its wines. So, delegating this job is a bit like handing over the steering wheel. Carolyn says the family did try to manage its own sales after it ended its relationship with its original distribution agent in 1988. But three years later, it signed on a new representative.

In the gap between agents, the Martinis struggled to get over their dislike of pushing and shoving. But learning to do a better job of marketing meant spending a lot more money than they felt they could afford—and, given the depth of their conviction that marketing was distasteful, more than they wanted to.

"I know more about marketing and public relations, probably, than anyone else in the family, having had it hammered into me by consultants and tutors and all kinds of classes. But none of this does much good if you don't have the instinct for it," Carolyn says. "I've known enough marketing people to know that they drive you nuts—if you are a production person, because they are immediate and sensitive to things the rest of us don't ever pick up on, details like—" A muffled gasp escapes her. " 'What does the color white on a package mean?' Or, 'I have a hunch we're going to "light is right"—to lighter colors, but not white, which connotes generic or cheap'! They are more driven than production people and everything is a crisis for them. They can sense a change in the atmosphere and jump on it even before it's a trend!" she says, as if describing beings as exotically talented as shamans or yak herders.

"Still, I suspect that if you really wanted to, you could get better at that sort of thing—couldn't you?" I suggest.

"Nah," says Carolyn, calmly dismissive. "You can be anything you want to, but if it's not your natural knack it takes an immense amount of energy. Okay, so then you're going to be divorced and your kids will never know you. Is it worth giving up your life for a bottle of wine? It doesn't even make *sense!*"

Clearly, being the head of a family business gives her some freedom to limit her work's distortion of her life as a woman. But I find I'm puzzled by her classifying herself as a "production person" when she has nothing to do with the winemaking—which is overseen by Mike Martini, two years younger than she. I ask why not. She says she doesn't have the gifted taste buds "you need for cooking, winemaking and so forth. Some people can taste things better and smell things better, but I'm not one of them."

"But then, if you weren't even interested in winemaking—in an Italian family, how on earth did you become the boss?"

She raises one arm, squares her jaw and punches the air with a tight fist. I laugh, taken aback by this naked display of power lust. "My brother Michael says I'm naturally bossy. And I had the general management skills—I have a master's in library administration. Mike has the training in chemistry and winemaking and so forth."

"So what was your childhood ambition?"

"To run something."

"But why?"

"Born that way."

She says she feels she is a mixture of many qualities of her grandfather, the founder, and of her mother, who is also intensely analytical. She reminds me more of tomboy playmates of mine from years ago than of woodenly self-asserting women executives in large American corporations—precisely because her bossiness is innate and natural-seeming.

She insists she had no interest in running the winery as a child even though she had her first job in it at eight, stuffing envelopes. As a teenager, she helped in her father's laboratory, in the tasting room, and on the bottling line. But then she chose to study humanities at Scripps College in southern California, specializing in arts and crafts, with faint enthusiasm. She traveled to the other coast in 1970 to Rutgers and used the master's degree she earned in a job that involved managing the cataloguing and tracking of library books for the university's nine campuses. In 1974, a traumatic year for the family, her grandfather died, her father fell seriously ill, and she felt she had to come home to help.

For all her undisguised pleasure in being *numero uno* at the winery now, she can also sound like a woman on a treadmill. When I ask whether Liz, her mother, had ever worked after her marriage, she says she believes she would like to have done so, but was too busy bringing up four children.

"I'd love it if somebody gave me about five years off," she says with an attempt at a laugh.

"To bring up your sons?"

"To do anything! I just need a break. No matter how much you like your job, getting up and doing it every single day gets to be a drag, and it's a long haul from the time you're twenty to the time you die."

"But surely you could take a sabbatical."

"One of the problems with running things is, you don't take sabbaticals because you could find out they don't need you!"

She is no less insecure, in her family's very own company, than a senior executive in a faceless, publicly owned corporation. I wonder about the aims of founders of family businesses.

"Do you think your grandfather set out to create a dynasty, with this winery?"

"Mm-mm. I think he gave it more lip service than he thought it would really happen. I think he really didn't think anyone would live past him—that anyone here would survive him, anyhow. Ha!" She pauses for a bark of laughter. "There was nothing wrong with his ego. Nothing!"

The Martini family's aversion to promotion and sales and marketing is only two generations old.

The first Louis Martini in Napa was a consummate salesman— prodigiously extroverted, buoyant, charming, overbearing, shrewd, contrary, quick-tempered and unpredictable. He was not above putting on airs. Carolyn remembers his having a crest on an early label for the winery that "had something to do with some idea of

European nobility that, being a good peasant boy, he'd always looked up to."

His son Louis Peter, his temperamental opposite, remembers himself and his sister Angiolina cringing with embarrassment at their father's flamboyant ordering about of bell boys in hotel lobbies on trips away from home. These jaunts were usually begun on impulse, with no warning given his equally strong-willed but quiet and semi-reclusive wife, Assunta. Clothes and toothbrushes were bundled into the family Chrysler as if for an emergency evacuation, and the journeys themselves were just as unsettling. On the highway, the older Louis would abruptly slow down to twenty miles an hour when he had something to say and, once it had been said, lurched within pounding heartbeats (not his) to seventy miles an hour.

His son remembers him terrifying timid young stenographers and bookkeepers by throwing tantrums at the slightest provocation. He was bored whenever the winery ran smoothly and peacefully and made sure these phases did not last long. But he was well loved in the Napa wine community in which he was already famous by the time André Tchelistcheff, fourteen years his junior, arrived from France in 1938. André remembers Louis Martini's wines being squarely in the Italian tradition, only more so: full-bodied, "with a great amount of personality," not unlike their maker—"they used to call him Napa Valley Mussolini!"

Whereas André, in keeping with that particular Californian convention, made wines based on a single variety of grape, Louis Martini's were blended—not, as in the great French châteaux, with a splendid, multifaceted aging as the goal—but for early drinkability. ("In other words," André explained to an archivist from the university at Berkeley, "if I believed in individual flower, he believed in bouquet of flowers!")

In the homely Italian tradition of winemaking, Louis Martini's aim was to make soundly constructed, inexpensive wines bought off grocery shelves and present on the table at every meal. Even so, André has described some of his wines as "outstanding . . . with entirely different . . . charm." Though posterity was not of particular interest to their maker, the wines have held up well. In *California's Great Cabernets*, James Laube noted that Martini Special Selection

Cabernets from the 1950s are still in excellent condition "and among the finest California Cabernets ever made."

The founder's success story was a classic of the immigrant genre. He was twelve when he arrived in California in 1899 to help his father, Agostino, with the clam-digging and fishing business he had started in San Francisco in the hope of making a modest fortune in a few years abroad.

The family came from Pietra Ligure, just west of Genoa, in the province of Liguria—chiefly mountains that plunge abruptly to the slender coastline known as the Italian Riviera. There can be no doubt that the Martinis long ago migrated to Italy from some distant Viking land. Being unusually tall, and blond and blue-eyed, they are impossible to confuse with the native Ligurians described in a vintage *Encyclopaedia Britannica* entry as "thin and wiry . . . short of stature and dark-complexioned . . . winning a difficult livelihood from the soil." In the seafaring Genoese tradition—Cristoforo Colombo and Amerigo Vespucci were natives—both of Louis's grandparents were marine captains, but Agostino was a cobbler until he went to America. Like other Italian peasants who got as far as California, the Martinis were prosperous by comparison with those who could only afford their passages to New York.

Agostino's seafood company prospered. In 1906, on a whim, he had his son help him make an experimental few casks of wine: some of the results were good, some execrable. Louis decided he would go to Italy to study how to make wine properly, at a university—not in the least deterred by lacking any formal education, having flatly refused to bow to his father's wish that he go to school. Later he would explain that he was an autodidact and a voracious reader— which helped him gain admission as a "guest" student to a school of oenology at Alba, where he mastered the essentials of winemaking in six or seven months and, soon after, returned to San Francisco.

He made small quantities of wine and sold it—mostly to other Italian immigrants—from the same wagon from which he distributed the day's catch of clams and mussels. Then, in 1911, he and Agostino rented a winery and vineyard land in Pleasanton, east of San Francisco. The venture was not a financial success and, seven years later, the Martinis gave it up. Agostino returned to Italy. Louis spent the next decade and a half in what, in hindsight, looks like preparation for the crowning creation of his career, his winery in Napa. He took a succession of different jobs with wineries in California's Central Valley, and in 1922 founded a company that survived Prohibition by selling grape juice concentrate to home winemakers, and by making and selling sweet and uncomplicated sacramental wines. In 1933, he built the St. Helena winery and gradually began buying vineyards.

Unlike ambitious Napa wineries of a quarter-century or so later, the new Louis Martini venture did not set out to match first-growth French wines in quality, but it did mean Louis had raised his sights. The Central Valley winery where he had worked, as well as his own winery there, at Kingsburg, had all been producers of unremarkable bulk wines—"California Burgundy," for instance, blended from grapes that are strangers to Burgundy. Had he stayed in that business, his Kingsburg operation might conceivably have been a serious rival of another Central Valley industrial (family-owned) winemaker, E&J Gallo, started at almost exactly the same time in another part of the same valley—and which produces more wine (in 1991, 48 million of the 173 million cases made in America) than any other company in the world.

Instead, in St. Helena, at forty-three, Louis set out to make inexpensive but crafted wines. He established a reputation as an innovator less for dazzling advances in the art or technology of winemaking than for successful adaptations to the (unorthodox) tools available in California of what he had learned of winemaking in Italy. For instance, even those of his wines that won the highest praise were aged in tanks made from redwood trees rather than the oak barrels traditional in France. He anticipated the change in the American wine drinker's taste from cloying, fortified wines to drier varieties.

His breadth of perspective meant he cared about the future of winemaking in the Napa Valley as a whole, and this led him to found the Vintners' Association in 1943. Today, this is a trade organization and lobbying group much like any other. But when Louis Martini was its animating spirit, it was a band of merry men that met to eat and drink superlatively well once a month, freely exchanged ideas about improving winemaking and solutions to technical problems—

and joined together to set quality standards and fight government regulations they thought misguided.

In his day, Louis Martini was to Napa what Robert Mondavi would become later—its most prominent Italian-American. Their shared qualities are a bon-vivant gregariousness, abundant vitality and charm—both men living exemplars of the fun-loving Italians of myth and cliché.

Neither man is typical in the least of the rest of Italian-American Napa. Modesty and a retiring disposition are most characteristic of the community—the Particellis with no sign for their grocery and no telephone listing; a sprawling tract of vineyard land in the heart of the valley that, at the request of the Italian-American family that owns it, is not identified on maps; a member of the Nichelini family, owners of a vanishing hundred-year-old winery, telling me they would certainly see me if I insisted, but would have nothing to say.

It is as if a classic peasant's caution about seeming to get above oneself crossed an ocean and a continent and has been handed down unchanged. Think of the patriarch of the extended family of peasants in the Bernardo Bertolucci epic *1900*, admonishing his cheeky grandson: "Remember this: you will learn to read and you will learn to write; you will go off to the army; you will see the world; but you will still remain Olmo, son of peasants."

This house like a small fortress in which the four Martini children grew up seems exactly the right place to be on the eve of Thanksgiving Day, that puzzling American celebration. It's true that harvest festivals have long been held all over the world, but so few Americans look as if they could have had pilgrims for ancestors, and harvests are abstractions to the urbanite majority.

Depictions of the original Thanksgiving feast in my schoolbooks sometimes included smiling American Indians bearing gifts, but the explanations of the day's meaning suggested that in succeeding years, the New England colonists were also celebrating the successful slaughter of "red" men. Even the day's modern meaning as the preeminent occasion for family reunions is wearing thin as the traditional family totters.

Perhaps a heightened awareness of families' fragility accounts for the wistfulness shading the joy of this week, a mixture of feelings that the outdoors also foments. To drive through a residential enclave of Napa on a crisp November day is to see festive red and yellow leaves on skinny liquidambar trees, as poised as adolescent mannequins; bushes thick with shiny red toyon berries; rows of exuberantly elegant white tea roses in full bloom. Yet some quality in the clear light cast by the milky blue sky becomes a melancholy reminder of the transitoriness of beauty and pleasure. In this particular Thanksgiving week, moaning night winds have been keeping people awake—"Oh, that wind, I can't stand it!" they complain, shuddering faintly, by day.

The stout walls of the Martini house at the western edge of St. Helena—a conversion of the valley's oldest stone winery, built in 1867 by a General Erasmus Keyes—proclaim protection from all the ambiguities and uncertainties without; protection of the family within. I feel snugly enclosed in this sanctuary furnished with capacious chairs and handsome, Brobdingnagian tables that, like the wooden floor, gleam under layers of polish. It is a home seemingly fitted to the scale of the kindly, shambling giant Louis Martini is, at seventy-two, but tiny, curvy, pink-cheeked Liz Martini looks overwhelmed by it. She greeted me affectionately when I arrived, wiping her hands on her apron, and asked if I'd like "a nice cuppa tea": she was born a Martinelli, but her mother was English.

Sweet, spicy smells fill the air. Liz has been baking five dozen cookies for their son Mike's wedding on Saturday. A glass-walled porch is like a miniature indoor meadow of pink, white and mauve dried flowers in pale straw baskets, Liz's contribution to the decoration of the disused stone winery in which the ceremony is to be held. It will be Mike's second marriage, and it's a reminder that, of course, even a child brought up in a family in business together, in a house that so powerfully recalls a stabler past in which divorce was rare and horrific, must live as a man of his time. In fact, Carolyn told me yesterday, the anachronistic closeness of the Martinis was partly responsible for the breakdown of Mike's first marriage. Once the subject was broached, she had run on at length, as if she had been waiting for a chance to air her views on it.

"Think about it," she said. "If you're married to somebody, then the two of you form a nucleus—it's kind of like putting you back to back and you face the rest of the world. But if you're a family business, besides that, you have—on the other side—relationships that go back to the time you were born. You're actually closer to the people you work with than the person you are married to. So there's bound to be conflicts of interest in there, if nothing more than just over time. Say you need to be home for dinner and you've got something going at the company. If you have no family work ties, it's easier to say, 'I've got to stay late or the boss will fire me!' In this case, the spouse is always looking at a situation where, 'You'd rather be with them than with me.'

"The people marrying in often do not understand the ramifications of what they are doing. They buy in and say, oh yeah, yeah, I'm happy to be a wife or a husband of someone in a family company. But they don't understand what that means emotionally.

"They don't understand what the commitment they have made means until they get stood up—until they see the advice they give their spouse not being taken because he's got allegiances on the other side.

"Then the in-laws do things like making comparisons between siblings—sometimes about things that have nothing to do with the business—and they don't understand the impact of that. Even if it does have to do with the business, the importance of things is weighted differently and, you know, it's complicated."

Though Italians and Italian-Americans place tremendous importance on maintaining family ties, it isn't as if their genes supply them with the ability to maintain these effortlessly. Louis says his parents' marriage was "rather rocky—they did a lot of shouting at each other." Yet he believes that beneath the discord, "they got along pretty well."

In her soft, deliberate way, Liz says that Assunta, her late mother-in-law, "was reticent to go out in public," but highly intelligent. "I always say that they were equally responsible for the success of the business. He was very, very bright and aggressive. But she was the systematic, orderly intelligence that kept things down on earth." She turns to her husband. "Don't you think so, Louis?"

"Yeah," says Louis. "He was more a dreamer, but he was also a doer. He didn't mind taking chances. She was a lot more conservative than he was."

Liz excuses herself, saying she "has some soup on," and disappears.

I look at Louis, his huge frame slightly hunched in his armchair, his blue eyes sleepy behind his steel-rimmed spectacles, thinking that he is more his mother's than his father's son. And his life, like hers, has been an adaptation to his father's whims and idiosyncracies.

Growing up, he tells me, he had never assumed he would work for the family winery, even as the only son. He was afraid he would not enjoy working for his father. Not until he enrolled at Berkeley in 1937 did he consider a course of study that would be helpful if he did indeed decide to join the winery. He chose to specialize in food technology, because it also opened doors to careers that had nothing to do with wine. Yet, still a student, he drew closer to the wine business. The university system allowed him to stretch his personal curriculum to include courses in oenology and viticulture at Davis—which, even then, had few equals anywhere for its teaching and research in winegrowing.

In 1941 Louis got his degree and, in the spirit of an experiment, had begun to work for his father when the Second World War broke out. He enlisted in the air force and was posted to England for two years to serve as a ground crew member.

He tells me he enjoyed his time in uniform and was strongly tempted to make a career of it. When I say I cannot imagine anyone trading in a life in a bucolic paradise for military servitude, he laughs shyly and insists that he enjoyed it just as much as the military academy he had attended for high school. "I didn't mind the structure. I didn't mind the discipline—which was easy, compared to my mother's."

In the event, it was in serving his father that his stoical temperament was tested. "He was the type of person that you couldn't tell him, 'I'm going to do this or that.' Most of the ideas had to originate with him. So what you did was, you made suggestions, and in a little while they came back as his idea. So that worked out o-o-kay!" he says with an ironic laugh.

"When I first came back from the service, we had a lot of people working there and we were doing *every*thing by hand. And I wanted to get a reasonably automated bottling line, but nah, nah, nah, he didn't want to change. Five years later, well, the union tried to come in. We had a union vote and of course it got voted down. But there were a number of people that voted for the union. And so my dad said, 'How many people can we eliminate if we go for this automated bottling business?' So I said, five. And he said, 'Go ahead and get a bottling line!' It took him five years to get the idea that we had to cut down on labor."

I tell him Robin Lail's father had always, in her childhood, said of Inglenook, "One day all this will be yours." Had his father ever said as much to him?

"No," says Louis. "You know, I never had the feeling of it being *my business*. I always had the feeling that I was to run it and pass it on to somebody else. It was making us a living."

"So it was more a responsibility than a pleasure for you?"

"Oh I enjoyed the winemaking part. I enjoy running the vineyards. I can't stand talking to salesmen very long."

He was thirty-six before his father let him take over the winemaking, and fifty before he was handed the job of president and general manager. Of the wines he made, *The Wine Spectator* has said, "His Cabernets through the 1950s and 1960s remain a benchmark in quality for the varietal in California." He also distinguished himself by finding and acquiring tracts of prime vineyard land for the family and by his work in improving the quality of grapevines—patiently searching for those capable of yielding wines of greater refinement and cloning them.

Still, he cheerfully takes responsibility for the errors of omission and commission in marketing that Carolyn had told me about. "My father was more well rounded running the business than I ever was," he says. "He was a real good salesman, a great PR character and a good winemaker. But if I don't like doing something, I just don't do it!"

Liz slips in bearing a tea tray painted with an English village scene and some of Mike's wedding cookies—oatmeal shortbread with cinnamon and a delectable coconut and custard confection.

"You want a cup of tea, dear?" she asks Louis.

"Yeeeeah," he growls, not unappreciatively.

I tell Liz I feel slightly as if I were visiting her and Louis in a time machine, and not just because of the age of their house and the hand-printed linen curtains in this room, made for the family that owned it in 1925. I say that a tightly knit clan and a family business that has stayed in place for three generations are a little extraordinary for our time. "I sometimes feel that way, too," she says, smiling. "Life itself is moving so fast that you don't build these roots. A company thinks nothing of sending someone across the country if they need a man there. And, look, we have television as an influence, the ease of travel . . ."

"Yes, but how has your family resisted all of this?"

"Speaking for myself," Louis breaks in, "I am *not* one that likes moving around. Things don't always look brighter on the other side of the fence. One of the reasons I didn't stay in the air force is I knew they would be moving me all over the world."

"But will the third generation carry on, do you think? Are Carolyn and Mike satisfied with the jobs they have in relation to each other?"

They exchange a quick sideways glance.

"Well, they seem to have kind of worked out a system," Louis says gruffly, looking down at his teacup. "They are getting along."

Oh no, Liz and Louis protest when I tell them I had assumed they inherited this house from Louis's parents. The older Louis owned another house and three hundred acres of land around it about a mile and a half away. It had a lake, about eighty acres in vines, two defunct winery buildings and a home that the family patriarch had built on it. But by the time he died in 1974, Louis and Liz had been in this house for twenty-two years and Louis is not, as he says, a mover. He says the property taxes on the estate were anyway too high in relation to its ability to generate income. Also, unlike the winery, which was registered in both parents' names, the house and its land were only in the older Louis's—which made it the one asset that could easily be sold to pay his estate duties.

"Do you think this house will stay in your family?" I ask.

"I don't know," Liz says. "None of them seem to be particularly interested in it at this point," meaning the children.

"Oh, they're interested in it," Louis says grumpily. "But they're interested from the standpoint of selling it."

"Yes, as an investment, not to live in," Liz adds, and they laugh long and heartily.

We discuss the fashion for building show-off houses among wealthy people who move to the valley from other places. I say that a man I'd had lunch with told me about a retired couple building an imitation château of twelve thousand square feet, even though the husband was already ill with a fatal disease when they began. It was a project that made no sense to me.

"Yes. I'm just amazed, driving around the valley," Louis says. "I wish we could go back to the way it was here in 1932. I don't know who they think is going to take care of those enormous places because getting domestic labor isn't easy—and good domestic labor almost impossible."

But, I say, I was astounded to learn from Carolyn that she and her husband were building what she called a castle, in Chiles Valley, northeast of Napa.

"It's Barry. It's his ambition, not hers. And he's building it himself, you know."

"But she said he's a lawyer."

"For some reason he finds building more attractive. Well you see, his undergraduate degree, before he went to law school, was in manual arts. So he'd rather be up there sweatin' away bricking, in the summertime, than in court."

I realize that Carolyn's Barry's passion for building made him a "production person," one who had the right stuff. After all she said about in-laws finding it hard to fit into large Italian-American families working together, I had asked her how the husband she married at thirty-three managed.

"Oh, I have a real hard-headed husband," she said, grinning. "He can take care of himself. *Easy*."

He had already made it clear, for instance, that he "was not necessarily sold on the idea" of their sons aged eight and two growing up and going into the wine business. And no, she said, there was no question of my visiting him for a chat because he drew a firm line between Martini business and his own.

You would think forty or fifty years had dropped off Louis Martini on a day we spend driving between parts of the family's scattered 1,300 acres of vineyard land. He is so keenly engaged—almost bubbly—that I would guess that the vines are his special passion even if he hadn't said as much.

Winding our way up to the most prized of the estates—the Monte Rosso vineyard in the Mayacamas Range separating Napa from the Sonoma Valley to its west—the scenery seems caught between acts of a drama. Around every other rising bend in the road is a vista of boiling blue-gray clouds, a retreating end-of-winter storm; in the strip of land at the bottom of the picture, riotous wet grass is sprinkled with lupines, wild mustard and a dainty white wildflower that Louis cannot name for me. The contrast between top and bottom in the scene is as if a saucy, lacy petticoat of many layers were peeping out beneath a dress of stiff gray wool.

We turn off Moon Mountain Road—after Jack London's Valley of the Moon nearby—onto a country lane: a vineyard can be glimpsed beyond its sweeping curve and tall green banks. This is the entrance to Monte Rosso. A sign declares sternly, "L.M. Martini. No hunting and trespassing."

I ask Louis why this and some other large Martini land holdings are not in the Napa Valley. "Oh, land in Napa has always been overpriced so far as we're concerned," he replies. "Even way back when we started."

I persist in wondering why the older Louis bought this vineyard the better part of an hour's drive from St. Helena when suddenly we turn a corner and the question needs no answer. We are only a thousand feet above the sea, Louis tells me, but there's a thrilling Olympian sensation as, approaching the top of our mountain, we are surrounded in every direction by other towering rounded peaks, the ones to the west misted and separated from us by the gaping expanse of the Sonoma Valley at our feet. The scale of the view is heart-stopping; the only buildings visible westward are fuzzy ant-sized constructions far, far below us. Vines cover 250 acres of steep slopes about us, perfectly at home in the Wild West.

"Oh, please stop!" I exclaim. "Those are the most extraordinary-looking vines I have ever seen."

He brakes beside them.

"That's because they are over a hundred years old. Zinfandel."

At this time of year the vines are leafless because they are dormant. The first thought crossing my mind is that this particular block looks remarkably human, exactly as you'd expect a nudist colony of centenarians might—gnarled, knobbly, craggy, and repeatedly twisted back on themselves at uncomfortable-looking angles.

"They look like that because, see, the new shoots come out at an angle to the old shoots," Louis explains. "So every time you prune, you're going in a different direction."

"They look like people—like characters."

"Old characters? Crabby faces? Yes." He chuckles.

But after we have looked at them in silence for a few moments, the idea of geriatric nudes no longer fits. They are dignified and serene, immeasurably wiser than the callow mustard around them—really rather like members of a religious order who have withdrawn from the world's turmoil.

There's a tightness in Louis's voice when he says, too briskly, "Obviously, this is going to be the next block we're replacing with new vines. Do you see that there are a lot of missing vines in there? You get individual vines that fail, and pretty soon you've got a moth-eaten setup." It's as if he's talking about euthanasia for beloved old friends of his. But production in this block and others of roughly the same age in this estate "is down about as low as it can go," he says.

Old vines must be replaced for the health of their owners' businesses, even though their increasingly scanty yield of grapes can make wines of exceptional richness and complexity. The great French châteaux save these more concentrated wines to blend with others from younger vines for their flagship labels. But an illustrious French producer, unlike most others, can command a high enough price for his outstanding wines to recover the cost of tending vines whose advanced age makes them poor producers (though even among these winegrowers, hundred-year-old vines are a rarity).

For all the praise heaped on, for instance, the silky 1979 Martini Zinfandel, made from the centenarian vines of Monte Rosso, the Martinis have to replace not only these but several blocks of vines—at this and other estates—in their forties, fifties and sixties. They own a far higher proportion of vines over thirty years old than almost any other large producer. "The value of the Martinis' vineyards is not as high as it should be because they are so far behind with their replanting," a San Francisco moneyman clucked disapprovingly, when I inquired about the winery's financial health.

Driving back down the hill with Louis, I consider the heroic range of tasks the family faces. Not only do the Martinis lack the funds to replant vineyards that are too old, but many others that have succumbed to the phylloxera root louse in the new plague that has been spreading through Napa vineyards.

These are Carolyn and Mike's problems more than Louis's, even though he is still chairman of the board, is party to all important decisions, and supervises the running of the vineyards. I wonder about the winemaker I have yet to meet.

"Is Mike much like you?" I ask Louis.

"He's much more a people person than I am. He likes production, but he really loves getting out with people. I never did."

I say I have been told that the three generations of winemaking Martini men have made markedly different styles of wine—that Louis's, the vintages between 1954 and 1976, are softer and more rounded than the "huge tannic monsters" his father made before him, and that Mike's, from 1977 onwards, are stylistically a sort of half throwback to his grandfather's.

"Well, Mike does make them heavier and more tannic than I would. Yeah. All of his red wines he makes on a heavier basis than I do."

Yet he is generous in praising the best results of his son's work, singling out a 1987 Napa Valley Reserve Cabernet as "really very, very good."

I say I have heard that some of his grandfather's drive and determination have come through in Mike—and perhaps some of his aggression, too.

"Well, Mike—if he were left on his own, he would be very aggressive. He would be a lot of good things but a lot of not so good things because he has a tendency to jump into something without thinking it out first. He doesn't have the experience to think about a backup position. Supposing it doesn't work, then what do you do? Maybe people stop buying a certain brand of wine—or supposing the government gets after you for something or other. You know, there are so many variables."

"Was your father like that?"

"No. He would move more slowly."

"Like waiting five years to put in the bottling line."

"Yeah. Right. For instance, if we had suddenly stopped expanding when we bought the bottling line, we'd have had a pretty expensive piece of equipment sitting there and no way to pay for it. And of course, I'm a little that way, too."

We wander off the subject of the winery and family for a while and discuss the difficulty of bringing up children, especially small boys, who seem to get into more trouble.

When his children were very young, Louis says, he once made a picnic table out of an old water tank. He sanded and varnished it and put it away in a basement.

"Well, one day I go and look at it and here's these saw marks all around the damn table. Sure enough! Mike had taken the saw—he was about five years old—and had gone around sawing here and sawing there." Even now, there's an unmistakable note of exasperation in his laugh.

"It's a wonder they don't saw off an arm or a leg when they get hold of tools like that," I say.

"Oh, not *theirs!*" he says acidly. "Another time, Mike was younger—about three, I guess, and I was at the winery and I get this call from Carolyn. Now Carolyn—ever since she was a little girl, has been quite composed. And she called up and said, 'Daddy, are you busy?' And I says, well, depends upon what you want. And she said, 'Well, can you come home?' And I says, what for? She says, 'Mike just set the sofa on fire.' So I tore home and it was kind of smoldering and I drug it outside and put out the fire. He didn't do much damage, but later it would have started flaming."

I see that in family businesses, people are apparently assigned their roles from infancy—Mike's being that of a reckless, heedless daredevil. I don't think I would like this pigeonholing myself. On the other hand, I reflect, I might be prepared to put up with a lot for a business that kept me out of cities and in the landscape through which we are passing.

Acacia trees heavy with raindrops and yellow blossoms lean into the road. Balletic white-tailed deer mincingly escape colliding with Louis's wagon. Glistening newborn lambs suggest rare black pearls set in verdure. The beauty about us is magnificently overwrought.

*   *   *

240

"The problem with working in a family business is that we've grown together and we have these stigmas from childhood. They play right into your professional lives and you can't help it," Mike Martini sighs amid the confusion of pronouns. He is dressed in a turquoise blue and white Hawaiian shirt printed with palm trees that conjures up beaches and warm water, and his manner never departs from folksy California bonhomie—but he's delivering a tirade all the same. "The result is tremendous communication blocks between me and Carolyn simply because we're siblings, you know. She's not willing to listen to me; I'm not willing to listen to her.

"She wants to dominate and run things and she's my big sister, but *I'm not going to have her run my life!* I'm makin' the wine, you know, and she has no concept of that—"

"But she admits that," I say, springing to her defense (a big sister myself). He appears not to have heard me.

"—and I don't have any respect for her when she tries to control a process she knows nothing about, has no education in! And besides, she's administratively trained, but she's not managerially trained. She is not a people person. And she has no flexibility. Now, guys work for me because we're a team of people that go out and produce a product. I like making wine. I'm like you—I do *not* want to be a manager!" he says.

I have told him that, unlike Carolyn, my experience of being an eldest child put me off the idea of being responsible for or managing anyone for the rest of my life.

"But she doesn't see it that way," he continues. "She just has this need to boss—an A type of personality. A classic A type of personality. And I'm much more of a C. A-type individuals are usually pessimistic and very vertical thinkers and so they don't allow themselves to feel and stuff. The C-type, people-oriented individuals are very optimistic and have a tendency to go forward and are usually very horizontal thinkers—much freer with ideas and variations on a theme to get to an end point.

"See, the classic difference between me and Carolyn would be Carolyn standing there telling me why we can't actually do something. So I say, here's an idea! here's an idea! here's an idea! I know I drive her *crazy* with all my ideas, so I throw a coupla hundred ideas at her and she'll shoot all but maybe one or two down. As soon as I open my mouth I get my case jumped on. So I stop giving her ideas. So then we have a barrier in communication."

He pauses and, perhaps because I look as stunned by his outburst as I feel, adds, "See, managerially, she has some very good ideas. She's been studying management, and she's a very bright lady and so on. But C-type personalities have a real hard time with her type."

He's the same height as his father, six foot four, husky, whiskery, ruddy-complexioned, has curly gray and blond hair and searching bright blue eyes that sometimes have a wild light in them. He's seated peacefully enough in his chair beside me at the restaurant where we are lunching but, as he talks about his sister, I have a fleeting mental image of a grizzly bear in full charge. He studies my reactions to what he says intently—unlike Carolyn and Louis, who demonstrate little interest in anyone else's opinion of them.

But, exactly like his father and sister, Mike, as a teenager, had absolutely no ambition related to working in the family winery. His childhood, he says, was not idyllic. Whereas most children of Napa winery owners were sent to schools a long way from the valley, he and his brother and sisters attended local establishments and suffered mild persecution by envious schoolmates. He was frequently taunted for being "a Martini," and then beaten up. Then there was the burden of having his parents constantly remind him that anything he did "reflected on the business and our label, because our name was on that label! And I resented it totally because it was not my choice."

He enrolled at Fresno State University—first, to study oenology, because of what he insists was a mindless assumption that that was what he should do. But his two years at Fresno coincided with the youthquake of the 1960s: contagious rebellion was in the air. On reflection, he found he had absolutely no interest in oenology. He switched majors five times without any sense of direction. He admits he was less interested in any course of study than in the Dionysian pursuits of the day.

Abruptly, in 1969, he served in the air force. He was posted to Germany and England. After his discharge, "I didn't wanna go to school or work in the winery and get pressured into anything, so that's when I went up to Nevada." By then, he was in love with an Englishwoman who did not enjoy living in American ranch country, so he brought her down to Napa at the end of a year and married her.

He was helping at the winery, working the mechanical harvesters, when he began to think about the job of a winemaker. It struck him that, actually, it had many attractions, creativity and travel among them. During this same harvest, a senior manager working under Louis told Mike his father was depressed—felt he had been holding the fort for his children pointlessly, because none of them showed any interest in joining the firm. The conversation decided Mike. He would go to the university at Davis and put in the four years it took to earn a degree in fermentation science (which includes oenology).

By the time he got the job of winemaker at Martini in 1977, Carolyn had relinquished her career as a librarian and was helping Louis run the winery. As Mike sees it, but for his return, the winery would have gone the way of the dodo. "To Dad, Carolyn's fine, and to Carolyn, Dad's her hero"—and their mutual admiration, according to Mike, compounded their biases and deficiencies and blinded them to the parlous state of things.

It wasn't just that the Martinis—who had long specialized in red wines—missed the white wine boom of the mid-1970s that had swollen the coffers of their Napa neighbors. Through the decade, the winery had continued to put out much the same wines in much the same style that Louis had made since the 1950s and 1960s. In the mid-1970s, a critic described the wines as "rarely exceptional" but "always priceworthy" and, until then, these characterizations hadn't hurt. But suddenly, the growing numbers of American wine drinkers wanted their taste buds titillated by exciting, unfamiliar flavors and they had begun to be intrigued by the idea of a quest for the extraordinary and excellent in winemaking, and its results. Some of them knew enough to want wines made with classic French techniques and tools, and to scorn the New World improvisations on which the Martinis relied.

Whenever Mike suggested to Carolyn that these changes in the marketplace called for a revolution at Martini, "she sort of said, well, Dad made the wine for all those years and you don't know what you're talkin' about. You're just a stupid brother!"

But in addition to his training at Davis, Mike had had other experiences that showed him his father's shortcomings as a winemaker. In 1981, for instance, he took an educational group tour of Bordeaux and Burgundy led by André Tchelistcheff. "To André, wine is a living creature, and I adore my dad, but he's a mechanic. He just doesn't have that sense about it."

In joint tastings organized by wineries for wine drinkers in California and all across the country, he tells me, "I'd stand there for tasting after tasting and nobody would come to our table and taste the wines because they were out of vogue, out of everything!" He insisted that Carolyn and Louis travel to more tastings and see this for themselves, but even when she did, he felt his sister listened to but did not hear the common criticisms of the wines.

Life at the winery became unbearable for Mike. Not only were sales declining in the early 1980s but "everybody seemed to be fightin' with everybody else." His and Carolyn's younger siblings, Peter and Patty, were also working for the family at the time—she in accounting, while he helped with marketing and sales-related tasks. Eventually these two would leave to make careers outside the winery and wine, but in Mike's first few years with the company, Martinis were tripping over each other, quarreling bitterly. "Nobody was addressing the important issues. I was trying to improve the wines and getting nothing but blocked. They wouldn't let me get oak, they wouldn't let me get grapes . . ." He trails off: sparks in his eyes speak eloquently of remembered anger and frustration.

Then, rather like the disconsolate hero of a fairy tale in his darkest hour, Mike found a rescuer. A marketing consultant employed by the family took his side in his disagreement with his father and sister about the need for a change in the style of the wines. In 1988, she advised him that the only way to convert Louis and Carolyn to his point of view was to have a panel of experts taste the Martini wines and comment on them. She helped him select and invite the group, whose members included André Tchelistcheff and the wine writer Bob Thompson. Carolyn and Louis and a winemaker working under the family's direction were present when the distinguished tasters "just sat down and tore apart" the wines, powerfully supporting all of Mike's complaints.

But even after the critics had tut-tutted over the wines tasting too strongly of the redwood tanks in which they were fermented, Carolyn and Louis resisted loosening the purse strings for a conversion to oak. So one day, Mike assembled Carolyn and Louis and Peter and Patty for a blind tasting at which he served three wines: a luscious Chardonnay from a winery called Morgan owned by a friend of his; a Martini Chardonnay; the Morgan Chardonnay doctored with a bit of sap he had surreptitiously scraped off the outside of a redwood tank. His tasters correctly identified and praised the Morgan wine, but erred in guessing that both of the other wines were their own. Mike confessed his ruse. "I just said, here's your proof! That was the only way to get through to 'em."

Actually, he had been sneaking in small numbers of French and American oak barrels for some wines soon after he took charge of the winemaking in 1977. He had unobtrusively introduced dozens of other minor technical changes even before his coups with the expert tasting and the redwood sap in 1988. In the middle of that decade, he had persuaded Louis and Carolyn to accelerate the jettisoning of the last of the generic jug wines from the winery's line. The Martini range of varietal wines was severely pruned, so that over two thirds of production now consists of Cabernet Sauvignon, Chardonnay and Merlot wines.

As the 1980s wore on the wine press began to single out Mike's wines for praise. His 1987 Monte Rosso Cabernet won a rating of 93—"outstanding"—on *The Wine Spectator*'s scale. It was described by the magazine as "very ripe and rich" and the finest Martini Cabernet for nearly twenty years.

Even in the economic recession of the early 1990s, there were clear signs that the family had been making the right moves. *The New York Times*, in a report in 1992, included Martini among large wineries that had been selling more wine than the year before—even though Americans had been buying less wine for the seventh year in a row.

Talking to Mike, I tell him I am much struck by his having had to resort to shock tactics and subterfuge to get his arguments across— even in the intimacy of a family business. He insists that, on the contrary, they were essential *because* Martini is a family winery.

*   *   *

For all Mike's relishing of his role as the family dissident, he is unmistakably a Martini, too much so to save it from what seems inevitable—a classic third-generation unraveling of his grandfather's legacy.

At our lunch, I notice signs of the second and third generations' preference for hiding their light beneath a grapevine. Though there are Martini wines on the list at this restaurant, Mike, like his father, makes a point of ordering someone else's wine. It is usual for Napa winery owners to make a great fuss about ordering their own.

When I ask about his future plans for the family wines he says he will be guided by what buyers of quality wines like to drink. It is usual for winery owners and winemakers to say they have a California equivalent of Mouton-Rothschild or Pétrus in mind.

He tells me how much he likes entertaining people and cooking for them. For moments, he sounds decidedly un-Martini and more like a trendy "foodie," describing how he likes to barbecue chicken. "You take garlic and rosemary and pancetta and chop it all up and put it under the skin of the chicken. Then you—I was at a chef's convention and a chef gave me this idea—you take a bottle of Chardonnay and put a bunch of herbs in it and you sprinkle the chicken with it. And then you take a bunch of oak chips and put 'em in Chardonnay and put 'em in as smokers in the barbecue pit to get, you know, the oak? . . ."

Being gregarious and extroverted and creative, I say, surely he would be good at marketing, if he chose to take on that task for the winery? After all, if he did, Martinis might keep more of the profits trickling away to their marketing agent. He gives me a look of bearish astonishment and shakes his head firmly.

"No. Because the *science* of management—I'm just not interested in sitting down logically to tackle it. See, I'm a basic horizontal thinker wandering across here and there. Vertical thinking is the logical, straight-down-the-line progression of thought, and I've been trained to do it, but it's an effort."

Yet it is soon clear that there are other reasons. He complains about winemakers being used as marketing tools—image-makers—for wineries. "This marketing of the wine-*maker*, more than the product, has made winemakers' lives miserable! Most of the winemakers

I know do not want to be on the road doing all the promotional stuff they do.

"There's lots of other things I like to do. I'd like to know my kids. I'd like to go skiing, scuba-diving and all this other stuff."

Because of the vending of winemakers' personalities, precisely because winemakers are seen more and more as a winery's most critical asset, Mike takes a dim view of his future. "It's been made very clear to me that the winery can't sell if I don't go with it. I'm trapped! Say we sell this thing and make a billion dollars. I can't go out and spend it."

He sounds just like Carolyn, telling me about her exhaustion, her longing to lay down her burden and rest. So much for *la dolce vita*.

Fatigue is one reason for the family's on-again-off-again wish to sell the winery. I consider the mighty struggle that Carolyn and Mike face at the winery after three taxing years in their private lives. Mike went through a bitter divorce, cared for his children alone for two years, and then remarried. Carolyn had her second son only two years ago, at the age of forty-two.

To stay in wine, the Martinis must be prepared to fight an unequal battle for years to come. Their Napa competitors alone include wineries with multinational monsters for parents—Beringer, for instance, owned by the Swiss giant Nestlé, or Beaulieu, owned by Grand Metropolitan of Britain.

Like other Napa winery owners, the family has found banks reluctant to lend it money to replant vineyards devastated by phylloxera. Napa land values that seemed as if they would go on roaring upwards forever in the last decade have been falling in this one, partly reflecting the oversupply of wine and the recession of the early 1990s.

"We can't sell even one of our seven vineyards for anywhere near its true potential worth," Mike says morosely. Among other reasons, the family would like to be able to sell some of its land to give Peter and Patty Martini cash for their shares of the company—to help them with the new lives outside the winery they have been trying to build.

Mike's frustration with the family's inability to do as it wishes has led him to change his mind about the position he took in Napa's critical political battle of the 1980s—in which the victors succeeded in preserving the county's winegrowing region exclusively for agriculture, and barring all nonagricultural development, until 2020.

In the heat of the debate Mike, like Louis, had supported the freeze. But he finds its consequences hard to live with. Once the land was no longer in danger from property developers seeking to make it a long-distance bedroom community for San Francisco, its rate of appreciation began to decline.

The family's liquidity crisis has led him to reason that since Napa is already altered almost beyond recognition, old-timers would be better off without the development ban, which makes it harder for them to sell out and resettle in simpler, sleepier, faraway farming communities resembling Napa twenty-five years ago. "You have to accept change. If you fight it, you're gonna mess yourself up. What's logical for this valley now is to have these new people move in. Let's face it, the agrarian lifestyle I grew up with isn't here anymore. It's the most cosmopolitan place in the world."

For all his feverish rationalizing, the decision to sell for the right price has been torturous for him, as for other Martinis. Battle-weary though he and his sister may be, every member of the family told me that the older of Mike's two daughters, twelve-year-old Jessica, rattles on merrily about doing her aunt Carolyn's job someday.

At first I wonder at my keen dismay over the likelihood that the winery will not be there for Mike's daughter when she grows up. Then I realize that it has something to do with my discovery, a few years ago, of the miraculous possibilities of actively practicing vicariousness—as a sort of minor mental discipline. Nothing I lacked could ever make me feel miserably deprived as long as I knew someone I liked who had what I didn't. I realized I was hoping, when I met the Martinis, that perhaps I would always know them—and so come closer in my imagination than I ever could in life to being born to a family with roots reaching deep into California countryside dear to me. I liked their having the quintessentially Italian knack for fighting furiously yet keeping their bonds intact.

I felt this was much too fey a train of thought to describe to any Martini. But at a juncture in my long talk with Mike, our conversation took a curious turn. He said there was absolutely no outside pressure for the family to sell the winery. Quite the contrary. "Most of the industry is rooting for us to stay and keep going."

One day, he said, he was chatting with the owner of another Napa winery—a relative newcomer, who used to be a lawyer—who confided that as a student at Berkeley, he had made a ritual of driving to Napa every weekend to buy a bottle of jug wine at the Martini winery.

"He liked what he saw so much that he decided to come up and build his own winery someday. And what I later discovered is that it was the old family wineries like ours that got many of these new people started.

"The old family winery was the dream they were seeking. And us staying here means that dream is still alive. By us going, *they* lose part of *their* dream."

CHAPTER NINE

Schramsberg: Carrying On

> Land is the basis of an aristocracy, which clings to the soil which supports it; for it is not by privileges alone, nor by birth, but by landed property handed down from generation to generation that an aristocracy is constituted.
>
> *Democracy in America*,
> ALEXIS DE TOCQUEVILLE

A POWERFULLY EVOCATIVE HOUSE stands on the first estate in America to make champagne that connoisseurs rank with the world's finest.

Picture a wide Victorian facade painted cream, dominated by a vast veranda that overlooks a jungle of greenery from which perhaps half a dozen lissome palm trees stretch skyward. At the jungle's edge the land drops away abruptly in a canyon-side on which giant cacti as well as fig, eucalyptus and oak trees thrive lustily.

Each time I return to the house at Schramsberg, images of other houses like it overlay and fuzz the picture. I see uniformed, turbaned bearers from Indian years-ago float back and forth across the veranda, carrying melodious trays of drinks: the scene might easily be Victorian Simla, the old summer capital of the Raj. When I approach the front stairs, I half expect a reception of chilly formality by a memsahib as pale as ivory.

One evening I am a guest at a dinner party at this place, the home of Jack and Jamie Davies. People who have directed me to them all marvel at the stubbornness that compelled these two to pioneer, in America, the making of champagne by the classic and exacting *méth-*

ode champenoise, when experts advised that the results would hardly be worth the candle. A form of madness like romantic infatuation carried this pair past all such obstacles to their plan—past the most glaringly obvious obstacle, that neither of them had ever made wine or formally studied winemaking.

They were urbanites who acted on their yearning for a different life, a life of passionate fulfillment, and so migrated to Napa from Los Angeles—he from an existence as a high-ranking, Harvard-educated big-company executive and she, an "interesting" corporate wife who had been part-owner of a small art gallery.

Frenchmen from Champagne still shrug disparagingly about even the best of the competition from California. But they can only shrug, too, about the irony that the Davieses' success exerted an irresistible pull on every *maison de champagne* of note. Twenty-five years after Jack and Jamie began, far from being able to recline on their laurels, they lose sleep worrying about holding their own against giant French rivals that have bought Californian vineyards and have begun to make sparkling wine nearby. Certain wine critics have taken to proclaiming that these copycats have surpassed the Davieses' much praised blends in refinement and delicacy.

But Jack and Jamie have persisted with their lusher, fuller-bodied style of winemaking and spurned countless offers to take Schramsberg off their hands—because they hope to be able to pass the business on to their three sons.

Family feeling is deepened by the handing down of land, the incisive Tocqueville said, over a century ago: "The family represents the estate, the estate the family, whose name, together with its origin, its glory, its power, and its virtues, is thus perpetuated in an imperishable memorial of the past and a sure pledge of the future." He predicted that Americans would find it hard to repeat this old European pattern, but it was primarily the wish to bequeath just such a legacy that led Jack and Jamie to buy Schramsberg.

Assuming that the winery continues to prosper, for this latter-day bid for landedness—no less than for a farm family many generations old—the ability to carry on will hinge chiefly on whether the Davies children are up to the job and can get on with one another.

All of this seems far from certain when I meet the children, still in their twenties—untested and unsure of themselves and of how they will negotiate the way ahead. So Jack and Jamie's labors at Schramsberg on their behalf are, truly, acts of faith.

People stand around chatting comfortably before we sit down to dinner. Jamie leads me to John, her second son, who looks less like one of the "wild Davies boys" of local legend than the golden youth you'd expect from the sheen of privilege that surrounds champagne. He stands beside the piano neatly dressed in a dark green linen blazer, fair hair short and sleek: the quizzical blue eyes boring into me arrest prejudicial thoughts about the dullness and predictability of young men in their mid-twenties reared in clover.

He directs our conversation. He names a string of famous wine writers and asks if I have met any of them. He smiles faintly, gaining confidence each time I shake my head no. One of them, he says, is especially good, and I should make an effort to meet him.

"But of course, he's a switch-hitter," says John.

"What's that?" I ask, amused. Am I to be subjected to an analysis of this man's talents as a baseball player?

He looks almost unbearably delighted by the question. "It means he likes boys as well as girls," he says, leaning closer, practically pop-eyed in his anxiousness not to miss the finest shade of my reaction. "That's the only unfortunate thing about him."

I see that his intense desire to shock comes not from any common species of rebelliousness but, principally, from assumed arch-conservatism.

"I think we all agree that the valley's been ruined," he continues, sipping at his Schramsberg bubbly with an air of contained rage. At first I am sympathetic. I think of Napa's principal artery, Highway 29, often so dense with traffic that on a hot summer day a grape grower anxious to get a gondola of grapes to a winery can wait a temper-fraying twenty minutes to cross it. He wishes he could turn the clock back twenty years to the time before it became "a magnet for people with really bad taste—mostly from New York and Los Angeles." They arrive, build their architectural "monstrosities," find the pace isn't fast enough for them, "and leave us these things we have to look at." As villains, this breed of newcomer may only be outranked by the Europeans, "whose attitude is, we're doing you all a great favor by teaching you how to live better."

I think: he is surely too bright to be oblivious of his own family's status as late arrivals—by the lights of, say, Dagmar de Pins Sullivan of Beaulieu or the Martini clan. John was a year old when Jamie and Jack and their elder son, Bill, moved up from Los Angeles, only in the mid-1960s. Better to listen to him and say nothing, I decide.

It seems his disapproval of those who came after the Davieses has philosophical underpinnings. He detests the idea of a melting-pot society. "You have your best chance of maintaining a particular way of life if you come from similar backgrounds." Since it must be as clear to him as to anyone else that he is speaking to a melting-pot of a person, I cringe inwardly. Outwardly I observe him, unblinking, only spurring him to greater provocation. He says he doesn't believe in "one of the basic components of the Declaration of Independence, that all men are created equal. I don't think that everyone should have the right to vote, or that people who can't afford them should be allowed to have six or seven children." He seems well aware that his button nose and expression of seraphic innocence make his opinions more startling—that, even so, I am finding it hard to take him seriously.

The tide of the party threatens to separate us. We set a date for continuing our conversation over breakfast on another day. Jack takes me in hand. A bespectacled, square-jawed man with iron-gray hair, he combines a precise professorial manner with a gruff directness, bordering on fierceness, a bit like an irascible old general. He introduces me to a couple with whom I exchange chitchat of the standard Napa variety. Yes, I have visited the valley before. How long have they lived here? It is indeed beautiful. Yes, I've heard that people have begun to get marvelous results with Merlot.

Talking to these two, I am free to keep wondering about the Davieses. I try to estimate the extent of Jack and Jamie's remove from their old lives. Watching them coast serenely between knots of guests it's plain that they are hosts by vocation. I can easily imagine them giving parties like this one in San Francisco and down in southern California, where they lived before, but the context is so different. If they were still in yoke as just a large-corporation-couple-with-a-difference, they would be defined by the decor of their house, the make of luxury car they chose to drive, their last exotic holiday and how the new exhibition at Jamie's gallery was faring. They would be another prosperous, upper-middle-class pair bereft of binding ties to any particular place, their identities mutable.

In Napa they are part of a sort of community even if, as Jamie has assured me, it no longer includes everyone who resides here: as the population has swollen, the valley has splintered into miniature subcommunities. There are other ways in which their new life is a dramatic departure from the old. Planting green growing things in earth brings people closer to rootedness, in the American West, in a way no other occupation—or provenance—can. And then, in this existence, in this room, the Davieses' guests are drinking something their hosts have wrought themselves—forged, like nearly all good art, from a struggle to be able to make it at all.

I wonder: if John is at all typical of the children of Napa's lifestyle émigrés, must one assume that their offspring tend to become romantic reactionaries? That the ownership of elegant country estates begets fantasies of neofeudalism—a wish for a new agri-gentry isolated behind high walls of wealth, privilege and, eventually, lineage?

I feel that if nothing else did, this oddly mesmerizing house must weaken the family's sense of connectedness to the rest of the modern world—just as it casts a spell of dislocation over some of its visitors. Halfway through the evening, I begin to identify the emotions wrestling to dominate me as relief at finding no tiresome memsahibs, and disappointment at the lack of fireflies, crickets and the trappings and pungent, cloying, sometimes putrid, smells and scents of India.

Yet, paradoxically, to Schramsberg applies that rarest of adjectives for Napa architecture: authentic. Like San Francisco's Italianate-Victorian mansions, it was simply built in the style of its day.

It comes as a shock when Jamie says she hates the color fuchsia. Or at least it does, the second time we meet. She is only slightly over five feet tall with a porcelain-like delicacy of form and build.

Evidence of passionate intensity in her startles because everything about her speaks of extreme restraint and refinement—more English than American. In Napa's scorching summers she dresses in white stockings, tailored skirts and white linen blouses, all cut with as much care as her cap of straw-blond and gray curls. The fine skin stretched over the impeccably ordered bones of her face looks barely touched by the sun. Her eyes are outlined in bright blue by a steady hand, her chiseled lips colored deep pink. She talks in complete sentences, the conversational equivalent of sound, considered prose.

Her opinion of fuchsia is part of an explanation of her and Jack's monumental obsession with keeping Schramsberg pretty much as it was when Jacob Schram—a wandering barber turned pioneer winemaker—built the house in 1875. When the Davieses bought it in 1965, they took on the work of restoring the house, which was collapsing, of returning the grounds to their original, quasi-civilized state and snatching back the vineyards from forest. All had been neglected by intervening owners after Schram's descendants sold out in 1921. Through their labors, the Davieses' guiding philosophy was that only changes for which there was a pressing need should be made, and that the past and present should fuse invisibly.

Fuchsia is the color of a peony that, so far as Jamie knows, has been reappearing beside the big veranda for every spring since Schram's day. That, she feels, is reason enough for it to be left undisturbed.

The same reasoning is behind the long-running battle she and Jack have fought to preserve the narrow, meandering approach to the main house and offices from the highway. It is just under a mile long and about twelve to fourteen feet wide; on both sides of it, the trees and brush press close together and lean into the road, their leaves and branches casting intricate traceries of light and shade below. Now and again, local county officials insist that the road must be widened to accommodate a car and a fire truck simultaneously.

Each time the issue is raised, Jamie reads to them in her unexpectedly dry, firm voice, from a fragment of world literature elevated in Napa to biblical status because the place's history is so short, its historical records scanty. The book is *The Silverado Squatters*, Robert Louis Stevenson's mini-travelogue about the part of his honeymoon he spent in Napa in 1880—in which he records his visit to the Schram household. Each time, Jamie manages to persuade the county that there is something to be treasured in the close coincidence between the approach as it is today and Stevenson's record of it in *The Silverado Squatters*:

> Some way down the valley below Calistoga, we turned sharply to the south and plunged into the thick of the wood. A rude trail rapidly mounting . . . on all sides a bower of green and tangled thicket, still fragrant and still flower-bespangled . . . through all this we struggled toughly upwards, continually switched about the face by sprays of leaf or blossom.

The Scottish scribbler also described the house that Jacob Schram built:

> . . . his place is the picture of prosperity: stuffed birds in the veranda, cellars dug far into the hillside, and resting on pillars like a bandit's cave: all trimness, varnish, flowers and sunshine, among the tangled wildwood.

The birds at Schramsberg are no longer stuffed. Half a dozen emerald-headed mallard ducks gravely waddle through the grounds like a papal procession. But there are stuffed—and faintly battered—children's toys on the veranda, next to the white-wicker peacock chairs.

Inside the house, there is no trace of professional decorator chic. The drawing room has a high ceiling, large, old-fashioned wire screen windows and doors; a few more dark corners and rather less light than generally considered desirable today. There is an antique French ormolu wall clock in a corner; an arrangement of blue snapdragons and purple hydrangeas rests on the piano; red roses in a pewter jug on the mantelpiece. There are bits of blue and white Chinese pottery and a Persian rug in pink, black and palest blue. Ordinarily, I think of Victorian interiors as oppressive and confining. At Schramsberg, I see that they were meant to be cocooning, sheltering, reassuring.

The Davieses do seem to belong here, but not in a scuffed-slippers-and-dressing-gown sort of way. Nor do they radiate the presumption of entitlement to elegance of people born to riches; nor do they have anything remotely nouveau or arriviste about them.

I decided, on my first visit to Schramsberg, that they were probably from cosseted, middle-class backgrounds and was astonished when I learned that this was not so. Kindly and frank as they are, they make me restless—because they themselves seem always to be, literally or figuratively, seated on the edge of their chairs. They seem less like the lord and lady of Schramsberg than like dedicated caretakers and preservers of its history, its ambience, its essence.

A highly selective admission of the new is also absolutely germane to Jack and Jamie's success in a style of winemaking little changed since its invention, probably, by the seventeenth-century monk Dom Pérignon.

In a time when the institution of marriage often seems hopelessly decrepit, Jack and Jamie would be insufferable if they were the least bit smug about their good fortune in being partners. They tell me separately and without ado that they think alike and need to say little to communicate. So there was a nearly effortless interweaving of lives and ambitions after they met in San Francisco in 1959, when Jack was thirty-five and Jamie twelve years younger.

Jamie's childhood in Pasadena, at that time a small town in southern California, had predisposed her towards a life of hard work and accomplishment set apart from the herd. Her mother died when she was eight and her elder sister, Dallas, just ten, and their stern puritanical father—a "hometown lawyer" (and later, judge) of German descent, who had been brought up in an orphanage in Iowa—rigidly required that the girls do all their housekeeping chores on time.

"As a little girl, I had wanted to operate as an independent person," she tells me on a choking-hot August afternoon on which we have taken refuge in the shadowy Schramsberg drawing room. She sits bolt upright and, though obviously exhausted, does not go in search of a cold drink or kick off her shoes, as I long to do myself. "I always felt I was much more in charge of my life than my peers. I'd experienced a lot more than they had," she says.

Her late teens and early twenties were a model for a constructive rebellion. She enrolled to study history at Berkeley, a "Commie" school to her father—where he never once visited her, on principle. After college and a year as a schoolteacher, she stepped up her revolt against him. She signed on for courses in driftwood sculpture and painting in the beguiling, then-bohemian seaside town of Carmel, where it struck her that the local artists were much too far from prospective buyers of their work. One day, she and a friend filled their cars with borrowed paintings and set off for San Francisco. They started an art gallery that grew and flourished and was reincarnated in various forms, and made them minor celebrities.

It was about then that Jamie met Jack, a close friend of her boyfriend at the time. At a dinner party at Jack's, a mere block from her own apartment on Telegraph Hill, she was pleasantly surprised. Unlike most good-looking men she had met, he did not seem vain and self-absorbed. And, "he had oil paintings on his walls, which was unusual. He had obviously chosen them himself, and some of them were by artists whose work we carried in the gallery." She doesn't say so, but I imagine that other facets of Jack, like his punctiliousness and conservatism, reminded her of a father of whom she was extremely fond—her mutiny notwithstanding.

Jack was a senior executive in an aluminum company—cut far adrift from his original dream of a career in sound effects and recording. That had had two promptings: a love of music and of "performing." His family moved from the South Side of Chicago to Beverly Hills in his second year in high school—when his father, a salesman, lost his job to the Depression. Jack's hope of a career in entertainment developed from a strong romantic streak—a legacy both of his mother's family, from the American South, and his father's Welsh forebears. As a child, he enjoyed public speaking and was an amateur magician and puppeteer.

He worked in a Hollywood sound studio after high school. After that, the Second World War interrupted his education in radio speech at Northwestern University. The road he took when peace broke out was less adventurous but also more demanding intellectually. He studied economics at Stanford, took a degree in business administration at Harvard, then proved himself a manager in a speedy ascent up the ladder in aerospace, aluminum—and later—packaging companies.

In his first encounter with Jamie he saw more than a fragile-looking twenty-four-year-old with a startling, incandescent smile. He saw a woman of ironclad determination and a natural entrepreneur, like himself. They married only months after they met and, soon after, Jack's new job in a packaging firm obliged them to move to Los Angeles. Jamie sold her art business: "I didn't give it a thought. Those were the days when you just followed your man." Her voice is raspy with sincerity—as if she is used to countering skepticism about this.

But it's a misleading insistence, because—as she herself observes—theirs was not the most conventional marriage. In brooding over possibilities for a small business that he longed to create, Jack "was very open to the idea of including me—which wasn't exactly commonplace at the time," she says. I point out that it is rare even today, and she nods and smiles.

Even before they moved to southern California, the seed of inspiration for the Schramsberg phase of their lives had been sown at a Dionysian lunch from which they returned at two in the morning. They had found models for a possible future in their hosts. Martin and Eleanor Ray owned a tiny but prestigious winery in the hills of Saratoga, near San Jose. He had a reputation as a cantankerous eccentric—had abandoned a career as a San Francisco stockbroker for wine.

The Rays were looking for twenty couples to co-invest in their vineyards. Jack and Jamie became one of them and, even after their resettlement in Los Angeles, returned to spend weekends in the Rays' guest cottage and observe and help a little with the work of the winery.

Jamie says she always had a keen interest in food. Even as a child, she had enjoyed taking over at the stove. She and Jack had found they loved the shared job of imaginative entertaining, and experimenting with exotic recipes. "And there seemed to be a natural link to wine."

The most successful Napa winery owners tend to have something of the hail-fellow-well-met charm of innkeepers. Jack's confidence and pleasure in being a host (part-magician; part-puppeteer) come from his aunt Tami Lue from Tennessee—his mother's sister, a milliner—who, when he was a child, lived in Los Angeles and took charge of security in the wardrobe department of Paramount Studios. Jamie tells me Jack caught the train from Chicago to spend several summers in a row alone with Tami Lue. She always bought him a little white suit so that he could help her entertain at home or tag along to her dinners with men friends.

About his attraction to Napa, Jack himself has told me: "I think wine struck me as a very individualistic way to make something—to sort of run up the flag and say, here it is!"

He persuaded a college friend to be a silent partner in Schramsberg—to match his own investment of $40,000 with an equivalent amount, and that was Schramsberg's seed capital.

One of the three Davies boys told me he was a Republican who only disagreed with the party line on environmental protection. But he didn't want to be identified with this scruple in print. I asked why not. "Because people will think I'm some kind of flower child—a throwback to the 1960s," he said disdainfully.

I found his parents nearly as leery of being identified as back-to-the-land romantics. Though the air was dense with this atavistic sentiment in the decade of the Davieses' move to Napa, and though the American bourgeoisie and intelligentsia were by no means immune to it, the attention-getting migrants to agriculture were indeed the peaceful moral anarchists called hippies.

Jack and Jamie emphasize instead that they were in the vanguard of middle-class Americans learning about fine living—of which wine was a part. Some of the men had got some inkling of all they did not know about the good life from serving in Europe in the Second World War. Wine drinking as an everyday indulgence had come as a glorious revelation to them.

But even though they had zeitgeist on their side, it took boldness for the Davieses to sink their savings into Napa. A woman who had grown up mid-valley, around Yountville, in the 1950s and early 1960s, told me it was such a backward place that she and her friends played their games in the middle of main roads and were hardly ever interrupted. A strange car driving by was an event—nearly cause for celebration—she remembered.

Jack and Jamie, convinced that there would be a revival in California winemaking, explored the remnants of the Napa wine boom in the late 1800s. Decaying shells of early wineries stood amidst vineyards largely reannexed by brush and forest. It was among these that, for many months, they sought a base—whenever they could steal time away from Los Angeles. Then a friend thought to take them to see Schramsberg. A single small vineyard survived—one given over to rootstock, or disease-resistant vines used for grafting. Instantly, they both felt they had found that special place that, until then, had eluded description.

The barber-turned-winemaker Jacob Schram had made sparkling wine. But the Davieses did not choose to make champagne to keep a tradition going. They wanted to find a specialization in which they could excel: the neighbors all made still wines.

There are people whose discernment and ability to recognize exceptional quality paralyze them—and then there are others, like Jack and Jamie, who are inspired to emulation. They were not deterred in the least by their own utter inexperience—nor by anyone else's perception of the absurdity of trying to make the drink of Europe's monarchs in rural obscurity on the more primitive of America's coasts; for countrymen whose idea of champagne was a sweet, fizzy concoction—intoxicating Pepsi-Cola—drunk at weddings. They set out to make a dry champagne by the same labor-intensive methods used by the most venerated *maisons de champagne*. Theirs would be aged sparkling wines, all but unheard-of in America, and they would craft these from Pinot Noir and Chardonnay grapes, expensive varietals with distinctive flavors—instead of relying on heavy doses of sugar and other additives to distract palates from a fundamental lack of character.

They came to these decisions on tours they took of the great Champenois estates, on which they made mental notes about flavors they would aspire to replicate. They were most drawn to the styles of the most traditional *maisons*, Roederer, Bollinger and Krug, whose wines tend to be more complex and have more body, and are aged longer. At home in California, they took courses in champagne making from the viticulture and oenology faculty of the University of California at Davis. For help with their very first blends, they hired as a consultant André Tchelistcheff's son, Dimitri—and so, as a bonus, frequently got free advice from André himself. Their trial batch of twenty thousand bottles of champagne in 1965 was made entirely from Chardonnay that had spent two years in oak barrels—not a recipe for sparkling wine that had been tried before in America.

They hired no salesmen at the beginning—indeed, had only one employee for the first two years. Jack himself hopped on airplanes, "with a couple of bottles in a bag," to call on prospective customers. For their debut, the Davieses priced their champagne at $6.25 a bottle, or three times as much as the closest comparable American wine. "From the first vintage, we've sold every bottle we've ever had for sale," Jack tells me, and I feel all but buffeted by the waves of pride surging from him.

In the publicity literature handed out to visitors at Schramsberg—as at other family-owned wineries in Napa—some of the early trials the Davieses survived are described in colorful detail. Apparently, it makes it easier for members of a still-puritanical society to loosen their pursestrings for luxuries when supplied with proof of their manufacturers' persistence, stern work ethic and pioneering derring-do.

Jack and Jamie, when asked what the beginning was like, trot out the same anecdotes repeated in one print profile after another. There's the tale of how, when they were planting the first five of their sixty acres of vines, the rumor flashing around the valley was that they had put the vine cuttings into the ground upside down. Jamie was eight months' pregnant when they moved into the house at Schramsberg, which was in such an advanced state of dilapidation that the Argentinian au pair who came with them excoriated Jack for bringing his wife to such a place. Jack nearly blew himself to pieces, trying to sterilize—with a burning sulfur wick—barrels that had been used to store not wine, as he thought, but brandy. Another time, he passed out from epoxy fumes, repainting the inside of a storage tank. There were also heartening episodes: in the Californian tradition, kindly neighbors helped them avert disaster more than once with timely advice and loans of equipment. And the first phase of their story had a spectacular happy ending: only seven years after they started in business, Richard Nixon made his toast to peace with Schramsberg champagne on his epoch-making visit to China.

The same Schramsberg publicity pack describing the Davieses' travails also contains a genteel manifesto, some of whose highlights are:

The Davies abide by traditional values of family, heritage and environment—the very reasons they went into the wine business.

. . . they wanted to run a business they could control: one in which their family and cultural interests wouldn't be compromised.

The Davies have . . . been prime movers in protecting agricultural zoning and stopping the construction of a freeway that threatened to spoil the Napa Valley.

Jack and Jamie want to pass the Schramsberg legacy on to their sons and grandsons. So far there are no grandchildren, but each of the Davies sons—William, John and Hugh, all in their 20s—is considering the wine business. Two, in fact, are now working in wine marketing for other firms.

This document, too, makes it plain that the Davieses are not merely selling expensive froth. They are giving visitors who make the trek to Schramsberg from days spent nursing Styrofoam coffee cups in impersonal offices a chance to join vicariously in an escape from the regimented, conformist world.

"People like the fact that this place was established in 1862 and is still doing its thing," Jack explains to me one day. "I think people have a feeling about the land—that they sense in farming and agriculture something that goes beyond themselves and the moment.

"I think people want to feel some kind of roots and that the absence of that is a source of trouble. Jamie and I are in some way contributing to a maintenance of . . . " Intensity of feeling stops the flow of words. "A continuation of . . . continuity, and some roots. That is a very, very powerful thing."

In the time I spend with them, I feel that if the Davies boys are to collaborate in carrying on where Jack and Jamie leave off, they will have to find their marked dissimilarities stimulating. These are clear even in the venue each son chooses for a tête-à-tête.

For the breakfast meeting we had planned at his parents' dinner, John picks a narrow, dark, greasy-spoon restaurant in St. Helena where vineyard workers and foremen roar at each other in conversations that seem hideously animated for seven A.M. It's a characteristically careful and shrewd selection: he remembers that I said I am trying to investigate parts of Napa off the well-traveled trails. He is pleased with himself, seeing me look around delightedly.

We order bacon and eggs and hash browns. He says his parents never took it for granted that he and his brothers would want to join Schramsberg someday. "They didn't ever discuss our joining in black-and-white terms—just provided us with the background and opportunities to learn about it. I think they are very happy that more than one, and possibly all three of us, have decided that that's what we'd like to do."

Later, every other member of the family will tell me that the question of how the boys might eventually divide the running of Schramsberg is wide open, but John has it all worked out—and, even as the second son, is unembarrassed about awarding himself the starring role. "I think Hugh could be chief oenologist and take care of the winemaking. Bill could take charge of property and vineyard management. And I could be in charge of sales and marketing," he says smoothly.

But then, with a brilliant, disingenuous grin, he adds, "None of this is carved in stone, of course. So it could get really ugly."

At least the winemaking son might have been chosen long ago if, in the tradition of Napa's long-established families, someone had been packed off to Davis—what West Point is to military clans. But Jamie and Jack had explained that it was important to them that their sons get a broad liberal arts education—or, as Jack put it, "If you come from an urban environment, your children don't go to an agricultural college." They don't see a new life on the land as entailing a relinquishing of one's separate identity. He said that Robert Mondavi, for instance, had told his son Tim, " 'We *need* you to go to Davis.' But Jamie and I feel that when you grow up in a small community, it's important to get experience on the outside."

John tells me that his elder brother, Bill, studied political science at a California polytechnic and at Boston University, where John took a degree in history—as did Hugh, a graduate of Bowdoin College in Maine. Growing up, the closest any of them came to learning about the wine business was in summer jobs both at Schramsberg and at châteaux in France and in Spain. At eighteen, John worked in Cognac, running tastings and giving tours "with a group of old Etonians," at Hennessy Cognac. His favorite European summer, when he and Bill were only eight and ten, was spent with the family that owns Roederer: "Basically, we hung out in a summer house in Normandy and played croquet and ate pheasant," he says with studied nonchalance.

John and I meet yet again, three months later, soon after I pay his parents another visit—on which I discover that they worry about him far more than about their other sons. Learning that I plan to see him in San Francisco, Jamie says, "I hope the atmosphere isn't *too* oppressive." She advises that I "try to laugh *with* him a bit—to lighten him up."

"Now, er . . . about John," I say to Jack hesitatingly. "He struck me as rather . . . well, really extraordinarily right-wing."

"Yes. Almost a fascist," Jack barks promptly, in his peremptory way.

"But how does someone so young turn out like that?"

"He wasn't always, of course," Jack says grimly. "I think that he maybe sees what he considers challenges to a way of life he values— and he finds those challenges unacceptable."

"You mean, like the threat of encroaching development here, and perhaps taxation?"

"Anything that intrudes—in other words, [in Napa] this is a life of very individualistic people. And the challenges of individualism bring out conservatism in people. The common wealth and individualism—they're not the same."

For our lunch in San Francisco, John has decided to impress me. I am invited to his University Club, hard by Nob Hill, on the sort of elemental, blustery day on which the city seems newly risen from the sea depths. Pale platinum light catching the planes of pastel buildings through sheets of rain turns stone and wood vaporous: the briny smells borne on the wind seem far more substantial. John and I take the elevator to the dining room floor and, from the stockbrokerish men seated at the bar, get looks usually directed at fish left out too long. A portly servant of the club whispers in John's ear: red-faced, John tells me we have to leave. He does not explain why, but apologizes handsomely. I later discover, by other means, that I have violated the dress code by appearing in slacks. Still, the purpose of this particular site for a rendezvous has been served. He wants me to appreciate that he belongs in this formal, exclusionary place. Again, he has calculated, correctly, that I'd enjoy looking it over.

We lunch, in the end, at a casual restaurant on Pier 23, where the snub-nosed, doll-like chef, who might easily be John's twin, turns out to be his girlfriend, Leslie.

Everything has gone wrong for him today, he says glumly. His job as a salesman for Gallo, the industrial wine giant—or what his father describes as "the school of hard knocks, for anyone who really wants to learn about marketing"—took him on a call to a disagreeable proletarian restaurant in the East Bay this morning. On the Bay Bridge, a car had overturned, slowing the traffic to a crawl. It's obvious that he is miserable in the famously regimented and authoritarian culture of Gallo.

I ask if he misses Napa.

"Yes of course I miss Napa," he says, glowering faintly. "I miss it very much."

"What do you see yourself doing, over the long term—and where do you think you'll live?"

"Oh, I'd like always to have a place in the city, but I'd like to make my home in Napa."

"Starting when?"

"Starting from when I'm offered a job there."

"Oh."

"Bill asked Dad for a job after he did two years with a public relations company in New York, and got turned down."

"Why?"

"I don't know."

He says that while he himself has never asked for a job at Schramsberg, he finds it "rather incredible" that his younger brother, Hugh, who graduated from college in the summer, had immediately been given a job in production. "Although I think it's great that he's doing it—because that's his interest."

I change the subject and ask what his hobbies are and have been in the past. He mentions riding, lacrosse, squash, archery—and, at present, principally "painting the lead figurines for fantasy role-playing games." No, he snaps at my question, not Dungeons and Dragons. It's a fantasy game he created with help from a group of young men friends—most of them scions of Napa winery owners—that meets at his apartment every Tuesday night. It's designed from sources as diverse as the writings of J. R. R. Tolkien, C. S. Lewis, Isaac Asimov and Arthur C. Clarke. He also "looks up things for the game in the Bhagavad Gita and the Satanic Bible and books on parapsychology."

"I'm the game-master," he says. "I run the game, which has evolved over many years."

He started playing Dungeons and Dragons in his early teens. I ask what attraction this sort of game holds for him now, as an adult. "I work now, and I'm glad to have something that makes me think," he says, a bit despondently. For every five or ten hours of game time, he has to spend between ten and twelve hours on preparation—compiling thick documents to which players refer to get to know the characters they are playing, and where, and when, in an entertainment that is mostly talked through. "You are creating whole worlds and societies, and there's got to be an underlying consistency in those worlds." For each lead figurine, he creates a "character sheet that describes the person's history, lineage, education, ability to withstand disease, ego size and strength, cultural traits, race and class."

For the session later tonight, he has been inventing a world "which on earth would be the Syrian-Babylonian world, where lives revolve around this enormous sea . . . " He continues at some length, eloquently.

I find it all fascinating—an admirable relieving of the *métro-boulot-dodo* tedium of a young businessman's existence, probably plumbing unconscious depths the way an artist might. I don't like John's politics, but I can remember flirting with the extremes myself, in my late teens. I look at his small, delicate hands as he tucks into his Dungeness crab and think: he is far more stimulating company than the average twenty-four-year-old, and with any luck, will someday discover the joys of tolerance and moderation.

I see why Jamie told me she worried about the game triggering in John "a level of excitement just as compelling as a marijuana high." This was worrying for a parent, "because it's a dream world." It was most definitely not the sort of dream she had in mind when, in another chat, she mused aloud, "If my children can't live out their own fantasies, it would be a shame." She is anxious that they should not feel like sacrificial victims of their parents' design for life. "If they chose to do something else, that would be *okay*."

John, my host on Pier 23, makes it obvious that he longs to run real life like his game. I say I have heard from Jack and Jamie that his brother Bill would like to be a cattle rancher out on the range. "But he would very much also like to be at Schramsberg," John says. "One of the great things about Bill having an interest in this is that it's a way for us to preserve the land and a lifestyle we're accustomed to." He'd like Bill to have a ranch in the Napa Valley—on some stretch of land unsuitable for grapes. This seems to me less than practical. I've seen no unused expanse of land in Napa that wouldn't look like a lady's pocket handkerchief in a rancher's eyes. And the valley no more resembles the open range for which Bill yearns than it does the Jardin des Tuileries. "By owning all this land no one will be able to build tract houses and we can preserve it as an agricultural environment," the game-master says confidently, though he concedes that the land is far too expensive for ranching on it to make much sense.

The last customers in the restaurant, we wait for my coffee to arrive. John's girlfriend walks over to our table, kisses him demurely on one cheek, and fixes me with a look telegraphing her opinion that, in my relentless interrogation, I am torturing her beloved. She continues to watch me narrowly, slipping into her raincoat, and then leaves. He says she's from Hillsborough, an opulent suburb south of San Francisco.

I ask him for his opinion of Jack's speculations about what has turned this son of his into a juvenile arch-conservative.

"What do you mean!" he exclaims, blue eyes sparking dangerously. "They *all* are—my dad, Bill and I are all definitely conservative. My mom is, too, but with a lot of humanitarian concerns. Then there's my dad's family. I never knew his parents, but my aunt and grandmother—they minded having to give up their slaves. They owned plantations in the South."

After lunch, after I have driven John where he has asked me to, I remember the genealogical explanation Jack had given me. He said he thought John was a throwback to "his grandfather on Jamie's side. People who create things for themselves tend to come to the conclusion that the world is built up of two kinds of people—builders and users."

*   *   *

Neither Bill nor Hugh is as candid or excitable as John; they are not fire-breathing visionaries. They resemble Jack and Jamie in their individual expressions of self-contained graciousness, revealing relatively little.

I give Hugh an account of the game-master's view of the future. "John thinks . . . big . . . things," he says, drawing out the words humorously. "He pictures this world with all of us involved in—I don't know *what*. But I'm interested in hangin' out. I like to use that pair of words," he says, a little belligerently.

He has chosen to talk to me on the rear porch of his parents' house on a sultry evening on which they are entertaining other visitors in the study. We peep in at the window on our way to the back of the house and catch a glimpse of smiling faces turned our way above glittering champagne glasses. We, however, drink mineral water with ice. Hugh, like most other American twenty-two-year-olds, is uncomfortable with the ceremony of wine drinking: one suspects his contemporaries think it a hobby and indulgence of the prematurely doddery. Actually, I'm glad to be abstemious because this has been one of those days on which I'm reminded of how poorly heat and wine of any sort mix.

Hugh is tall, gangly, coltish, and has curly dark hair. His eyes beam trustingly behind stout-lensed tortoiseshell spectacles. I don't for an instant doubt the sincerity and lack of calculation in his telling me he always goes to Jack for advice in crises and is "fascinated" by his parents.

He admits that he carefully avoids conversations about touchy subjects with his brothers, especially John—because, "talking with him, you express your true feelings and all of a sudden you might get shot down." That Hugh is the family's lone Democrat does not exactly encourage him to open up.

Yet there are grounds for violent agreement between the brothers— since all of them not only bemoan the changes in Napa since their childhoods, but are dedicated to fighting any future defacing of the valley. Hugh says, "This is where my roots are. This place gave me everything I've got. I'd be a lost person if I left it behind me for good."

He got a foretaste of environmental activism earlier in the year in a sojourn in Washington, D.C., in which he worked as an intern for a Democratic senator. He tells me the experience helped him to order his priorities. "The things that bring a smile to my face are not big business, dollar signs, trade bills. These eucalyptus trees, for instance," he says, waving at a glaucous pair standing a few yards away from where we sit. "They just grow, boi*iiii*ng! . . . like, you know, a Jack and the Beanstalk kind of deal. Right there is enough— just a *lot*, to me."

He sees no irreconcilable contradiction between opting to be a Democrat—for the classic reason that "they have a better grip on what life is like for most people"—and helping to manufacture nectar for the affluent.

"We are a family, farming," he says earnestly, his long frame tense with anxiousness to win me over to his point of view. "Being a farmer is just making good use of the land. Other than that, we're simple people trying to make something the best it can be."

Yet he says, only minutes later, "It's a rural community, but it's not removed. It has all kinds of influences from faraway places and I'm *fascinated* by faraway places."

Brother Bill is slim, stocky and the shortest of the Davies brothers— roughly five and a half feet tall. More striking than his stature are his big, pale-lashed, light blue poet's eyes. There's a soft haziness, a remoteness, in them; an expression of someone absorbed in goingson on distant spheres even as he does his best to be present with me.

He is not a conservative cast in John's mold—is seemingly more dove than hawk, and more the nostalgic than the exclusionary kind. Unlike John, he expresses no wish to see the Napa Valley peopled chiefly by people as much like his own family as possible. He says he especially likes the rednecks in Napa; he likes the Mexicans. He likes the old-timers, like the descendants of Italian immigrants, who "don't compete well" in the new, fashionable Napa, and whose involvement in grapes and wine is "a romantic, hobby, personal interest kind of thing."

But, even to these folk, he prefers the rednecks and ranchers of cattle country. If he and his brothers are successful at Schramsberg, he says, he would like to own a ranch in Montana or Wyoming someday. "Cowboys, just like the field-workers in Napa, seem to have a better understanding of what it's all about, even if their range of experience isn't all that great. And there's a different style about cattlemen. They live close to the deer and the wildlife, and close to the land."

Bill himself is an unusually gallant twenty-seven-year-old. Unlike John's, his meditations on the matter of where we should lunch are guided not by my work nor by any sort of self-advertisement, but by his determination to help me feel at home. Since I am British, he has concluded I must be dying for a pasty or a plateful of bangers-and-mash. So, with each of us in our separate trucks, he has led me to the outskirts of Calistoga—to the Lord Derby Arms, which I have already spotted in the Napa Yellow Pages, where it says of itself: "Authentic English pub-restaurant—Dine on our deck overlooking vineyards." I'm moved by this gesture of Bill's, even if I do find an "English pub" without red-faced, smoke-begrimed patrons fortifying themselves against chill and damp about as reassuringly familiar as I would a bald cat or a winged pig.

He is on a short holiday from his job as a salesman for a wholesale distributor of wine and liquor. He could be competing for the same customers as John, he says, except that his territory is in southern California, near Los Angeles. The job is giving him invaluable practice in salesmanship: these days, Napa wineries stand or fall on their ability to find customers for their wares.

But surely it's a mistake for him and John to be acquiring virtually identical work experience, I suggest—something that will only make it harder to decide who should do what at Schramsberg in the future. "It's too early to see how the pieces will fit together," he says. "But I do think you need to have things precisely divided. You can't just say, well, let's all get in here—that could make trouble."

Certainly it might simplify matters if Bill were to go off and be a cowboy, but he's been told by a rancher friend that he will have to sell an awful lot of champagne to find the funds he'll need to sink into cattle ranching. Besides, he's not ready to leave the valley.

"I love these hills. I just can't pull away from here. I love the business—it's been a great thing I grew up around, an excellent thing my folks created. I just can't imagine selling the winery. I want to keep things rolling—do whatever it takes to keep a good thing going."

*   *   *

Watching Jack and Jamie at work one Sunday morning sharpens my appreciation of the cliché that links the words "success," "bitch" and "goddess."

Like the twelve-dozen-odd others here—a cross-section of mostly middle-aged, middle-class, quasi-sophisticates from the cities around San Francisco Bay—I've been invited to a "Grand Frog Dedication and Cinco de Mayo Celebration" at Schramsberg. It's the Mexican national holiday, which the winery's workers from across the border are commemorating privately, elsewhere. Beside the pond between the house at Schramsberg and the barnlike building that houses the offices, Jack has been contorting himself into a variety of uncomfortable positions to photograph giggling guests who take turns paddling in a small boat to a frog statue in green bronze.

It's a charmingly soigné, anthropomorphic frog that the Davieses have commissioned from a local sculptor. It is dressed in a bow tie and tails and balances on one hind foot in mid-sauté, holding a champagne glass aloft, and a bottle in its other fist.

The invitees, mostly drawn from Schramsberg's customer mailing list, are perfectly happy to quaff their bubbly, pass around their Polaroid portraits-with-frog, and attempt something like conversation before they leave. Let me quickly say that I'm in one of those churlish, irritable moods into which people from the Old World and East Coast occasionally work themselves—in scenes of dappled light and shade on perfect, softly sunny California days. Why, we ask ourselves, are Californian conversations so often flat and flabby even when the lean, taut-bodied participants are highly educated and hold demanding jobs? Surely, surely, if you are lucky enough not to be in Northern Ireland or in, say, Hanover, on a grim day in February, you can make some effort to say *any*thing with cerebral bite in it, offer any proof at all of a *mens sana* lodged within a *corpore sano?*

I stand eavesdropping on the periphery of groups gathered around, first, Jamie, and later, when he has put away his camera, Jack. It's virtually the identical conversation over and over and over again. "Gee, Jack (or Jamie), how are you doing? You look great! Everything around here looks terrific! Hey, listen, I've got to get myself a case of this Reserve!" A potbellied mafioso type in dark glasses and Bermuda shorts assaults Jack. "Remember me? We played golf on that————trip in '84. I'll bet you can't guess what my handicap is now!" It's clear that Jack no more remembers meeting him than he does Garibaldi or Leonardo da Vinci but, gamely, pretends he does and claps the man on the shoulder. Even as a mere listener, I soon feel as if I'm about to explode from boredom.

Week after week, the Davieses fly—sometimes separately, sometimes together—from one promotional affair to another. A reception in Copenhagen for the Danish-American Wine Society. A wine seminar on a cruise ship in the Baltic. A wine festival in Holland, organized by Schramsberg's Dutch importer. A promotional tour of Puerto Rico. On and on and on. Virtually the only craft (as opposed to industrial) wineries that can afford advertising campaigns for their wines are owned by multinational monster-companies. Advertising is anyway seen as déclassé—a measure to which no Mouton-Rothschild or Domaine de la Romanée-Conti would ever stoop. In the American wine trade, winery owners must appear in person and press flesh enthusiastically enough to engender rave reviews by word of mouth, and in the columns of wine writers.

All over the Napa Valley, friends of Jack and Jamie have shaken their heads worriedly over the increasingly frenetic pace of the Davieses' lives as Schramsberg's success has attracted yet more competitors. Jack and Jamie have looked me in the eye and assured me that they are still enjoying themselves. I have strained to believe them, despite the tremendous contrast between the peaceful pastoral existence they told me they once envisaged and their present, in which they dart about like hummingbirds on speed—but always, wherever they are, projecting tranquil self-assurance.

It isn't only for themselves and their sons that they work so hard. Twelve families invested in the winery after their original partner bowed out, and these newer partners must be rewarded with a decent return on their investments. But this is not easy to do with Champenois rivals—almost every vaunted name in Champagne, including Moët et Chandon, Roederer, Mumm, Taittinger and Piper-Heidsieck—acquiring Californian vineyards of their own and pushing locally made sparkling wines, frequently at heavily discounted prices. They have been squeezing down Schramsberg's allotment of space in articles recommending champagnes for Christmas and New

Year's Eve; elbowing the Davieses' wines off the lists at some fashionable restaurants; waging vicious price wars.

And then, quite shamelessly, they have repaid the American hospitality that allows them freely to compete on American soil, snap-
ping up parcels of prime land—something Americans may not do in
France—by going to extremes to cast California-made champagne,
for all time, as inferior to the French kind. American producers, like
everyone else, are legally barred from using the word "champagne"
on their bottles in the European community. They were forced to
remove the words *methode champénoise* from their labels, however
faithfully they imitated the techniques of Champagne.

I once had a telephone conversation with Count Chandon, a high-
ranking executive of a sprawling conglomerate that includes the
world's largest champagne-maker, Moët et Chandon. "The champagne
in France is more elegant, more *raffiné*," he intoned in his impeccable
Franglais—didactic, but striving not to sound condescending. "California wine is, how shall I say, more fruity and round, because the grapes
are more fruity and rich." Never mind that sweet wine was all that
Frenchmen—including Louis XIV and Napoleon—ever drank until an
English wine merchant virtually invented dry champagne in 1848; that,
to this day, the English drink drier champagne than the French do.

Jack takes every chance he gets to tell the world about the infuriating Champenois: "The finer California champagne has become, the
more vigorous the French effort to formally define it as inferior."

Though Schramsberg has legions of American customers proud to
have "discovered" an all-American marvel of winemaking early on,
an oversupply of champagne could end the Davieses' dream of a family carrying on.

The Schrams were not granted this wish. Jamie told me that while
he was alive, Robert Schram, a grandson of Jacob—the barber-
turned-winemaker from Pfeddersheim, on the Rhine—paid an
annual visit to Schramsberg. Each time, he was in tears by the time
he and his wife had driven up to the veranda. His father, Herman,
had been forced out of business by Prohibition.

One of my quaintest discoveries in Napa is the incipient countrifica-
tion in some of the children of the nouveaux farmers. The day of our

lunch, Bill Davies tells me—not with resentment but with keen regret—that his father never took him hunting. Jack and Jamie did take the boys hiking and camping in the Sierras all through their childhood. But Bill speaks of not having hunted with Jack as if deprived of an accepted rite of passage. As Jack himself had a quintessentially urban upbringing, this seems a most curious expectation.

The Davieses reflect other rural-urban paradoxes that define Napa. For Jamie, the valley's halcyon days were when entertainment chiefly took the form of pot-luck dinners with neighbors who shared their quixotic winemaking ambitions. Then, there were no stylish—and impersonal—gourmet restaurants for social gatherings. Many of the neighbors grew to be close friends. There was a much stronger sense of community. "Life was simpler," she says.

Both she and Jack have fought to retain that simplicity, having witnessed the ravages of urban sprawl in southern California. But as feelingly as they laud the pleasures of rusticity, they have been nudging their fellow-Americans towards elevating their standards for stylish living.

Some examples. In one issue of a newsletter that goes out to Schramsberg customers, the featured article was a transcript of a conversation with the owner of a restaurant in Santa Monica about the formative experience of staying in a château in Brittany at the age of fifteen. His tone is that of an enthusiastic advocate:

> Madame Brandeley . . . and her sister, the Countess, and Bernard, the Count, all lived the good life. They had no money but they did have the great château, the beach house, the whole nine yards . . . every occasion called for a party!
>
> The neighbors brought game—pheasant or venison—and we went to the coast to dig clams and oysters and dig for lobster. Then all would cook.

In another issue, a customer contributes a meditation about the life and death of a yachtsman friend. The penultimate sentences read,

> Each year, on the anniversary of his death, I buy a bottle of Schramsberg champagne and go off alone to Point Reyes. I sit on a high dune and stare out across the ocean. Each sip of champagne raises a different memory of the man, and the moments we shared together.

Before leaving, I always pour the last of the bottle on his realm: the waves.

There's a hankering in all of this, and for what? Possibly, the *savoir vivre* of an aristocracy: never mind that the hankerers are citizens of the greatest democracy.

CHAPTER TEN

Weekenders

The way God would live if He had money, unquote: the new Napa
Valley was unveiled in all its gaudy glory last Sat. by Dr. Bruno
Ristow and his wife, Urania, who put on a major fling in their new
"weekend cottage," which contains more marble than the
Parthenon and is in much better shape. Designer Richard Tam
arranged for a full moon to rise behind the Roman columns overlooking the pool and Peter Mintun's orchestra, a group aug-
mented to the size of the Santa Monica Symphony. . . .

SUMMER'S END: A crescent moon and a shining star in the
luminous dusk above the jagged Mayacamas mountains. "Islam
rises," murmured Walter Landor. There was a party going on, of
course. There always is, in the Napa Valley. . . .

Herb Caen columns,
The San Francisco Chronicle

By seven o'clock the orchestra had arrived, no thin five-piece
affair, but a whole pitful. . . . The air is alive with chatter and
laughter, and casual innuendo and introductions forgotten on the
spot, and enthusiastic meetings between women who never knew
each other's names. . . . I had taken two finger-bowls of champagne, and the scene had changed before my eyes into something
significant, elemental, profound.

The Great Gatsby,
F. SCOTT FITZGERALD

I'M BEING CHASED down Mount Veeder by a screaming March squall that swirls and slams into my truck's windshield with ferocious blasts of rain. Limbs bright with sprouting leaves torn from trees dancing like dervishes whirl giddily into the fast-curving tarmac. Mounds of collapsed stones and wet earth along the mountainside edge of the road are reminders that stretches of this country can and do vanish in mudslides. In gaps in the forest a maniacal creek races itself, swollen with muddy water.

At the base of the mountain, I turn north onto Highway 29. Except for the tremor in the tops of tall trees, the flatland of the valley is peaceful under its pelt of bright mustard. At intervals, the gray sky is interrupted by vertical filaments of light pale and softly brilliant as young champagne. The abrupt transition from the wildness of the higher terrain to nature becalmed in the files of dormant vines below feels like an experience of schizophrenia in landscape.

On this particular journey I'm finding it hard to make the switch. Leaving the house of a friend halfway up Mount Veeder, my jeans and shoes got soaked when I struggled to stop a puppy from barreling through a heavy wrought-iron gate as the wind made a lunge for my umbrella. Perhaps it has something to do with the fungal smell of wet denim, making me feel only half human—and half mold—a hybrid as bizarre as those clams that ingest and partially become the algae that sustain them. Or perhaps it's because of the incommunicable glee storms induce in me. Whatever the explanation, the crazed harmony of the squall is still more real to me than the change of scene.

I don't feel a tremendous enthusiasm, in this state, for what I'm about to do, which is enter the Napa of smooth polished surfaces.

There are people who live in San Francisco or within a radius of hundreds of miles of the city and, though they hardly ever read the wine pages of its newspapers, are devotees of their society and gossip columns. They know Napa chiefly as a playground for the rich or famous, or people both adjectives fit, something vaguely like a northern Californian approximation of the Riviera.

Some of the Napa subjects of the society reporting have moved to the valley (or bought second homes in it) from places far away: the ballerina and actress Natalia Makarova; the writer Paul Erdman; the

actor-comedian Robin Williams; the actress Julia Roberts; the director Francis Ford Coppola and his writer-director wife, Eleanor; Graef
Crystal, the Berkeley industrial relations professor famous for revela-
tions of the inflated earnings of some top American executives (some
of whom, as you might expect, also have Napa homes).

Having got used to the idea of people with money moving to
Napa from places as distant as Switzerland to live out fantasies of fulfillment, it was not the super-rich-and-famous-from-far-away that
interested me. It was the super-rich from San Francisco that did—
San Franciscans possessing what passes on the West Coast of America for "old money." With proximity a minor, mundane consideration
in this age of the Concorde and private airplanes, these folk granted
practically unlimited choice picked the Napa Valley for their second
homes.

Oddly, most of their large and dignified Napa houses are grouped
in a loose enclave on a flat stretch of land within about four miles of
Rutherford. There's a stately separation of tens of acres of vineyard or
pastureland between them and yet they seem close—a notable
departure from the tendency of other wealthy residents or quasi-res-
idents to create miniature kingdoms unto themselves in isolated
locations in the foothills or mountains.

I arrive at the mailbox that is the critical landmark. Following
instructions, I take not the short, straight drive to the long rooftop
visible above the trees but the curved, unpaved one mostly sub-
merged in puddles and turned to the consistency of wet fudge—so
that my truck mulishly disputes the direction in which I turn the
steering wheel. José Cebrian, the chatelain I am here to see, wanted
to make sure I took the more romantic approach.

He stands waiting for me beneath the front porch of his converted, two-story stone winery. He immediately suggests an overgrown choir boy—a matter of large blue eyes with an expression of
absolute innocence startling in a fifty-seven-year-old, and a spherical
body clothed in a dark blue velveteen sweat suit. We shake hands
and he gracefully motions for me to precede him into the house.

Someone else hovers just beyond the doorway—a slender gray-
haired man with a thin, fine-boned face and sensitive dark eyes. He

wears a V-necked, gray cashmere pullover perfectly coordinated with a burgundy-colored shirt, buttoned at the collar, printed with a gray paisley pattern.

José introduces him as Boz Scaggs. I know this to be a name I have seen in newspapers and magazines, but not for many years.

"We were just finishing lunch," José announces in his deep voice, with characteristically mannered delivery—a conversational equivalent of copperplate.

There's an uncomfortable silence as I rack my brain.

"Er, your name. Boz Scaggs. I seem to have seen it somewhere. Something to do with music?" I have a fuzzy mental picture of a leather-clad, wolfish figure associated with the name—but find it hard to reconcile it with the man before me.

"Yes," says Boz, shy and almost apologetic.

"Well, I'm embarrassed because I'm sure I should know more—but I'm deeply ignorant of a lot of modern music."

Boz and I scrutinize each other, politely wary.

"Boz is also a part-owner of Slim's—the restaurant in San Francisco," José says.

"Oh yes. I think I've heard of it. Uh—are you, perhaps, in rock music?"

"Ye-es. *Yes*," says Boz, nodding earnestly and staring into my eyes encouragingly.

A short, slim, thirtyish woman with a radiant complexion, aquiline nose and formally waved, chin-length blond hair lightly descends the staircase in formal tweeds. We are introduced, but I'm distracted by her intensely interrogative eyes and instantly forget her name.

"Thanks, José. Great lunch," Boz says, and slips away with her.

José follows me up the staircase in sandals that go flippety-flop. He says Boz and his companion, his fiancée, came to lunch to plan their wedding—which is to take place in this house in a few weeks. Boz's intended, he confides, is a vast improvement on an erstwhile female friend, who would "go to the opera and sit with her legs wide apart and you'd think, can't she even pretend to know how to behave?"

They will rent the entire house for their honeymoon for a fortnight, and José hopes they end up owning it. Only last week, he got a notice informing him that the Internal Revenue Service intends to set in motion a foreclosure sale of his estate, an attempt he means to foil with the help of lawyers. He says he will use the house—bought from his mother, Katharine de la Viaga Cebrian in 1964—as collateral for a bank loan. Then he will pay the back taxes he owes. No, he has no philosophical objection to paying his taxes, it's just that he "got a bit behind."

In the meanwhile, the house is for sale. "Boz told me his group will have a new release in a few weeks. He said, 'José, if it's a smash I'm buying your house.'" Unless José gives him a discount, or Boz is a shrewd negotiator, he can expect to pay $4.9 million for twelve acres of land, six bedrooms, six fireplaces and five bathrooms. The feature that José most emphasizes, however, is that "the flow is so good. Mamma designed it and she laid it out. It's lovely in the summer because, for a party, you just *flow* into the ballroom and these other rooms," he says, with a magisterial sweep of one hand.

The house was the principal setting for another romance in José's circle. I've been told that before their marriage, it was the trysting place for Danielle Steel, queen of the best-selling novelists, and her husband, John Traina, the former San Francisco shipping magnate.

I've accepted José's offer of a cup of tea, so we are in the rather small kitchen, a museum of antique, round-cornered, windowless appliances. José makes it clear that he is seldom here. He delves through the many boxes of tea bags in the cupboard suspensefully, as if on an Easter-egg hunt.

We leave the kitchen with our cups of tea. The impression the house makes is of a downsized castle that might be oppressively gloomy without the California sunshine pouring in through the modestly proportioned windows cut into two-foot-thick gray stone walls. One sign of the dominant Spanish aesthetic is the shade of apricot in which the inside walls are painted; another is the chiaroscuro paintings on chiefly religious themes in heavy gilt frames. José calls my attention to a shadowy work by the seventeenth-century Spanish painter José de Ribera: St. Francis holds a crucifix and reads from a book propped up on a skull. José says his grandfather acquired the Ribera when he bought the art collection of a former director of the Bellas Artes, or Museum of Fine Arts, in Spain.

Despite the grandeur of its scale, the house has a lived-in quality—the dark pine floors are well scuffed—and it is spared from boring perfect taste by, for instance, a florist's standard green glass vase stuffed haphazardly with pink camellias from the garden. Almost every object has an uncommon history: an attractive clock framed in something like a pewter sunburst belonged to Stella Wheeler Bishop, the grandmother of José's first wife, Celia, who died; José is divorced from his second wife, Gretchen, and now lives alone.

Soon after I notice that the house seems somewhat underfurnished, José mentions a fire in 1970 "that destroyed all Mamma's beautiful furniture. We were having a party, playing charades, when one of my children came running in, shouting, 'The house is on fire!' The caterers had been barbecuing on the balcony and sparks flew up into the shingle roof."

I have seated myself in a large, comfortable chair beside the drawing room fireplace in which a small, smoldering log does unequal battle against the chill and damp. José reclines on one elbow on a deep, golden brown sofa, like a Roman voluptuary.

I ask him why he has never been more than tangentially involved in the wine business even though he was not yet ten when he first set foot in the winery-turned-house—soon after his mother bought it in the early 1940s, with one hundred acres of vineyards attached to it. Later, she purchased other great tracts of Napa land and was the last owner of Schramsberg before Jack and Jamie Davies took it over. She had wanted José to run Schramsberg after her divorce from her second husband, for whom she bought Jacob Schram's creation as an occupation. But José, then in his twenties, "was afraid Mamma would continue to lose money on Schramsberg and I wanted her out of there."

Instead of a winery owner, he became—"by a sort of accident"—a real estate agent with the enviable specialization of selling Napa's poshest houses to wealthy San Franciscans, a coterie to which he himself belonged. The family of his father, Luis Cebrian (who died when José was a small child), once owned the ninety-thousand-acre Cuyama ranch in mid-coastal California, on which oil was discovered in the 1930s, while it was still in the family's possession.

John Traina, who declined to let me ask his wife about Napa, had

offered me José's name and telephone number as a sort of concilia-
tory gesture, advising me to get in touch with him immediately. He
said José was the key to understanding San Francisco society's
lengthy flirtation with Napa. In the 1950s and 1960s, John said,
"José's mother gave wild parties. That was how the San Francisco
scene started going to Napa.

"There was a time when everyone wanted José to find them a
wooden Victorian house or a stone winery or some other sort of
grand house. Of course he's done nothing but drink all the old wine
in his cellar for some years."

There's none left now. José says, with a look of infinite regret, that
he wishes he were able to offer me some of the "delicious wine with
a beautiful label, which has a picture of Charlie's father's house in
France on it." He speaks of Charles de Limur, a member of the
Crocker clan—virtually the only name among San Francisco's "old
families" that East Coast Brahmins will occasionally recognize. This
de Limur, José says, makes a tiny quantity of wine every year with
the help of friends, and has given him some cases of it. But they, too,
have gone the way of everything surpassingly drinkable here.

When dusk falls José fetches me a glass of a chilled, sprightly
Chardonnay from the Franciscan winery that is familiar: it is so reasonably priced that I occasionally buy it myself. There's something
far too vulnerable about him for me to risk hurting his feelings by
telling him that what I really need now is a glass of red wine, to
warm my bones. The little oak log continues to make a show of hiss-
ing and I'm only four feet from it but Nigel, José's spaniel, came in
and shook his dripping coat onto my still-damp jeans. So I've had to
put my jacket on, to ward off pneumonia—though, presently, Nigel
makes amends for the unexpected cold shower, warming one of my
feet by practically going to sleep on top of it.

José has only lived in this house for seven years after twenty-one
years of using it as a weekend retreat from a far more imposing house
in San Francisco. He has nothing to say about the growing of grapes
or collecting of wine, but he has a trove of tales of intimate encounters with Napa's most illustrious figures that not even André Tchelistcheff could match.

"I'll never forget. Once, Mrs. de Latour, she gave me—Mamma

used to dress me in short pants, and I'd have to kiss the women's hands, you know? And one night, Mrs. de Latour, who was a very regal woman, was coming to dinner. She was tall and sort of—with a big bust. And she came upstairs and I bent to kiss her hand and she kept *shaking* her hand and I kept trying to kiss it. And she gave me *a bloody nose!* My nose was big in those days also!

"And so I went to my room, *crying*. I was about nine or ten years old. And Mrs. de Latour came in. And she sat down and said, 'I'm sorry I gave you the bloody nose. I knew you were trying to kiss my hand. I want to make a point to you and your mother—that you're an *American* now.'

"I've never forgotten her for that!"

Fernande de Latour called him "Foo," his mother's nickname for him.

It was certainly hypocritical of Fernande, living in the little-France-in-California that she and her husband made of Beaulieu, to insist that José—who had spoken Spanish before he learned English—be an all-American boy. Actually, the question of the degree to which José was Spanish or American was beside the point. The strand missing from Napa's cultural plaid that I finally found among the elite from San Francisco was British. Such ancestral ties as this group does have to the British Isles are eagerly displayed.

In my first conversation with José, over the telephone, I had said I connected the name Cebrian with a photograph of a grande dame with an unforgettable profile I had seen in a San Francisco magazine many years ago. I said very few people could live up to such a profile, but this lady seemed as if she might. "Yes! That was Mamma!" he exclaimed happily. "She had an archbishop's nose. It started growing when she was sixteen. She's ninety-eight now and has had to be put in a nursing home, but when she could, she loved to talk about how you could look up her family in Burke's Peerage—her family seat—the Croftons who lived in Mowhill Castle in Ireland in I don't know what county."

I found it surprising to discover only in José's circle, imprints of British culture—on people. Surprising, because giant British corporations like the Grand Metropolitan Group and Allied-Lyons own more Napa land (through local subsidiary companies) than do American corporations or foreign firms of any other nationality. But they administer their Napa holdings from afar, largely through American executives.

British aesthetics—represented in wine connoisseurship, a British invention—is the ghostly guide, or at least, influence, for almost everyone concerned with winemaking in the valley. But there are only one or two small, intimate wineries run by British expatriates and it takes special effort to track down Brits in any wine-related occupation.

On the other hand, you can meet, for instance, Austin Hills. He grew up in San Francisco but had a Scotch nanny whose rearing of him has marked him strongly; in any case, it seems as if any dilution of the culture of his ancestors, who sailed from England in 1638, has been firmly resisted by every generation down to his own. In spite of having attended neither an Eastern prep school nor Ivy League college, he speaks with the precise yet languorous patrician drawl of one that has.

In the course of an afternoon I spend with him, I find myself transfixed by his shoes. They are plain black loafers, shone to a high gloss, with the squashed look of very old and very expensive soft leather. They speak of restrained good taste, modesty and frugality.

Austin is the first and only member of San Francisco society since John Daniel of Inglenook to get involved in Napa wine on a large scale. Not that you'd guess this from the strikingly simple buildings—pleasing in the way barns are—that house his winery, Grgich Hills Cellar. The cluttered office in which Austin and his short, flamboyant, Croatian partner, Mike (from Miljenko) Grgich, have desks looks like a cross between the order-processing room of a tire-manufacturer's warehouse and an untidy, indigent college student's study.

My visit to Grgich Hills overlaps with one from the art director and photographer of *The Wine Spectator* for a cover shoot. Austin is a slender, shy, shrinking presence beside Mike, readily conceding center stage to him. Somehow he maintains a mien of studious expressionlessness, listening to his partner—a famously compulsive rake, looking the part with his purple beret and insinuating dark eyes—speak to their women visitors. Yet it is easy to detect that behind his mask,

Austin cringes. "You have good *body*!" Mike growls gutturally to one woman. "Your eyes, I *never* forget your eyes," he purrs at another.

But Mike is a superb winemaker: *The Wine Spectator* article on Grgich Hills, when it comes out, places him in "the top rank of California winemakers," praising his "taut, intense Chardonnays" and "sculpted Cabernets, Sauvignon Blancs and Zinfandels." He and Austin have been in business together for fifteen years, happily united by their complementary personalities and shared passion for thrift.

After the photo session, Austin and I travel the short distance to another part of Rutherford, to his all-white wooden farmhouse built in 1910 in what he calls the "post-classical" style. The furnishings define this as a large weekend cottage. Flouncy slipcovers, in jolly floral prints, look as if they might have been sewn by his wife. In a collection of family photographs by the staircase, Austin points her out: an attractive, limber figure on skis, long blond hair streaming behind her.

I ask him how he has managed to avoid the architectural *folies de grandeur* of other Napa wineries—resist the temptation to attract more tourist traffic to Grgich Hills with some marvel of design and construction.

The question draws a short laugh from him.

"Well, I think if you look at Europeans who have been making wine for a long time—they make it in what are basically very simple utilitarian structures."

"You don't mean the châteaux, do you?"

"The châteaux are residences. They don't make wine in the châteaux. That's a distortion by Americans. They see these châteaux and sort of assume they make wine in them. The wine is made in the *chais*, which are simple structures. You know, our winery has internally financed its growth—we borrowed very little money. And that's the most enjoyable way to go about it.

"What has happened in the Napa Valley is that a lot of people made fortunes in other businesses and therefore are building monuments to themselves. Like Captain Niebaum—he made a fortune in fur trading and decided to retire here."

The pauses between his sentences are of such staggering length that I'd be restless without the diversion of observing the penetrating intelligence—and a youthful desire to please—in his huge azure eyes. He has alabaster skin and thinning brown hair straggling down to his collar; overall, he looks exactly like a shrewd medieval scholar-monk.

I suggest that he himself has his "château" a long way away, in San Francisco—a house bounded on one side by the French consulate, and on the other by the singer Linda Ronstadt.

"Yes! That's right!"

I ask him why he has got as involved as he has in the wine business. I know that in 1976, he negotiated a brilliant price for the sale of the Hills Brothers Coffee company to a Brazilian company—after which he could have settled down to a life of leisure. But he was forty-one at the time of the sale and, admirably, someone apparently possessed of a strong desire for accomplishment for its own sake.

This he hides behind the upper-class conceit of never allowing oneself to be seen to strive for anything. "I thought it would be nice to have some sort of investment in land," he says languidly. "Originally, I'd got involved in rice growing near Sacramento. But that wasn't so interesting. I enjoyed wine and I bought a vineyard just south of Calistoga to grow grapes in 1970 and sold it. Then I bought this vineyard." Between Grgich Hills, which he owns with his sister, Mary Lee Strebl, and Mike Grgich, and Hills Vineyards, owned by himself and his sister only, Austin has a controlling share in six hundred acres of Napa land.

He bought his post-colonial house with the help of José Cebrian, a classmate of his at the Towne School in San Francisco for a while—before José's Mamma dispatched him to a Canadian school, because she worried about him not speaking English properly, and then to a school in Peru, when she despaired of his Spanish.

Austin tells me only that, having bought the vineyards surrounding the house from a descendant of the Fealy family—whose ancestor had in turn bought the land from George Yount—"I thought it would be nice to have this old farmhouse right next door."

The house happens to be in the same prosperous neighborhood as that of José, who gave me a far livelier account of its acquisition.

"I'd sold Austin sixty acres of vineyards which belonged to Mrs. Grigsby. But then Austin came to me and said he wanted the house. And you know Austin—well, he's very nervous, so he didn't want to ask her himself. So I went along and said—Mrs. Grigsby was ninety-six at the time—'Have you ever considered selling your house?' And she said, 'Oh no, dear, I don't own it. My sister does and I rent it from her.' And I said, 'How much rent do you pay?' And she said, 'Fifty dollars a month.' And I said, 'Mrs. Grigsby, your own sister, and she charges you *fifty dollars?'*—knowing full well that Mrs. Grigsby had money but was *extremely* parsimonious and used to hardly eat at all, so that I used to have to send the Mexicans over with meals for her.

"I said, 'Mrs. Grigsby, do you know that this porch is rotting and you are liable to fall through it anyday and that that, at your age, could be serious, and that your bathroom is crying out for repairs? Well, Mrs. Grigsby, I have a buyer who will let you live in it rent-free for the rest of your life and *he* will make all the repairs at *his* expense.'

"So there's Austin, like a vulture, *waiting* to get his house, and Mrs. Grigsby continues just as chipper as ever and in full command of her faculties. Then one day she fell ill with something relatively minor that needed proper attention, only she was too stingy to go to a proper doctor. And she died. Not at a hundred and one, but at a hundred. And Austin got his house at last. He wouldn't want me to tell you what he paid for it, but it was very little."

I ask Austin why he continues to live in San Francisco when he has his pretty white house in Rutherford, and all his Napa vineyards, and Grgich Hills.

"We-ell, I'm *from* San Francisco," he says uneasily, as if he wishes he could say more, but can't.

He suggests I refer the question to his wife, Erika—reverentially pronouncing her name, "Ur-ka."

It occurred to me that more monied San Franciscan men might, like Austin, exchange their floating weekender status in Napa for a fuller engagement with the place—if the idea had greater cachet with their wives. I had an impression of how a San Francisco beau mondaine might view the valley from a book by a writer I had never read before I met her husband. John Traina told me that a novel by his wife called *Thurston House* was set partly in Napa.

No sooner does Danielle Steel's newly wed and ravishingly beautiful but petulant Camille Thurston first set foot in Napa than she misses the San Francisco parties and balls, the chance to "show off her new clothes," and is "disturbed at how far they were from town." Her reaction distresses her adoring, fabulously rich husband, Jeremiah:

> "I had hoped you would like the Napa Valley, Camille. It's important to me."
>
> "Well it's ugly and boring and stupid. . . ."
>
> . . . He wanted her to settle down to his country life in Napa. He couldn't be in San Francisco all the time, and he wanted her with him.

The book reminded me that the face of Napa I love best—a simple, shared cherishing of the land and its produce—is precisely what women of Camille's predilections detest. But I was astonished to discover that her sentiments about the valley precisely coincided with Danielle's own—not least because this fictional creation turns into a sort of she-devil-on-wheels as the book progresses.

"You can't satisfy every need here," John tells me over a lunch at Piatti at which his partner in Napa real estate development, George Altamura, will soon join us. "My wife treats it almost as a prison sentence when I bring her up her for the summer. She grew up in Europe—in France—so she feels this is more 'country' than other people do."

He tells me he himself likes "being a farmer and escaping to the Napa Valley and worrying about oak root fungus and not enough rain—a totally different set of circumstances." Since 1968, he has bought and sold various small vineyards—twenty acres, four acres, twenty-five acres—and now, according to José, is closely involved in the management of a model vineyard. He does not make any wine, but sells his grapes to the highest bidder.

He says: "The Napa Valley tends to cut people down to size more than most places, and I think that's because it's farm country. It's fine if you have a fancy house or a fancy garden, but what most people want to talk about is food, wine and the grapes. I enjoy evenings in the valley at which there might be a local judge or a retired winemaker present, and they all have their stories. Everyone in the valley is houseproud. They bore you to death telling you their house was built in the 1880s and was the first house on the road. Of course our own house was built in 1860!

"There are some people who come here who think of it as a fancy place, but luckily they are still in the minority. Some relatives of Austin's see it that way—they want to sell their house in Lake Tahoe and come here.

"I don't even wear a necktie in Napa. And some fool gave a black tie party recently and we all just laughed at him."

He did, in fact, look quite unlike anyone else I met in Napa when I had my first glimpse of him—a short, slight silhouette gliding proudly on the backs of his heels, through Piatti's patio garden, in spring sunshine. Behind him was a fittingly fantastic backdrop of hairy pastel Iceland poppies and water trickling out of lion's heads in a terracotta fountain. He wore dark glasses with aviator frames and a greenish gold alligator skin jacket that intensified the amber of eyes that turn adamantine when he speaks of business, or when a question threatens to breach the walls around his family's private affairs. Mostly, though, they glow with affability.

I remark between forkfuls of risotto with truffles that businessmen are usually conventional animals who fear the unusual, that it therefore takes an odd sort of businessman to marry a writer. "True," he says, keenly amused. "But I *am* an odd sort."

This is incontestable. He took an adventurous route to rebuilding the fortune that his grandfather, an immigrant from the Aeolian Islands, made in chocolates in San Francisco. His father's generation of the family had been lotus-eaters. At nineteen and twenty—in the summer holidays from Stanford, where he was working towards a degree in economics—John worked as a purser on ships traveling to the Far East. He made his pile through an unfashionable interest in a shipping line that he eventually relinquished. Now, in his late fifties, he spends much of his time managing the $25 million a year his wife is estimated to make from her books, as well as a tour company and his real estate development firm.

I say that Napa's vineyards seem to attract many businessmen seeking a purpose for their lives more fulfilling than the mere making of money; that other businessmen obey creative promptings vicariously, through marriages to women working in some branch of the arts. Men without these channels often seem to take mistresses to gratify the same urge by other means. His face lights up with surprise and he warmly agrees: "My first wife was a socialite and that got boring rather fast. If I were still with her, I'd have to have several mistresses." He says he and Danielle discuss the progress of her books in detail. "She has immeasurably improved the quality of my life."

Apparently he once led a far wilder existence. He drinks very little wine now—only orders a glass of Pinot Noir to keep me company, explaining that in his youth he drank enough "for several lifetimes." It was in that phase that he started going to parties at José Cebrian's: at the most memorable one, an especially decadent reveler drank a toast from a glass with a goldfish in it.

The entire set is more sober now. The change seems to have begun around the late 1970s, when some floating weekenders began to acquire a social conscience. A then prominent member of the coterie, Pat Montandon, found herself and her then husband (now married to John Traina's ex-wife) the subject of increasingly hostile muttering among locals about a large, ostentatious and often raucous party they gave at their Napa house every year.

Robin Lail—who worked for Robert Mondavi at the time—had told me that it struck Pat that she might disarm her critics by converting her annual bash into a charitable event. She mentioned the idea at a lunch with Robert and his wife, Margrit Biever, who had recently undertaken to raise a million dollars for the St. Helena Hospital and were hoping for a large contribution from her. Margrit had been toying with the possibility of starting a Napa version of the famous Burgundian charitable auction of the wines of the Hospices de Beaune. Serendipitously, Pat's and Margrit's separate ideas were combined into the first annual Napa Valley Wine Auction, organized by Robin in 1981. Its form has changed little over the years: a great bash one night is followed the next morning by an elegant sale of wine, usually by an auctioneer lent by Christie's. The thirteenth auction, in 1994, raised $1.6 million—the most ever.

At the one auction dinner I went to, I was seated between a smiling but uncommunicative grape grower's wife and a towering blue-rinse beehive hairdo that housed a woman with a Grand Inquisitor's style of interrogation. Had I met?—she reeled off a list of names of Napa notables and her eyes widened in wonderment whenever I nodded. "What is he like?" she demanded. "How well have you got to know her?"

The entire affair was a sort of mutual gawkers' convention. The non-residents like Ms. Beehive had paid the hundreds of dollars it costs to attend to watch the winery owners and Napa celebrities, whom I found on that evening to be poor conversationalists—distractedly jerking their heads this way and that. They, in their turn, had paid the fee to put in an appearance, to maintain their standing as members of the club—and to see who had come to see them this year. Was it a bigger crowd than last year's? A more or less sophisticated one? Were enough people on the dance floor or should a different band have been engaged?

I tell Erika Hills about the conundrum to which I'm hoping she will have an answer. When wealthy people from halfway across the globe choose Napa to fashion "lifestyles" as different as possible from what they are used to, why don't their counterparts in San Francisco venture further afield—further than, say, Napa—and construct fantasy lives of their own? Or, might they in fact go somewhere far away I don't know about?

"Oh no. San Franciscans don't really go abroad," she says quickly in her broad-voweled, German-inflected English. "They don't feel the need, because they have it all—the most beautiful setting—right here.

"And they don't feel comfortable not being recognized somewhere else."

Several of her friends predicted this forthrightness. Her bluntness and common sense are found refreshing in her circle. José Cebrian said: "She's a wonderful Mother Earth. And she makes Austin bring his better wines up from the cellar when he begins to pour others—she says, 'Oh, Austin, we can't only serve people these wines. People *know* we are wealthy!' "

When the subject of Grgich Hills comes up, she tells me she had to take Mike Grgich out to lunch last week "to tell him his life is a mess! Why doesn't he hire a woman to keep house for him? He won't spend any money on himself—like a typical Serbo-Croatian." I mention someone else she knows, another divorced bachelor, and she says, "I told him he should get a girlfriend just to release his physical tensions, but he said it was against his religion—he's a Roman Catholic—and that he has no desire, in any case."

She is all ablaze with animal vitality. At the Buckeye—across the Golden Gate bridge from San Francisco—where I am her guest at lunch, the funereal light of a heavily overcast day bleaches the colors in the flowers and trees outside and filters reluctantly through tall, wide windows. Outlined against the restaurant's somber dark paneling, Erika is a powerful countervailing force. She is buxom and blond in an olive green jacket with a stiff round collar whose seams and shoulders are generously decorated with gold braid: she looks like a winningly androgynous officer of some dandified regiment of the Austro-Hungarian empire. Her practicality shows in her strikingly disproportionate tiny, square hands that appear far too young for a woman in her late forties.

Though Austrian, she has lived in America uninterruptedly for twenty-three years. "I'm from Graz. Arnold Schwarzenegger and I are from there," she says with a sinuous torso wriggle. "It's an intellectual city. There's an arty circle and then you have the haute-bourgeoisie and the old people."

No, she doesn't miss it—"because my memories of my young years are not happy." After much time as an airline stewardess and a long romance with someone handsome, wealthy, Argentinian and Jewish, she met Austin at an art gallery opening near San Francisco.

She says she runs their household quite unlike any other in the San Francisco establishment. She has Austrian au pairs to look after her two small sons and a Mexican housekeeper. Yes, she says, other wealthy San Franciscans have English nannies and their houses are run approximately along upper-class English lines: "They are almost overly proper. Because the forefathers were adventurers and the moment you had money and power, you thought that was how you had to live. They looked back to England and saw how those people had to live."

She and Austin don't use their Rutherford house much, she says, because "we live a fuller life in San Francisco. We're very involved in the cultural life there. We help support the San Francisco Art Institute and the American Conservatory Theater and the University Art Museum in Berkeley.

"Austin is fourth-generation San Francisco and he runs everything from there. But I *wish* we lived in Napa—we wanted the children to grow up in the country so that they could be exposed to the values— have closer relationships with others, see how a small community works. The perfect combination would have been school in Napa for the first eight years."

I believe I would miss sports cars and black tie dinners and diamonds the size of pigeon's eggs if they were mysteriously eliminated from the world—even though these things form no part of my life or aspirations. On the other hand, in anyone but the very young, I think of any interest in leading a glamorous life as a sign of the wrong sort of immaturity. While still in my early twenties, I did work that occasionally put me in luxury hotels, limousines and the first-class cabins of airplanes, but when these experiences failed to transform me into a magical being forever liberated from bondage to the humdrum, my disillusionment was profound. Although I could not then have put it quite like this, it was as if I had been given an understanding of glamour in its archaic meaning of *something done to someone else*—as in the *Oxford English Dictionary*'s example of eighteenth-century usage: "When devils, wizards or jugglers deceive the sight, they are said to cast glamour o'er the eyes of the spectator." It did nothing to change me or my lot.

Still, a little glamour does unquestionably add grace notes to life, temporarily relieves monotony, stimulates the imagination, acts as a sort of perfume for cerebration. Wine has much the same role—and can also be a powerful tool of glamouring, in the old sense.

Glamour attaches itself naturally to Napa's haute weekend crowd from San Francisco. The older money in the set, which cultivates understatement, scorns display and treats the valley as a place for undemanding pleasuring. Newer money works hard at a deliberate cultivation of the connections between glamour, wine and wealth.

Before I knew I would be scrutinizing Napa to write about it, I had clipped and filed in a collection of miscellaneous curiosities the Herb Caen item about Bruno and Urania Ristow.

Four years later, a man with the massive silhouette of a retired football player and the large, round, balding and bespectacled head of a frighteningly cerebral scientist stands waiting for me in a circular drive. Dr. Bruno Ristow is San Francisco's most famous plastic surgeon and, waiting at the door of his pale pink weekend house is a fine advertisement of his handiwork, his wife, Urania. She is built like a dainty, finely proportioned flower—a freesia, say—has long dark eyes, brown hair and a marvel of a nose that is straight, but with the suggestion of being fractionally retroussé. She looks as if she has stepped out of a page of *Vogue*—wears a brown cashmere cardigan, a garnet red length of silk wound twice around her neck, brown and gray striped slacks in a men's suiting fabric and black moccasins decorated with a curly appliqué pattern. She is a Nicaraguan of Spanish descent who left her country at seventeen for America and a career as a model, which she gave up for a first marriage; after a divorce, she married Bruno, who had been married twice before.

His ancestry is northern German except for one Portuguese grandmother, and he is from a small town in Brazil. In 1967, at the age of twenty-six, and at short notice, he left Brazil for New York in search of treatment for the cancer diagnosed in his first wife, who later died of the disease.

He is dressed in woollen trousers and an Ultrasuede trompe l'oeil cardigan in which a diamond-knit pattern is mimicked in green and brown on a tan background.

When he goes down to the cellar to fetch a bottle of the delectable 1989 Château Woltner Estate Reserve Chardonnay, Urania gives me a discourse on her husband in her slightly imperious tone of voice: "I'm a person that likes aesthetics, but I would say that Bruno has a tremendous sensitivity to beautiful things. He likes a very organized closet. He likes a beautiful pant, a beautiful shoe. I mean, he will go out of his way to *find* this perfection in objects. And he *surrounds* himself with it. And I admire him a lot—because when I'm staying here, I put on my gardening pants, but this man is dressed to the teeth! He's not trying to impress anybody. This is not when we have company. This is when it's only the two of us. It is fascinating!"

When I thank her for letting me disturb their weekend peace, she reassures me. "Bruno has just been exercising his cars, one at a time, and today we went to lunch at our neighbor's." Bruno's vintage car collection includes two Ferraris, a Bentley and a Jaguar. "Just toys," says Urania with wifely condescension.

Bruno explains—in an accent part-Latin, like Urania's, and part folksy American—that they are here in Napa, quite simply, "because it's such a wonderful lifestyle." Napa, he explains, is deeply relaxing. "It's such a pleasant drive from San Francisco, through Marin County and the cow fields. Usually on a day like today, which is cold-ish, we have a fire. And my wife cooks a boeuf Bourguignon, or tonight she has coq au vin—typical winter dinner, you know, with some of our fine wines. We are ourselves planting a new vineyard and I think this place is really a paradise!"

The house was decorated—in a style that might be described as sub-rococo—by the late Richard Tam, who switched from designing women's clothes to interior decoration and then died of AIDS. Urania once worked for him as a model. It's clear that his aesthetic sensibility was heavily influenced by his view of himself: Urania tells me he was the only son of adoring, rich Chinese-Americans from San Francisco, "and when Richard saw the movie *The Last Emperor*, he said, 'That is the only child that has ever reminded me of me!'"

I am given a tour of the house. It has ceilings that seem easily fifteen feet high, which, Urania says, mislead people, "because it's really a *very* small house." Bruno says, "It has only 4,500 square feet! Right now we have a house in San Francisco that's twelve thousand square feet and even has elevators, I mean." Through that house, Bruno unexpectedly exceeded one of his most cherished dreams. It seems he was working in New York as a surgeon and might have remained there, had not "the door to California opened through *Architectural Digest*. In all the photographs, California looked so beautiful. Yes, it's absolutely true!" he says with characteristically boyish enthusiasm. "Little did I know that I would also have my home in *Architectural Digest*—the one in the city—in 1983!" The walls of a small sitting room are hung with mementos from the Ristows' holidays abroad: they ride to hounds in England and go on African safaris.

In the drawing room I find my attention riveted by a large chandelier constructed of deer antlers turned pale gray by a chemical wash. Urania thinks the deer they came from were American: Bruno insists that because the antlers are so generously endowed with points, the deer must have been European. There is a gleaming grand piano, a shiny marble fireplace and, at the top of marble columns by one door, twin busts of strikingly handsome black-amoors that "Richard picked up in Venice," Urania says. The sofas are covered in a tiny floral print and the house plants are intimidatingly tall and lushly leafed.

The long views from most of the plate glass windows are of gently sloping vine-covered terrain at the southern end of the Napa Valley. From the upstairs bedroom, close to the horizon and in the direction of San Francisco, the San Pablo Bay is visible as an expanse of glimmering wetness; massed above it are malefic clouds, pregnant with drama, in shades of intense violet and pewter. We are allowed a short stroll past the miniature lake and swimming pool before fat, heavy drops of rain begin to fall.

There is just enough time for Urania to show me the trellis painted verdigris on which she has been trimming wisteria canes and, on the lake, against the weeping willow tree on the far bank, not merely mallard ducks and canvasbacks but a "rare South American swan—they live only in Argentina," Bruno says; the bird has a black head and neck, red beak and a white body.

Urania tells me that their avian visitors eat "about $400 of cracked corn *a week*."

"Can you imagine!" says Bruno. "We call it the Ristow Diner."

Bruno calls my attention to a specially commissioned arrangement of decorative tiles on the floor of the swimming pool. This, he says, "is a piece of Napa history because the College of Art in Napa, which is very modest and small—well, to paint these tiles and bake 'em in their ovens. . . !" Later, listening to my recording of our conversation, I will wince at the insincere "Wow!" his announcement elicits from me.

Then as now, thinking about the Ristows, a debate begins in my mind. Well all right, a kindlier version of myself reasons with another, there is inevitably something silly-sounding about people expressing a passion for aesthetics at length. And, since beauty does matter to you, too, why not be glad that such people exist to keep designers and artists and craftspeople in hot dinners? But a less tolerant self stubbornly persists in its ambivalence—chiefly because of the frequency with which the comparative form crops up in all the Ristows say. It is not enough that they themselves like what they have to derive pleasure from it: it must also be explicitly or implicitly better than what others have.

There is the location of the house, for instance. The first Napa house that he and Urania owned—and bought through José Cebrian, who told me, "I dated her before Bruno removed her one mark of distinction, a bump in her nose"—was near Rutherford, on the edge of the gilded enclave. Watching me stare at the view from the present house, bought after that earlier Napa dwelling was disposed of, Urania says, "You should see it when the fog comes down. Now, Erika Hills's house is so Napa, so Victorian, but it's so *flat* in Rutherford!"

"This is really a magnificent site if you compare it with the valley," Bruno says. "We were the second people to build a house of some significance in this area. Other people think Rutherford is a choice area, but for Urania and I it's not."

Urania says Bruno plays the piano beautifully. "A Steinway?" I guess unimaginatively.

"That's better than a Steinway!" he exclaims. "It's a concert grand Bösendorfer, as a matter of fact."

His cars? Well, one of the Ferraris "is one of the most beautiful cars ever made. It has been involved in complete mystery. It surfaced in an auction in South Africa in the 1960s, but I have been pursuing its history *relentlessly!* Because a racing car with a luxury interior—I know nothing like it was made before!"

The devil's advocate in me is roused.

"If you leave out reconstructive surgery," I say, "your profession is about the cultivation of beauty—yes?"

"Corrr-ect!" says Bruno.

"And you live in this house, surrounded by natural beauty and drink luxurious wines, and you can go out to dinner every night and eat fabulous meals. But can there be too much of a good thing—of all these good things—do you wonder sometimes? Can there be such a thing as an overcultivation of beauty in a place like this?"

Bruno chooses to discuss the question in the context of plastic surgery. There have been scientific studies done, he tells me, revealing an appreciation of beauty to be innate—"genetic." In different rounds of an experiment in which a woman pretended to faint in a

subway, people walked by when her face was painted with a disfig-
uring scar, but she was overwhelmed by solicitous attention when
made up to look lovely. He says that in other studies, boy babies only
three months old spent far more time looking at pictures of beautiful women than of plain ones.

Yes, indeed, one *can* go too far in aesthetic surgery—for instance,
remove so many wrinkles from women that "they look like China
dolls—but that is not good taste! Good taste has to come in."

Scarcely a day passes in his practice without some woman patient
two or three weeks past her operation telephoning to say something
to this effect: "Dr. Ristow, I'm bumping into every piece of furniture
in my house, because I'm looking in mirrors all the time! I never
thought I was *sooooo* beautiful!"

Urania chimes in. "I think—"

She pauses. Lightning pulses suddenly through the room and
there is an almighty clap of thunder. We all laugh in nervous surprise. "I think it's incredible that, before, you had maybe ten good
years, or twenty years, of looking your best. And now you can have
thirty or forty!

"I have had a face-lift," she announces, as if hoping to startle me
out of the skepticism I am finding it hard to hide.

"Urania is forty-eight," adds Bruno.

Well, yes, she is extremely beautiful in a way forty-eight never was
before the invention of cosmetic surgery. But I also find myself
thinking, she couldn't pass for twenty-nine or even thirty-nine—
eyes, voices and even demeanor often give the game away. And,
knowing her to be the wife of a plastic surgeon, I wouldn't have
blinked if he'd said she was sixty. Bruno and his kind, wielding their
knives, are merely transforming the movement from youth to old
age into a graduation from youth to an artificial agelessness. A century from now, I find myself thinking in some distress, will there be
no faces deeply grooved with the kindliness, with testimonials to the
value of sheer endurance—the reassurance about the end of the journey of life somehow conveyed in faces of old, old people in my memories of my Indian childhood?

Who operated on Urania, I ask, too caught up in my dismay to
acknowledge a second flash of lightning.

Bruno says he did; no, he didn't find it difficult to cut into his wife, and he has in fact "given both my parents face-lifts. My father called me from Brazil and said, 'Bruno, you've got to do something!' His retirement as dean of his college had been covered by the newspapers and he saw the photographs and said, 'I don't want to look like this for the rest of my life!' "

Bruno himself looks the age he is—fifty-two—in spite of having a face apparently wrinkle-free. Collagen injections, I wonder, or a benefit of his being slightly overweight?

He and I argue politely about the desirability of surgery that is not correcting disfigurement of any kind. "People with highfalutin and unrealistic desires are very rare," he insists. "The people I see have their feet planted on earth and it's a very *happy* practice. Plastic surgery is a *very* happy practice."

But can a happiness composed of pleasing surfaces go very deep, I wonder aloud in different ways. Bruno tells stories about romance entering the lives of customers lonely for years, after he has gone to work on them. He seems not to see that this is beside the point of my question. I'd be getting depressed, listening to him, if the storm outside hadn't been gaining force—rain drumming on the roof, wind shrieking shrewishly and ear-splitting thunderclaps announcing imminent doom.

We pause at a muffled thud in the tumultuous darkness. Bruno changes the subject. He tells me how one night, he and Urania saw fourteen wild turkeys at the door—yes, that door right there—their beaks against the glass, peering in.

In cities, I think—making my way up Mount Veeder afterwards in a downpour so heavy and mist so dense that I pull over twice to let bolder drivers roar past me—most storms pass virtually unnoticed. But however many well-heeled sophisticates Napa attracts, it will retain a feeling of countryside for as long as foul weather can crash in on conversations in the most opulent temples of materialism, restoring these to their properly insignificant proportions.

CHAPTER ELEVEN

Epilogue

A SUNDAY AFTERNOON. In a high reach of the Mayacamas, in the lacy shade of a wisteria arbor, a grape grower friend and I have drunk with our lunch of sausages and grilled vegetables a Pinot Noir made by her Napa dentist, a part-time viniculturist. The food and wine and other members of her household are making me sleepy. When respectfully addressed, the miniature black cat stretched out in a deck chair opens a single yellow eye in flickering acknowledgment; the slumbering Alsatian, her back pressed against a cool stucco wall, groans and sighs operatically. The June air is redolent with the scent of banks of star jasmine. My friend disappears behind *The Napa Register*; I try to bring my notes up to date but, as if hypnotized, do no more than scribble, over and over again: the scent of jasmine . . .

So I propose that I rouse myself from my trance by mowing the tiny lawn. Lawnmowing is a chore I shirk at home, but the green patch here is extraordinary. Seemingly afloat, it rests on the edge of a terrace jutting out over Pickle Canyon, whose steep sides are sumptuously embroidered with vines. The scale of the highlands around us is grand enough for the outlines of individual vines and trees to merge, halfway to the skyline, into a blur of deep green velour, turning indigo on the horizon. Only one other house is visible—a mysterious silhouette on the summit of a faraway knoll. Working in the garden in this spot offers the illusion of penetrating the surrounding magic; of joining in.

My friend is trailing me, raking grass clippings, when we hear the syncopated drone of a helicopter. She interrupts herself in mid-anecdote to gaze at the sky. "Oh, that's—you know—the man who used to be married to . . ." She names a famous citizen of San Francisco and, drawing on my meager store of society page expertise, I suggest a name for the pilot. "That's right! He's probably had lunch in the valley and is on his way back to the city." She waves at the emerald green bullet-shape. "When he sees me, he usually makes a loop and comes back." A German joke, I think, and smile indulgently: this friend is the least fanciful of women and although we rarely discuss the Napa Valley explicitly, I count on my visits to her to restore a sense of proportion to my experiences of the place. We are far too small to be seen from a helicopter.

She returns to the story she was telling me and I launch a fresh attack on a wiry dandelion clump that has gotten in the way of my mowing. Suddenly, there is that sound again: the glistening bullet is back, a little lower in the sky, and it describes a jaunty circle around us like a trained sky poodle, showing off. I stare at my friend, thunderstruck. She laughs delightedly. "There you are, I told you he'd come back!"

Napa's distance from ordinary life has far more to do with the wealth of its inhabitants than with wine or winemaking—whose mere mention sometimes earns a curled lip from urbane American neo-Puritans I run into. One such intellectual told me it was unfortunate that I had chosen to write this book—to waste an ability to communicate on such a frothy subject, when it could serve worthier causes.

But, smarting a little from his reproof, I remembered clipping for my files a *New York Times* pulse-taking report from Lithuania, whose early bid for independence had met with a crackdown ordered by Moscow. Soviet tanks patrolled the streets of Vilnius after an attack on unarmed crowds. Other calamitous consequences seemed imminent. The reporter, Francis X. Clines, described Lithuanians staunchly carrying on, beginning with a bride at her wintry wedding, "a study in white against white, hope against hope." His dispatch ended with a family defiantly celebrating a birthday in the midst of the menace and dread—with champagne.

The story testified to how potent a symbol the champagne was, just as much as the bridal white, of hope and life triumphant.

The clearest statement I have ever read of wine's intrinsic power, as a thing quite distinct from connoisseurship or snobbery, is in one of Marguerite Yourcenar's exquisitely imagined meditations in *Memoirs of Hadrian*:

Wine initiates us into the volcanic mysteries of the soil, and its hidden mineral riches; a cup of Samos drunk at noon in the heat of the sun or, on the contrary, absorbed of a winter evening when fatigue makes the warm current be felt at once in the hollow of the diaphragm and the sure and burning dispersion spreads along our arteries, such a drink provides a sensation which is almost sacred, and is sometimes too strong for the human head. No feeling so pure comes from the vintage-numbered cellars of Rome; the pedantry of great connoisseurs of wine wearies me.

I hope my book has offered glimpses of how Napa's well-heeled, well-educated, well-traveled people—wherever they come from—have been attempting to give contemporary significance, in the New World, to this substance with its tremendous, tremendously old mystique. They express some of their ideas in the way they choose to conduct their lives in the valley—and most of their choices are remarkable for how much they borrow from the past, or from the Old World.

It is as if these cultural sculptors have been straining to use wine's links with archaic tradition and facets of its fashioning to compensate for or restore what has been lost in modern life: stability, a sense of continuity, close ties within extended families, religious faith—and ceremonies affirming all of these; things crafted, not mass-manufactured; things whose making requires patience and a willingness to suffer Mother Nature's whims.

Though these aims are laudable, their execution is frequently quixotic or distractingly dotty. It makes for bizarre entertainment, watching Napa's denizens assiduously spell out the connections between wine and art and culture and the life well lived, starting with the design and decoration of their wineries and houses and extending to—of all things—croquet. They grab at the trappings of permanence, seeking to found lasting dynasties on country estates intended as monuments to posterity, taking every chance to be written about and photographed as they try.

There is pathos and irony in all of this: though the valley's future as winegrowing country seems assured, no like stability can be expected for the people in this landscape. Intrinsic problems of management and succession plague families striving to carry on. Some family wineries are bought by large corporations and virtually disappear; even without this phenomenon, families must contend with all the other modern forces of discontinuity, including a freedom of choice unknown in centuries past: no one who "returns" to the soil today is ineluctably bound to it. So it seems certain that the vineyards and wineries will continue to be the backdrop for a stage on which a constantly changing medley of dramas is performed by a changing cast of players drawn from all over the world.

Which means, as far as I can see, that Napa always will have much less a sense of place than of *places*. Unlike those of other cosmopolitan parts—Manhattan or cities of the Old World—the valley's hybrid society is unlikely ever to stay still for long enough to allow a cohesive and unmistakable local culture to form.

In this way Napa is only a microcosm of California, that cultural equivalent of a perpetual motion machine—an especially fantastic one that moves haphazardly. The metaphor is as true for the state today as it was ninety years ago, when one Arthur Tysilio Johnson set down his mostly acid description of the place in *California, an Englishman's Impressions of the Golden State*. To a devotee of the region's landscapes like myself, some of them are all but unrecognizable in his travelogue.

For instance: the oak-strewn hills, like many in Napa, that turn a sublime pale gold in the summer he presents as "a yellowy-grey cheese-rind dappled with round spots of green mould." He writes of the leeward Coastal Range's "dismal ribs of . . . arid mounds of sun-baked soil and withered grass"; the famous orchards of the Santa Clara Valley, now Silicon Valley, he finds dull, "naught but rows of trees set out with mathematical accuracy."

Still, take what he calls "character" as virtually the equivalent of culture—or lack thereof—and his overall impression of California and America is almost exactly the same as my own about Napa. Only, what he sees as temporary, I believe to be a permanent condition.

> To attempt any exact analysis of the American character, especially in the West, seems altogether impossible. Your average Westerner is such a parcel of conflicting natures, the result of a mixed and recent origin. . . .

. . . The truth is . . . the individual, like the nation, is only in the making . . . it is too soon yet to make any safe conjecture as to what the people are, or will be.

It is in mutable, fungible, ever-aborning—culturally shallow—places like this that dreamers thrive. Dreams readily take root and blossom extravagantly.

Index

About the Author

CHERYLL AIMÉE BARRON was born in Bombay and grew up in India and England. She was first sent to California from London by a former employer, *The Economist*, and has lived in the northern half of the state since 1981. *Dreamers of the Valley of Plenty* is her first book.